ALSO BY JENNIFER ALLEN

Better Get Your Angel On

FIFTH QUARTER

FIFTH
QUARTER

The Scrimmage of
a Football Coach's
Daughter

JENNIFER ALLEN

RANDOM HOUSE

NEW YORK

RANDOM HOUSE and colophon are registered trademarks
of Random House, Inc.

Library of Congress Cataloging-in-Publication Data
Allen, Jennifer.
Fifth quarter : the scrimmage of a football coach's daughter /
Jennifer Allen.
p.   cm.
ISBN 0-679-45202-8
1. Allen, George Herbert, 1917—Family.   2. Allen,
Jennifer, 1961—Family.   3. Football coaches—
United States—Family relationships.   4. Allen family.
I. Title: Fifth quarter.   II. Title: The scrimmage
of a football coach's daughter.   III. Title.
GV939.A53 A37   2000
796.332'092—dc21
[B]
00-029062

Random House website address: www.atrandom.com
Printed in the United States of America on acid-free paper
2 4 6 8 9 7 5 3

First Edition

To my husband, Mark,
for absolutely everything

FIRST QUARTER

Dinner, New Year's Eve, 1968

DAD SAT AT THE DINNER TABLE, sipping his milk. We all watched him sip his milk, his first and only drink of choice. Then he set his glass down on the table where my three older brothers and I sat, while Mom scowled as she stirred a pot of boiling spaghetti on the kitchen stove.

"Listen," Dad said, "a guy who goes out after a loss and parties is a two-time loser." Dad was referring to his ex-boss, Los Angeles Rams owner Dan Reeves. "First, he's a loser for losing, and second, he's a loser for thinking he doesn't look like a loser by partying it up."

Dan Reeves had once said, "I'd rather *lose* with a coach I can drink with and have fun with than *win* with George Allen." Reeves had been drinking all Christmas night at a Hollywood bar when he called my father at home from the bar telephone, the following day, at 8 A.M. "Merry Christmas, George," Reeves had said. "You're fired!"

That was a week ago. Now, on New Year's Eve, Dad sat in his pajamas, talking to us kids at the dinner table. Mom stood in her bathrobe, clang-ing pots and pans on the stove. This was a rare dinner with Dad since he had taken the job as head coach of the Los Angeles Rams three years be-fore. For my father, getting the Rams to the National Football League Championship meant drinking a tall glass of milk at the office for dinner, then spending the night on his office couch so that he wouldn't waste valuable work time driving home, eating with his family, and sleeping with his wife. The long hours paid off: the 1968 Rams defense had set a new fourteen-game record for fewest yards allowed on offense. But the team finished second in the Coastal Division, falling two games short of reach-ing the championship play-offs. A week later, Dan Reeves fired Dad. Since then, we had been keeping the TV volume turned down low so as not to disturb Dad's weeklong monologue, which had begun the day after Christmas.

"Heck," Dad said, "Dan Reeves is dying of cancer. Maybe that's his problem. He's drinking to forget he's alive!"

We all knew what came next. When talking about drinking and dying, our father always cited his own father, Earl, who died an unemployed alcoholic. To our father, the only thing worse than losing was dying without a job. "I want to die working," Dad told us all. "That's the only way to die!"

"Dying," Mom said, setting down Dad's plate of spaghetti. "Who's talking about dying? I thought we were going to have a nice dinner together for once in our lives."

"I'm trying to teach these kids a lesson."

"They've learned enough as it is."

"You know," our father said as our mother finished serving dinner, "you kids have a lot to learn about life."

We kids nodded. We twisted our forks into our spaghetti as Dad told us again about his other kids, the players he'd recently coached at the Rams: Deacon, Lamar, Roman, and Jack. Deacon Jones, Lamar Lundy, Roman Gabriel, and Jack Pardee had organized a team strike against Dan Reeves the day after Reeves had fired Dad. Thirty-eight of the Rams' forty players signed a petition saying they would quit if my father was not rehired as head coach. "We won't play if George don't coach" was the slogan they chanted for the television cameras. Dad was so moved by this display of support that he could barely manage more than a few words for the reporters before stepping down off the platform to lean against the shoulders of his men. Dark sunglasses covered his eyes as one by one the players took the microphone to speak for their former coach, whom some called their best friend.

"Now, *those* are men to aspire to," our dad told us. "You kids need something to aspire to." He said television was turning us all into wallpaper. He said we needed to have daily goals besides watching television all day long. "Show me a person without goals and I'll show you someone who's *dead*!"

"Please, George," Mom said, "it's New Year's Eve. Can we please eat a dinner in peace?"

But my father now directed his gaze at the little black-and-white television perched on a stool over my shoulder. A local Los Angeles announcer was summarizing the past year's events: the assassinations of Senator Robert F. Kennedy and Dr. Martin Luther King Jr. and the recent firing of Los Angeles Rams Head Coach George Allen.

"You know," my father said, not taking his eyes off the television, "I'm disappointed in each of you kids." He said there was a lot to be done around the new house and no one was doing anything about it. A few weeks earlier, we had moved into our large new house. It was our third home in three years as we followed Dad, moving from team to team in the NFL. Sealed boxes still filled every room of the house. Pointing to a box in the kitchen, Dad said, "You see a box like that, you unpack it!" Pointing to a scrap of brown paper on the floor, he said, "You see a piece of paper, you pick it up!" Peeling away a strip of packing tape stuck to the edge of the kitchen table, Dad said, "You see a piece of tape, you toss it out!"

We leapt from our dinner chairs to unpack boxes, pick up paper, toss out tape.

Mom stopped us all. "Not now," she said. "Sit down, it's time to eat. Let's eat."

"You know," Dad said, "it would be nice if someone said a little grace for a change."

"I said it last time," my oldest brother, George, said.

"*I* said it last time," my middle brother, Gregory, said.

"*Bull,* you did," my youngest brother, Bruce, said. "I always say it!"

"*Grace!*" Mom shouted. "There. I said it."

Dad shook his head. "Boy, oh, boy," he said, "here I am fighting to get back my job, and my own family cannot even bow their heads to say a few prayers."

Everyone looked to me. I was almost eight years old. When no one else wanted to say grace, I said it. I bowed my head and closed my eyes and thanked the Lord for our food and shelter and asked the Lord to help Dad get his job back with the Rams.

"Amen," we all said together, and Dad thanked me for my special grace, and George called me Ugly and I called George a Moron and George called me a Dog and I told George to Shut Up and my father said,

"You know I don't like that word," and Gregory said, "What word?" and Bruce screamed, *"Shut up!"* and Dad just shook his head, ran his hand through his thick black hair, and said, "Boy, oh, boy, you kids."

"*Now* can we eat?" my mother said.

"Who's stopping you?" my father said. His gaze returned to the television. The announcer was now giving a play-by-play of Senator Robert Kennedy's assassination in the kitchen of the Los Angeles Ambassador Hotel.

"Now *there's* a leader," Dad said. "There's a man this country will never forget."

My father was talking about Rosey Grier, a former Rams defensive lineman who had tackled and helped capture Kennedy's assassin, Sirhan Sirhan, moments after the shooting.

The telephone rang.

"Uh-oh!" said Dad, sitting up. "Uh-oh!" meant "Oh, *no!*" Every time the telephone rang since Dan Reeves called the day after Christmas to say, "Merry Christmas, George, you're fired," my father would say, "Uh-oh!" and refuse to answer the telephone. We knew the call would invariably be for Dad, but still we all sprang to answer it, saying, "Hello? Allen residence? Hello?" and then we would force the receiver into our father's hand. It would usually be just another sports reporter calling to ask Dad about his "uncertain future." Our number was unlisted, yet every sportswriter in the country seemed to have it in his Rolodex.

Earlier that day, our mother, who is French, had intercepted one such call.

"You Americans are so brutal!" she laid into the guy, "so different from the French. At least when a man is standing at the guillotine, we give him a cigarette before cutting off his goddamn head!"

Mom hated reporters. She said reporters were vultures preying on Dad. Dad liked reporters. He often talked to them as if they were long-lost friends, confiding in them recently how much he loved coaching the Rams. That's all Dad wanted, he would tell reporters. Dad would tell them, "I just want to coach, you see?" But this time, tonight, when the telephone rang, Mom answered it. *"Enough!"* she screamed into the receiver and slammed it down, then took it off the hook.

"You think those goddamn reporters care if we're trying to eat our goddamn holiday dinner in peace?" she asked. I looked around the table.

Gregory was pouring himself another glass of milk, Bruce was slurping up the last of a long spaghetti strand, and George was licking his plate clean.

Dad hadn't touched his food.

"Starving yourself isn't going to get your job back, so *eat,*" she said. Then she said to all of us, "Your father thinks chewing is a distraction. Your father's afraid chewing might take his mind off football."

Dad nodded his head and sipped his milk. He'd lost fifteen pounds during the last season: skipping meals, getting vitamin shots, drinking milk for dinner. He had two bleeding stomach ulcers: one that acted up during the season and one that bled off-season. He believed milk calmed ulcers. His love of milk was so well known that he became the spokesman for a local dairy that sponsored his weekly pregame radio show. Instead of regular payment, Dad made a deal with the dairy to deliver hundreds of gallons of the stuff to our door daily.

"You know, football was the only thing that didn't bug me," our father said. I knew of a few things that did bug him, beginning with his childhood during the Depression in Detroit, where he and his parents and sister lived in a two-room shack with a single-seat outhouse. His father, Earl, a failed musician, suffered a severe injury on the Ford assembly line that left him with a metal plate in his head and shakes so violent that even alcohol could not sedate his pain. After that, Earl could not keep a job. At ten years old, my father went to work to support the family by planting potatoes for pennies a day. What really bugged my father was allowing his brilliant younger sister, Virginia, to convince him that she should take over the care of their aging parents so that he could pursue his dream of coaching professional football. Only in later years did he realize the depth of her sacrifice when he discovered she had hidden the menial nature of her clerical work in order to allow her brother his rise to fame. These were some of the things that bugged my father.

"Apparently," my mother said.

"That's right," said my father. He said we kids needed to find out what we wanted to do with our lives and then follow that dream. Dad said without a dream, well, maybe we kids weren't really Americans.

"So you better drink your milk, Jen," Dad said to me, "if you want to grow up to be big and strong like Mike Ditka." At such a young age, I had visions of growing up to be big and strong like Mike Ditka. "Iron Mike" Ditka was a solid, six-foot-three, 225-pound tight end who played in five consecutive Pro Bowls, the first tight end selected to professional football's highest honor: the Hall of Fame. My father had drafted Ditka to the Chicago Bears the week I was born in 1961. Our simultaneous entrance into my father's life linked us forever.

When I drank my milk, I envisioned my frilly ballet tutu transforming into sleek football pants, my tight leotard into a loose jersey, my satin slippers into stiff cleated shoes. My long brown hair streamed out of the back of my helmet as I ran onto my field of dreams, and I thought I could hear the announcer scream, "The former Miss America, now the first pro-football girl in the NFL! Jennifer! Jennifer! Jennifer!"

"Jennifer! Sports!" everyone around the table was shouting at me.

It was my job to time the turning of the channels on the TV to the sports reports of local television stations. Starting with KTTV Channel 11 at 5:32, I then spun the dial as quickly as I could to catch the 5:35 report on Channel 9; 5:37 on Channel 4; 5:39 on Channel 7; and 5:44 on Channel 2. As one announcer wrapped up hockey, my brothers would shout channels—9! 4! 7! 2!—and I'd get nervous and lose precious seconds of sports news turning to the wrong station. Then I would be called an Idiot, a Moron, and an Ugly Dog, and my father would shake his head, disappointed, once again, in one of his children.

In the days following my father's firing, sports reporters asked the questions we dared not ask: Where was George Allen headed next? Buffalo? Pittsburgh? Washington? How did George Allen, one of the most successful coaches in the league, get fired by Dan Reeves, one of the most respected owners in the league? And most important, would Dan Reeves reinstate George Allen as head coach of the Rams? Just as the morning sports pages might brighten our breakfast, the nightly sportscast could cloud our dinner with new insights we could not expect from our father. Without the media, we kids might never have known which NFL city we would end up in next. An entire day passed after Dad's last firing before I learned about it on the news. Dad had not been able to tell us; Mom was too busy crying. That night after Christmas, I watched my father tell a TV sports reporter, "I haven't told my children yet." So on this New Year's Eve, we all listened attentively to the sports reports.

The first reporter said, "It looks as though George Allen is going to take a year off from football to write the great American novel."

Though this was certainly news to us, it did not sound implausible. We did not even look to our father for any kind of response before I switched channels on the TV. Dad had already written three books. With a master's degree in physical education, my father was known as the resident intellectual of the National Football League. His five-hundred-page master's thesis, "The Technique and Methods Used in Game Scouting by Outstanding Football Coaches," received an A at the University of Michigan. My father often showed me his thesis, letting me feel the weight of the neatly typed and numbered pages. The text spoke a language I would never fully understand—the 34 tab statue right, the 44 tite blast fielder, the 78 ax up and out—but I understood the work that went into making the book. He had typed the entire thesis himself on an old Royal typewriter that he had just given me for Christmas. "To Jeniffer, love, Daddy," read the note taped to the space bar. He always misspelled my name. Sometimes Jeniffer, sometimes Jenifer. Mom said that with over forty men on his Rams roster and over three hundred plays in his playbook, I was lucky my father even remembered my name. I remember wondering that night if my father would want his old Royal typewriter back to write his great American novel.

The next sportscaster said that two years remained on George Allen's contract with the Rams. It would be easy for Dan Reeves to reinstate Allen with the same financial terms. But, the sportscaster wondered, how could Allen know that he would not be fired again? Though the firing of George Allen shocked many, no one was surprised, he said. The sportscaster reminded us that Dan Reeves had once said, "George Allen is the last coach I will hire." But hadn't Reeves said that about every coach he ever hired—eight in the last twenty-three years—and then given every one the ax?

"What makes George Allen think he is different from any other coach in the National Football League?" the sportscaster asked his viewers. "Coaches are hired to be fired."

"Rot in hell," Mom said to the TV.

Dad rubbed his forehead with the heel of his hand.

Bruce said, "Turn that moron *off!*"

I turned off the little TV.

Now Mom demanded to know the truth. Mom said to Dad, "Do you mind telling me what you plan to do?"

Dad sipped his milk. He gazed at the blank screen of the television.

"Hey, George Allen!" Mom screamed. "Hey, I'm talking to you! Hey, I'm not some goddamn reporter! I'm your goddamn wife!"

Dad finished his milk then. He set his milk glass on the table. He got up from his chair and said, "For cripes sakes, sweetie, all I want to do is coach, you see?"

"Thank you for your insight," Mom said as she got up from the table.

Dad put the telephone receiver back on the hook and said he was going to watch some game films in the basement. One by one, the boys followed Dad down. George followed first. At seventeen years of age, George had a tall, solid build that towered over our six-foot Dad. Gregory followed next. Gregory was only fifteen years old, but his round, hunched shoulders reminded me that Gregory was already burdened by the same posture as Dad. Bruce followed last; with his quick, agile, thirteen-year-old body, he effortlessly raced his father and brothers down the stairs. I stayed upstairs, helping Mom clean the pots and pans. Mom muttered to herself, chain-smoking, flicking ashes into the soapy water that filled the kitchen sink. When we were done, Dad called us down to the basement, where he had set up a PROPERTY OF THE LOS ANGELES RAMS 16-millimeter projector to watch a tall stack of Rams highlight films. Dad wanted us to understand why he was never home for dinners or birthdays or even Christmas. He wanted to teach us the beauty of the sport of football. He wanted us to know the plays as well as he knew them, so well that even with his eyes closed he could decipher what play was run by merely listening to the rhythm of colliding helmets and crashing pads. Remote control in hand, Dad slowed entire games so that we could see, in slow motion, forward, and reverse, the perfection of a particular running back, how his torso remained steady while his hips turned this way and that, faking a defender, twisting out of a tackle, all to gain an extra inch on the grass. Once Dad reran a play so many times that he burned a hole in the film and it caught on fire.

After watching Dad's favorite plays of the 1968 season, he asked us all, "Who wants to watch *The Impossible Dream?*"

We had watched *The Impossible Dream* possibly a thousand times, but we were always willing to see it again. *The Impossible Dream* captured what seemed to be a perfect time in all our lives—our father's second season as head coach in Los Angeles. He had transformed the last-place Rams into a first-place team that led the NFL in defense, earning him his first NFC

Coach of the Year award. *The Impossible Dream* was a record of that season set to the music of Dad's favorite Broadway show, *The Man of La Mancha,* a musical about Don Quixote.

Even at my young age, I knew the lyrics were corny: "to reach the unreachable star, to right the unrightable wrong." But every time I heard that music while watching those men—Deacon Jones head-slapping his way through a thick mass of linemen, Lamar Lundy making a game-saving tackle, Roman Gabriel gracefully dropping back to pass, Jack Pardee making a diving-interception end-zone catch—my heart would race and my throat would tighten and my legs would curl up under my nightgown and I felt as if we were one family dreaming together in the dark.

The film ended with the next-to-last game of the season: the Rams versus Vince Lombardi's world-champion Green Bay Packers at the Los Angeles Coliseum. Lose, and my father's team would be knocked out of the play-offs; win, and they would be one game closer to entering the play-offs. With fifty-four seconds remaining in the game, the Rams were behind by three points, and the Packers were prepared to punt. My father placed all eleven players on the line to block the punt with not one player back to receive. It was a wild play my father had the Rams practice for days before the game. He determined the only Packer weak spot to be the team's left-footed punter, and he believed that the game might come down to this very moment—a Rams gamble to block a Packers punt.

The Rams miraculously blocked the punt, and even more miraculously, they recovered the ball and scored a touchdown to win the game.

Seconds later, the film showed my father on the sidelines, crying, shaking his head, as if to say "No, no." My father cried when he lost. He also cried when he won. As he cried, his players toppled him over, lifted him up, and carried him on their shoulders off the field. In another week, he would lead the team to their first play-offs in twelve years.

Watching the film replay these events, I would remember how that night, after the victory, my father was so wound up he needed a sleeping pill to get to sleep. I would also remember how my father awoke the next morning so exhausted that he could not even remember if he had won or lost the game. Still in bed, I could hear him ask my mother, "Did we win or did we lose?"

Now, on New Year's Eve, after *The Impossible Dream,* we all clearly remembered these events. When Gregory turned on the lights, I could see that each one of us had been crying.

When Dan Reeves fired our father, he fired our whole family.

Dad rubbed his eyes.

Mom lit a cigarette.

Gregory rewound the film and carefully placed it in its gray metal canister until the next night's screening.

We all kissed Dad, said "Happy New Year" and "Sweet dreams," and headed upstairs. As I got in my bed, I hoped that maybe what one reporter predicted would come true: that Dan Reeves would change his mind and reinstate my father as head coach of the Rams. More than wanting Dad at home, I wanted to see Dad happy. He just seemed so unhappy to be home with us.

Lying in bed, I listened to my parents talk. Our bedrooms shared a wall. Mom was blaming herself for Dad's firing. She said she knew all along that taking the Rams job had been a mistake. Mom said the moment she saw the Rams colors—gold and blue—she knew we were doomed but didn't dare say anything to Dad then.

"How can you trust a team with such flaky colors?" she asked Dad now. Then she told him, "Look, something good will come out of this—you'll see."

My father kept saying what he had been saying since the morning Dan Reeves had called.

"For cripes sakes, sweetie, don't you understand?" Dad said. "All I want to do is coach. You see?"

The Repossession

ON THE FIRST WORKDAY after Dad was fired, a Rams executive from the front office called to inform us that he would be coming to repossess our car. Our car was a brand-new, two-door 1969 Oldsmobile Toronado, white with golden Rams horns painted over the front fenders.

Royal blue racing stripes stretched the length of the car on either side, underscoring the huge gold medallions emblazoned on both doors that proclaimed, "Official Team Toronado of the 1969 Los Angeles Rams." The Rams executive who called was a short fat man I had once watched roll down an entire level of the Los Angeles Coliseum steps, drunk. He'd been caught at least once by the Dallas Cowboys spying on their practice. We heard that he had brought champagne to work on the day Dad was fired. Now he was coming to repossess our car.

"Maybe he'll drive off a cliff on the way to our house," my mother said. Until then, she said, the Toronado would remain ours.

Mom loved to drive the Toronado. She liked to lay on the horn several times when dropping me off and picking me up from school. She would lay on the horn and an entire playground would run up to the curb to see the Batmobile, as they called our car. The Toronado did feel like the Batmobile, with its huge froggy headlights, its roaring engine, and its sculpted bucket seats that flipped all the way back. But the first school day after Dad's firing, the car felt like an old, dumb joke. When Mom picked me up, I slumped down in the bucket seat.

"Did anyone bother you about Daddy today?" Mom asked.

Mom was barefoot, wearing a bright Hawaiian muumuu and bubble-shaped wraparound sunglasses. Two cigarettes burned in the ashtray.

"You know," she went on, waving and smiling at the people watching our car fishtail out of the school parking lot, "a lot of people are jealous of Daddy."

I couldn't understand why anyone would be jealous of a father who had been fired the day after Christmas, but I didn't say anything to my mother. I didn't tell her about the boy who had punched me in the stomach that day after I had kicked him for calling Dad, then me, a loser. I didn't tell my mother how I had decided to change my last name to Alan and how the teacher had made me write "Allen" on the blackboard one hundred times. I had tried to tell the teacher in my childish way that George Allen was not really my father, he was just this guy who stopped by our house every once in a while, a guy who we took in over the holidays because we felt sorry for him. I didn't and couldn't tell my mother any of this because my mother always told me, "Remember, whatever you say and do will be seen as a reflection on your father."

"Listen," my mother now told me, "if anyone ever bothers you about Daddy, ask them, just you ask them, 'What does *your* father do for a living? Sell *shoes*?' "

Hot Santa Ana winds off the desert had dried our canyons into fire hazards and littered the roads with debris. Long twisted strips of eucalyptus bark and large gnarly limbs clawed at the Toronado as we drove home. When a branch caught the underside of the car, Mom whipped the steering wheel back and forth until the branch fell away broken in the road. Weaving over double-yellow lines, Mom skidded through turns as our tires skimmed the edges of unguarded cliffs. Her ancient broken-handled hairbrush slid back and forth across the car's vinyl dashboard. Mom tossed her burning cigarette out the window and then listed her attributes as she ran the four-way stop sign near our house.

"How many American women pay the bills, file the taxes, build the houses!?

"How many American women go to the hairdresser, have their nails done, hire maids? All of them! All of them pay for the things I do for myself for free!"

It was true: Mom cut her own hair, did her own nails, cleaned her own house.

"How many American women play bridge all day while their children eat hot dogs and their husbands have affairs with their secretaries?" Mom lit another cigarette.

"How many? Tell me, how many? I want to know!" she demanded.

Mom was now yelling to hear herself above the radio station that gave us "*all* sports, *all* the time."

Mom prided herself for being un-American. She prided herself on the fact that she had built our house without the help of an architect and that she had raised four children without the help of a husband. Now, with Dad fired, Mom held on to one of the last things she had left to feel proud about: her naturally curly hair.

"How many of your friends' mothers get permanents to have hair like mine?"

I told her that I didn't know—I didn't have any friends.

But my mother didn't hear me. Even without the blaring radio, my mother was quite deaf. The bombs, she said. From the war. During the war, the Germans invaded the French colony of Tunisia, where my mother and her family lived in the city of Tunis. First the Germans invaded, and the Nazis took away my mother's father. Then the Allies bombed Tunis. Bombs fell in her neighborhood. Bombs blew out her family's windows. While the rest of the family hid under their beds, my mother, a teenager, calmly went out and swept up the glass as it shattered around her. My mother said the bombs that fell on her childhood home ruined her ears.

It took three years for Mom to re-create the home she had grown up in in Tunis. She built our house on the highest point of land on the Palos Verdes Peninsula, overlooking the entire city of Los Angeles and the Santa Monica basin. P.V., as it is called, is an exclusive oceanfront community, which was accessible at that time by dead-man curving roads along cliffs that often crumbled into coves during earthquakes. During the winter landslide rains, Mediterranean-style mansions, offering spectacular ocean views, slid several hundred feet down to the Pacific Ocean. During long hot summers, highly flammable sagebrush canyons caught on fire, burning several houses to the ground. Wild peacocks roamed throughout the peninsula's hills, and at night their woman-killing, Hitchcock-screaming calls made me tremble in my bed.

My mother selected every doorknob, toilet, faucet, and socket for our new house. She had the stairs designed to match the width and height of those in the Louvre. She hand-selected the stone for the den fireplace, spending days in the deep bottom of a nearby quarry. Unable to find the perfect keystone for the mantel, she ordered the quarry to blast for more rock. She eventually drove our building contractor into early retirement. Once, when Dad suggested that Mom hire an interior decorator to help her, she yelled at him, "Mind your own business, will you? Do I tell you how to run your team?"

After Dad's firing, I'd spot reporters at the foot of our driveway in dusty, fender-bent cars, taking notes. They had called our house "imposing" and our lifestyle "majestically impressive," though for the three years prior to moving into our new house we had lived first in a motel off the 101 Freeway, then a run-down cliffside rental from which my brothers got us evicted. My brothers had broken the rental's roof by installing a sixty-foot antenna so we could reach every sports station in Southern California. When Dad was fired, a reporter told my mother that we could remain in sunny Los Angeles in our lovely new home living comfortably on an annual Rams severance pay of $44,000. My mother had answered, "If one is frustrated in paradise, one may as well live in hell."

Everyone knew where we lived. Except Dad. He would get lost trying to drive himself home from the Rams office in Long Beach and have to stop at a gas station and call for directions. Once he got lost driving us home in dense ocean fog after buying us cones at a local ice-cream shop. None of us offered to guide Dad back to his new home. We all ate our treats in silence, watching him steer with one hand while the other hand held open the driver's door so that he could see where the double yellow line turned in the road. When a truck zipped by, nearly decapitating him, Dad said, "Cripes sakes!" and quickly shut the door. We were a block away from our new home.

Every time Dad changed football teams, Mom built another house. She had built three in the last five years. Change a team, build a house. Mom called every house her final pièce de résistance. "I'm an optimist," my mom said. "I keep thinking if I build a house, your father won't change teams." Once, after losing a game by one point, Dad offered our new house to the pool man. Dad told him, "Heck, I'd trade all of this to you, the whole house, this lot, this view, all of it, to you, for a *tie*!"

Turning onto our street, Mom and I passed the Green Bay Packers fan's house. Often his mailbox lay smashed in the street, a casualty of my brothers' drive-by to school in the morning. George would swerve his Mach II Mustang while Gregory held the baseball bat out the window to clear the mailbox off its post. The Packers fan would nail the battered mailbox back to the post; the next morning it would be in the middle of the street again. Lately, the Packers fan had resorted to stapling a Kleenex box to the mailbox post to receive his mail. Another neighbor, a San Francisco 49ers fan, owned an aging, yellowed, yapping poodle. He complained that our dog, a German short-haired pointer named Hilda, bullied his dog. Once I watched Hilda roll the poodle on its back in our front yard and stand over it, pinning its ears to the ground with her paws. Hilda stood barking over the poodle for so long that the dog went limp and I thought it was dead. Another neighbor, a Baltimore Colts fan, said Hilda's barking at night was causing him to have marital problems. Hilda barked all night at her own echo into the canyon below our house. The Baltimore Colts fan approached my mother and informed her that he was going out to buy a gun. My mother encouraged him. She said, "If you think a dog's bark can ruin your marriage, then please, do your wife a favor, shoot yourself."

After Dad's firing, our neighbors would walk out onto their front lawns and see if it looked as if we were moving. None offered condolences. Some called their realtors and happily told them our house would be going up for sale soon. Every day we would find realtors' cards and notes in our mailbox—"If you need any help, give us a buzz!"

"I'll be damned if I ask anyone to help me sell my house that I built, me!" Mom said, finding a FOR SALE sign someone had staked into our newly sodded lawn. She skidded the Toronado to a halt, threw the sign into the street, and backed over it with the car several times. Two of our neighbors watched from behind a neatly manicured rose bed. Mom waved a friendly wave and said, "Vultures," before burning rubber down our driveway.

She pulled us up just inches from a wall of moving boxes that had been stacked outside along the garage wall for weeks now. The boxes were starting to collapse and fade in the sun. Each box was marked in thick black Magic Marker ETTY, my mother's name. These boxes were filled with my mother's things: French piano books, French schoolbooks, French art books, and, later, I learned, love letters from a French fiancé killed on his way to a wedding during the war. When I once offered to help my mother unpack these boxes, she asked, "Why? Where's the room? On the shelf next to the trophies and footballs and plaques? No, thank you, I know who I am. I don't need some goddamn medal to tell me who I goddamn am!" I always thought of my mother's life before my father as a moving box she never unpacked.

We sat in the car, looking at the boxes. Mom took the broken hairbrush with bent bristles off the dashboard and lifted a curl of her naturally curly hair off her forehead. My mother had kept the hairbrush for as long as I could remember. She never threw anything away. Nothing. She saved, saved, saved. She had learned to save during the war. She said you never knew when one day you might wake up and have nothing. Now, lifting the curls off her forehead seemed to help my mother regain her composure. She looked at herself in the rearview mirror. On good days, she looked a lot like Elizabeth Taylor. On days like today, she looked like my mom.

George's red Mustang screeched up beside us, the Packers fan's Kleenex mailbox speared on the antenna. My brothers were home from school. Gregory slid barefoot out of the car. He surfed every morning and often forgot his shoes at the beach. George got out of the driver's side and unlocked the trunk. Out crawled my brother Bruce wearing a Rams T-shirt, a cracked football helmet, and muddy football cleats. Junior-league football had ended weeks earlier, but Bruce still wore this uniform to school.

"Are you out of your mind?" Mom screamed at Bruce.

"George said my shoes were dirty," Bruce said.

"Filthy," George corrected.

George's car was also Rams property. He didn't want to be held accountable for any dirt or damages. Mom asked Gregory why he didn't stop his idiot brother from hurting his baby brother, and Gregory said, "Big deal, keep your pants on!" None of us knew what "Keep your pants on" meant, but it never failed to make us check our zippers.

"Did you hear about Dad?" George asked, and I said, "What happened?" and Bruce said, "God, are you as dumb as you look?" and I said, "Oh, shut up!" and Gregory said, "Dad doesn't like that word," and before anyone could say anything else we all scrambled, elbowing each other, charging in to turn on the color TV set in the den. Mom sat in the only chair the movers had brought into the den—Dad's worn leather recliner, covered in beach sand and alive with Hilda's fleas. The rest of us sat on the unpacked moving boxes. Mom lit a cigarette. She smoked L&Ms. L&M, the football programs advertised—"When a Cigarette Means a Lot!" Cigarettes seemed to mean a lot to my mother. She kept several cartons stashed in the pantry, a few under the living-room couch, and a couple more in the kitchen cupboards. "I always like to be prepared," she once told me. "If an earthquake strikes, I'll have plenty of cigarettes."

There was Dad on the TV. The title under his image said so—GEORGE ALLEN, FORMER HEAD COACH, LOS ANGELES RAMS. Dad was standing at a microphone-covered podium in his blue sports blazer, white shirt, and striped tie. A well-dressed man stood beside Dad. "Who's that?" I asked, and George replied, "*Reeves*, you moron!" It was the first time I had ever seen Dan Reeves. He looked like a nice man to me; his hair was perfectly combed and his clothes were neatly pressed. He didn't look as if he were dying of cancer. "He doesn't look like a drunk to me," I said.

"All millionaires look perfect," Mom said. "You think they keep their millions by looking like drunken slobs?" Reeves had been a millionaire at birth and, when he was twenty-nine years old, he owned the Rams. Now he was in his fifties, only a few years older than Dad.

"Owner—I hate that word, 'owner,' " Mom said when the TV showed Reeves with his title, DAN REEVES, OWNER, LOS ANGELES RAMS. "Nobody owns me," Mom said.

"The thought of firing Allen had been in the back of my mind and built up over a period of time," Dan Reeves told the reporters. "It started before the season, and it grew. It has been difficult for me to get through to George Allen."

My mother grunted and lit another cigarette.

"Allen works fourteen hours a day," Reeves continued. "He doesn't care that much about anything else. He is single-minded of purpose. Of course, that's what makes him a great coach."

As soon as I heard the words "great coach," I knew Dad had been hired back to the Rams. I looked at Mom and saw that it was news to her, too. Reeves said the "falling out" had been due to lack of communication between owner and coach. Reeves said he and Dad had met only twice during the season, and that they had miscommunicated. Reeves thought that any future problems could be resolved with better communication. He said he and Dad were going to make an effort to meet at least once a week, and if anything was wrong, they would discuss it immediately and not let it "fester."

The sports reporters had a lot of questions for Reeves. Wasn't it true the real reason Allen had been fired was that he had traded the same draft choice twice? Or raised players' salaries so high that the Rams now had the highest payroll in the league? Or had spent almost $10,000 in monthly phone calls beyond the budget? Or promised prospective players new cars if they'd sign with the Rams? All without Reeves's permission? Wasn't Allen really fired because he was running the team like its owner and not like its coach?

Reeves said that was all behind them now, and he wanted to make one last point; the Rams player revolt had *nothing* to do with the decision to re-hire my dad. Reeves said, "Allen's intense loyalty and devotion are the sole reason I rehired him," adding for the third time that Allen would be the "last coach I will hire."

Dad stood at the podium. He said he was very happy to be returning as the Rams coach. And then he said, "I'm back because my players stood up for me."

Dad excused himself from the podium, said something about having to prepare to coach the Pro Bowl, and tried to slip away. Dan Reeves had to run after him, and for a moment the television camera lost them both. Then the camera found them standing under an EXIT sign. The owner wanted a televised handshake with the coach. The two men paused, mid-shake, for a smile and several flashes of newspaper cameras.

"Your father thinks he's Jesus Christ," Mom said, stubbing out her cigarette, "always going back in for more." Already she knew that my father had accepted the same terms of the original contract: same pay, same shaky clauses that would not ensure that he could not be fired again.

"Your father loves to suffer," she told all of us, dragging herself upstairs to get dressed for the night-out celebration with Dad.

FOR DINNER THAT NIGHT, Mom left us hard-boiled eggs, burnt calves' liver, and cold buttered noodles. A handwritten note warned us: "If you don't eat your dinners, I won't take you to the dentist!"

My mother used to trick my brothers into drinking cod-liver oil, taking naps, and eating cow's tongue by telling them that if they didn't, she wouldn't take them to the dentist. It no longer worked on my brothers, and it had never worked with me. I was only hurting myself, Mom would tell me. "Look at you," she'd say. "How do you expect to grow up to be big and strong like your brothers if you refuse to eat?"

Besides the fact that my brothers would all grow up to be over six feet tall—a solid six feet four for George—eating bored me. I tossed my dinner to Hilda and she'd vomit it all back up in the laundry room as a welcome-home surprise for Mom.

That night, Gregory and Bruce tried to force me to eat by pulling a long carving knife out of the drawer and threatening to surgically insert food tubes directly into my stomach. When that didn't scare me into eating, they called me "Mrs. Wolf." Mrs. Wolf was the wife of the manager of the motel where we had lived while waiting for our new house to be built. We all knew Mrs. Wolf was dying in the manager's suite on the second floor. We only saw her once, when she stepped out onto the balcony and looked down at us splashing in the motel swimming pool. She was ultrathin, with towering, stark white hair that looked like it was ready to topple her over the balcony railing and into the pool. When my brothers said I was going to end up like Mrs. Wolf, I dreamily imagined being married to a motel manager, with the sun too bright, and fainting to my death into a Valley motel pool somewhere off the 101. But that didn't scare me into eating, either.

Instead of eating, I filled my baby bottle with milk. I was still nursing a couple of bottles of milk a day from my Gerber bottle. No one could break me of the habit. No one even said anything about it anymore. I sat between Gregory and Bruce with my bottle in front of the TV to watch *Laugh-In*.

George came charging in, demanding to know who had touched his Kramergesic.

"Not me," Bruce said.

"Never use it," said Gregory.

George didn't suspect me. I was a girl. What would a girl do with Kramergesic? Kramergesic was a sticky, bright orange vaporous balm that my brothers George and Bruce stole by the gallon from the Rams training camp. I used to open the tub of it that my brothers kept in their bathroom and study their fingerful scoops of the stuff and wonder where they put it. I thought maybe they put it *everywhere*. I knew before playing in football games they rubbed it on their shins and calves and arms and wrapped each limb in tight cloth adhesive tape so that they looked like mummies before they put their uniforms on. Game days, our house reeked of Kramergesic, and on any day there were Kramergesic fingerprints along the stairway railing, car doors, refrigerator door—*everywhere*. After a while, George and Bruce would start to turn a weird, semipermanent sickly orange as they continually rubbed the stuff into their muscles to soothe the sprains, soften the bruises, mend the tears. That night I had rubbed Kramergesic on my arm muscle to make me strong enough to wrestle my brothers. But George didn't even suspect me; to him, I was just an ugly dog, as he called me, sucking on a baby's bottle.

"What are you morons watching?" George asked as he changed the channel to *Hee Haw*. George loved *Hee Haw*. His favorite character was the big, slow-witted Junior. Junior tried to tell jokes yet always failed to re-member the punch line. There was also something mildly country-thuggish about Junior that I think George felt akin to. After *Hee Haw,* we watched *Mannix.* Mannix investigated a car burning at the bottom of a steep oceanside cliff. We'd watched the *Mannix* television crew roll the car off one of our cliffs the previous summer. Our cliffs were famous for sui-cide car crashings through guardrails, both televised fictions and real. Whenever I saw Coast Guard and Fire Department and Police Depart-ment helicopters hovering, I never knew if it would be for *Mannix* or my mom or maybe even my brothers. The wrecks would stay down on the rocks for a few days and then they'd be gone, as if they had never hap-pened. Even whatever windshield glass or suicide note I'd think I'd find in the tide pools would be sucked out by a strong undertow. Once Gregory swallowed an entire bottle of aspirin and walked to the cliffs to jump to his death. Too sick to even jump, he came home and passed out on the couch, where Dad found him. Dad took him to the emergency room and Greg-ory had his stomach pumped, and Dad promised to spend more time with him, teach him to pitch a baseball, shoot a basketball, kick a football. But once Gregory returned from the hospital, Dad went back to work, and as with the car wrecks at the bottom of the cliffs, everyone at our house acted like nothing like that had ever happened there.

When *Mannix* ended, George said, "It's late, morons, time for bed!"

We all obeyed George. If we didn't, we knew he would kill us. Once, when Bruce refused to go to bed, George hurled him through a sliding glass door. Another time, when Gregory refused to go to bed, George tackled him and broke his collarbone. Another time, when I refused to go to bed, George dragged me up the stairs by my hair. George hoped some-day to become a dentist. George said he saw dentistry as a perfect profes-sion—getting paid to make people suffer. Instead, George became a lawyer and went into politics.

We all went upstairs to our separate bedrooms. George slammed his door so hard it shook the house. Bruce's bedroom was closest to mine. I could hear Bruce listening to his miniature Rams-helmet radio. He had the radio tuned to "*all* sports *all* the time"—hockey, baseball, basketball, football—and I could hear him quietly impersonating the announcers, mimicking their rising and falling voices as they broadcast the play-by-play.

My brother often whispered himself into a deep sports-trivia sleep, and I would get out of bed and go into his room and pry the helmet out of his arms and turn off the dial. Sometimes when I couldn't hear the radio, I'd think he was asleep, and I'd peek in and find him eating from a box of Hilda's dog biscuits. He would offer me one. That night, I could hear Bruce, between whispers, digging around in the dog biscuit box. I couldn't get to sleep, so I wandered into Gregory's room, where I always could.

The lights were off, but I could see Gregory by the red light of his stereo. When I came in he took out a flashlight and shined it on the glow-in-the-dark designs he had hand-painted on his ceiling. He clicked off the flashlight so we could lie back and admire the words of his handiwork—PEACE, LOVE, ACID. He had an extra bed that fit next to his, and I lay down in it and listened to the Doors. Gregory dropped his hand over the side of his bed, and I cracked each knuckle in his fingers while he explained the lyrics of "The Unknown Soldier" to me, and the gunshots from the twelve-man firing squad at the song's end. "Here's a guy who fights for his country," Gregory said, "and then he's blindfolded and shot to death by twelve men."

"Like the guillotine in France?" I asked, but Gregory didn't answer; he had fallen asleep before the guy was dead, moments before the record needle lifted off the turntable and the stereo light went off.

The smell of Shalimar perfume and cigarettes let me know my mother and, hopefully, my father, were home. Mom led me out of Gregory's room down the dark hall into my own bed. "What's that smell?" she asked me. "Kramergesic? What have I told you about snooping around in your brothers' bathroom?"

Deeper into the night, the screaming peacocks in the canyon sent me into my father's twin bed. Dad always let me crawl in. All I had to say was that I was scared, and my father would lift his blanket, slide his pillow, put an arm around my waist, a hand in my hand, and I would fall asleep.

In the morning, Mom was snoring in her bed that was pushed up against Dad's, and Dad was gone. He was back on the practice field, coaching the West for the upcoming Pro Bowl. All that he left us that morning was the sound of his bathroom faucet, dripping a slow drip into his sink, the *drip, drip, drip* sounding like the wooden metronome he kept on his office desk, reminding himself of the steady passing of time.

George Allen Day, 1969, Pro Bowl

I DREADED THE PRO BOWL. The annual, end-of-season, all-star players led by the "second-best coaches" game always fell around my birthday. A birthday card from my father with my name spelled correctly would have been enough. But instead, my dad would make some kind of public announcement, either having the announcer blast birthday greetings to me on the P.A. system or making Mom drag me to the field during halftime for a few fans to join the end-zone bandleader in singing "Happy Birthday." Often I cried and couldn't stop. When I turned six, the bandleader tried to console me and held me up to the microphone, which only amplified my sobs so loudly throughout the entire stadium that he almost dropped me. I cried even after my mother had dragged me back to my seat.

That year, in 1969, with my eighth birthday just days away, I shuddered at the beginning of the game, when the announcer said there would be a special halftime ceremony for George Allen and his family.

During the first half, I missed the amazing passes of our West quarterback, Roman Gabriel, that would earn him the Most Valuable Player Award. I just remember watching the clock tick away the quarters as I tugged on the hem of my fake leather skirt, pulled up my stretched-out kneesocks, and chain-chewed my chocolate cigarettes downwind from my mom's L&Ms. At halftime I slumped along out onto the field behind my brothers and my mother. I was so relieved to find that the man waiting for us on the fifty-yard line was not the end-zone bandleader but actually Sam Yorty, mayor of Los Angeles. Yorty had the ruddy-cheeked grin of a con man. Earlier in his administration, Yorty had blamed the Watts riots on Martin Luther King, saying that Los Angeles had some of the "best" slums in the United States.

Mayor Yorty now said Head Coach George Allen was the most important man in the city of Los Angeles that day. The way Coach Allen had taken the Rams out of a several-year losing streak to have the best two-year record in the National Football League, the mayor said, was a boost to all the people of Los Angeles. For Dad's contribution to the spirit of the revival of Los Angeles, Mayor Yorty declared January 19, 1969, "George Allen Day in Los Angeles."

Unfortunately for the mayor, my father was not there to accept the award; he was in the locker room pumping up his players. Mom accepted the award on his behalf, and the plaque got passed along by my brothers for me to carry, and we returned to our seats, where I held the thing on my lap the rest of the game, studying the seal of Los Angeles, marveling at its many colors, reading the proclamation with all of its *whereases, therefores,* and *heretofores,* feeling like it was some sort of phony certificate issued from the wizard of Oz.

Our West beat the East, 10 to 7.

Dad was awarded the game ball, which he later gave to the newly inaugurated president of the United States, Richard Nixon.

After the game, all along the dark stadium tunnel leading down to the locker rooms, fans huddled, waiting to spot the most important man in Los Angeles today. Ivy covered the tall walls on either side, opening to a California winter sky above us, the mildewed, mossy concrete ramp slick beneath our feet. A gas lamp burned above the locker room doors where I watched and waited, wanting to be the first to spot one, two, three brothers and finally my dad. As soon as I saw Dad, I tried to run through the crowd to him. My mother stood back. She knew better than to crowd or rush in on my father. Once, when she had, my father mistook her for a fan. "You'll have to get to the back of the line if you want an autograph, Miss," my father had said to her.

I tried to push through the crowd with the Most Famous Man plaque. Fans elbowed me in the head as they closed in, waving rolled-up programs, torn ticket stubs, empty peanut bags, anything for my father to sign. "Hey, George! Coach! Allen!" they screamed. "Can you sign that?" My father never once turned down an opportunity to sign an autograph. He used his own felt-tip pen, one he always kept tucked in the inside breast pocket of his Rams blazer. I stood crushed between the backs of jackets and belt buckles. I couldn't see my father's face, yet I could hear his voice, asking his fans "What's your name?" and "How do you spell that?" I could almost reach through some arms and touch his playbook, but I doubt my father even knew I was there. One fan looking down at me saw the plaque and asked, "Is he your father? Are you his daughter?" Before I could answer, the fan shoved his baseball cap at me and said, "Have him sign this, will ya?"

I handed the fan's cap up to my father. My father took it, looked around the crowd, and still not seeing me, asked, "How should I sign this?"

My father signed the cap and moved on. I watched him and his swarm of fans slowly make their way up and out of the tunnel, leaving me holding his plaque.

My father had won his Pro Bowl. He had been rehired at the Rams. Our family would stay in our big, bright new house on top of the Palos Verdes hill forever, or until he got fired again. For my birthday, what more could I want? Still, watching my father unthinkingly walk away from where I was standing alone in the gaslight, I never felt so uncertain about my place in this world of football and men and fans. More than that, I never felt so uncertain about where in the world I stood with my father.

SECOND QUARTER

Friends

AT SCHOOL, I had trouble making friends. At recess, I didn't want to play with the other girls on the jungle-gym bars, spinning skirts upside down for all the boys to see. I didn't want to play with the girls in the sandbox, trotting the little plastic horses around, making them neigh and buck and gallop. I didn't want to play with the Brownie girls sitting in a circle in the grass, playing secret Brownie games. I wanted to play with the boys, but the boys wouldn't let me. No kickball, no basketball, not even a marble shoot. At recess, I walked the edges of the playground alone, counting the hours until the school bell rang and told me it was time to go home.

Home, I'd sit on the worn-out basketball on the oil stain in the driveway, waiting for my brothers to return from school. When George's Mustang skidded just short of running over me, I'd toss the ball at the first one out of the car and say, "Game of Horse?" They'd drop their books, take the ball, shoot a few hoops. I'd lose, paying the price by getting swung upside down by my feet and then hoisted up on a high narrow branch in an olive tree, where I'd have to try to get down by myself.

One by one, my brothers' friends drove up, parking their parents' cars all along the street in front of our house. George's friends had the same pork-chop sideburns, greasy-haired scalps, and almost the same broken-toothed look as the inmates on George's favorite album, *Johnny Cash, Live from Folsom Prison.* Gregory's friends were tan, with long, chlorine-bleached hair and hip-hugging bell-bottoms. Bruce's friends sported crew cuts, button-down permanent-press shirts, and white sneakers. They all looked different, yet they all had one thing in common: football. They all played on the high school's varsity, junior varsity, and freshman football squads. I knew them all by their surnames—Mitt, Smith, Clark, Finney, Bragg. Birth names—Johnny, Jim, Mike, Matt, Frank—were insignificant. The only name that counted was the name the game announcer shouted into our stadium's P.A. system: Mitt, Smith, Clark, Finney, Bragg. I knew each boy's height and weight and starting position. I memorized their vital stats in the program during time-outs in the games my brothers played. Now that football season was over, these boys kept in shape by playing ball on our front lawn.

Our lawn was forty yards long, thirty yards wide, a perfect playing field for a game of short passes, quick cuts, tight tackles. There were no rules, no time-outs, no referees. Whoever had the ball was *it*. The object of the game was to get the ball and run, dive into the concrete driveway end zone, and score a touchdown. After a skin-scraping score, the boys then charged down to our side yard, where Dad had installed a regulation-size goalpost to kick some extra points.

Sometimes, for a play or two, they'd let me in the game. Somebody would toss me the ball, shouting "Allen!" and I'd make the catch and tuck the football into my body the way my father had taught my brothers, the way I had seen the receivers do it watching game films all off-season long. I'd try to think on my feet, read the defense: that guy's there, that one's *there,* where's the hole?

"Move around!" they'd shout at me. "You're killing the grass!"

I'd run for the open hole, there! Run! Go! *Now!* But then I'd feel a hand slap my arm, and I'd pull the ball in tighter, and a gang of legs and arms would wash over me and drown me down to the ground. I knew each boy's touch: one grabbed me only by the ankle, his hand skinny and cool and mean, dropping me to my knees. Another one swept a big fat arm around my waist, lifting me off my feet, flipping me over his back and upside down while another slapped the ball out from my arms while I tried to hold my dress down.

"Fumble!" I'd hear someone call out. No one likes a fumbler. Fumblers are kicked off the field.

Couldn't I have just one more try, please?

They'd laugh, then designate me "ball girl" for the rest of the end-less game. I'd sit again on the worn-out basketball on the oil stain in the driveway, waiting to retrieve any stray footballs.

When a carload of high school cheerleaders slowed past to watch the boys on the Allen lawn, the boys poured it on all the more—hitting harder, tackling tougher, tearing apart our newly laid sod. All the boys—greasers, surfers, crew cutters—were toughs. A couple of them ended up in jail, a few in detention homes, and one in a federal prison in Arizona. My brothers led each pack, never having to call home from jail, always playing injured. George played the best game of his high school career with a vomit-inducing, memory-lapsing concussion. Gregory survived four broken collarbones, three broken noses, and one dislocated shoulder. He once jogged four miles on a fractured ankle before realizing that a bone was tearing through the skin of his foot. Bruce was injured often but never let on. A broken jaw kept him from eating but didn't keep him off the playing field. Bruce was the most difficult brother for me to watch. When Bruce had the ball, he ran head-on into one of George's mountain-sized friends. The mountain stopped Bruce by grabbing hold of one of his ears to bring him down. Bruce got up, ran ear-bleeding off the field, dove into the swimming pool, and within seconds, returned, laughing, dripping, fully clothed, ready, willing, begging for more. They pounded Bruce the hardest, I think, because he was the youngest, the smallest, and the most athletically gifted. Over the years, Bruce's room filled with trophies from three sports. Maybe that's what made Bruce Dad's favorite. I know it's only part of what has made us all love Bruce the most.

These boys on our lawn claimed to be friends, but I could tell that deep down in their hearts they hated each other's guts. That's what made them such good football players; they were motivated by an extreme sense of competition, not by loyalty or love. In my short life I knew already that none of them would remain friends with my brothers through our next move to our next town and our next team. For now they claimed to be friends for life, as they tried to maim each other on our front lawn.

"Hang on, hold it, stop!" one would shout, and then the boys all begrudgingly stopped, put hands to hips, wiped sweat off foreheads with forearms. The one holding the ball stood cocky, spiraling the ball up in the air, saying, "Hurry up, queer bait." The one who shouted "Stop!" would still be doubled over, one hand on a knee, the other hand blowing bloody snot out of a nostril. After a few gut-wrenching coughs, he'd spit up a stream of pink bile onto our lawn. Then, spotting me watching him, he'd smile. Another one winked. Another one shot me with a thumb-and-forefinger gun.

I returned the smile, the wink, the bullet. I was madly in love with each of the boys in turn. Sometimes the love lasted for as long as a play; sometimes the love lasted the entire afternoon. I couldn't join them, so my love instead roamed among them on our lawn. All a boy had to do was run, score, bleed, barf, or spit, and I'd be in love. Back then, I thought I knew what love was all about.

When the Official Rams Team Toronado pulled into our driveway bringing my father home, the game came to an abrupt halt. The boys tucked in their shirts. The boys wiped their noses. The boys snorted down, coughed up, and then swallowed their own thick snot.

Double O was driving Dad home. Double O was a five-foot-six, 135-pound, sixty-seven-year-old retired police detective Dad had hired to throw spies out of Rams practices. Double O also drove Dad to and from work so he could study his playbook instead of spending time driving around, lost, looking for our home. Double O, named after James Bond, carried Dad's playbooks out of the car. Then came Dad, carrying canisters of game films under each arm. Dad stepped to the edge of the playing field lawn and asked, "Are any of you boys out for any sports?" The boys quickly formed a single-file line and stepped forward one by one to answer Dad's same daily questions: Sport? Position? Time in the forty? After this ritual, Dad had all the boys downstairs in the basement to look at the new stacks of Rams practice films.

"What do you think the Rams need to do to improve this year?" Dad asked them afterward.

Dad was always asking people "What do you think the Rams need to do to improve this year?" Dad asked waiters, car-wash attendants, hotel bellhops. When Dad asked strangers this question, it sounded like he had no idea what needed to be done with the Rams. Once I offered Dad some unsolicited advice and sketched out a play on a dinner napkin. "Have the receiver *stand* in the end zone," I informed Dad, "waiting, just standing there, waiting for the ball, and then all the quarterback has to do is toss him the ball, and *touchdown!*" Dad thanked me for my suggestion and tucked the napkin into his back pocket. It was the same response he gave to President Nixon when Nixon offered a suggestion on the implementation of a new shotgun offense. Dad listened to the advice of the common man more than that of a man as notable as a president, or a person as unnotable as a grade school girl. I think Dad preferred the common man's views because Dad saw himself as a common man, one who had once worked as a waiter, a car-wash attendant, and a hotel bellhop, a man who had worked hard to earn his place in the profession of coaching American football. I watched him listen to each boy's suggestion for the Rams season ahead—improve special teams, use draft picks wisely, strengthen the offensive line.

Then Dad made his usual pitch for the national boys' Punt, Pass, and Kick Competition. Each year, countrywide winners competed in finals during halftime of an NFL game. I'd seen countless boys choke—short, high punts; wobbly, dwarfed passes; low, two-yard kicks—while drunken fans booed them off the field. Dad thought all my brothers' friends should take the opportunity for this possible public humiliation, which was not open to my brothers; anyone related to the league was not eligible. Dad said the event might pave a path into professional football. Dad then handed out application handbooks to my brothers' friends. On the cover was a cartoon rendering of Dad standing outside the gates of the Hall of Fame in Canton, Ohio. If a boy worked hard enough, he could someday be inducted there, my father told them. Dad was working hard to get inducted into the Hall himself.

Dad read aloud from the program:

"Bear down, boys, sharpen your punting, passing, and kicking skills and then compete against boys your own age in a real fun contest for great trophies!"

The boys followed along, silently mouthing the words they knew so well.

Dad handed off the program, playbook, handbook, anything he was holding when he was talking and needed to use his hands, to me.

"Listen, boys, football is the greatest sport we have to instill discipline and teamwork! It helps boys like you learn to take life's knocks and teaches you how to play with pain." Dad said "play with pain" in slow, measured tones. He squinted, and I saw his lips moisten with saliva the way they did when he became excited. He wiped it off quickly with the back of his hand. "Listen, boys, the world's getting so that today, nobody wants to pay the price! Everyone wants to take it easy! Kick back, drop out, get high! Nobody is willing to bleed a little! It's all about bleeding, boys. Only by *bleeding* can a man ever feel alive."

The boys nodded their heads soberly. Even Gregory's acid-head friends nodded their heads and said, "Right on."

Then Bruce talked about how great it was to earn a trophy. Bruce's trophies filled the deep bookshelves in his room. They all looked the same to me: a gleaming, solid gold figure in action—baseball, football, basketball—mounted on a thick block of polished wood. On the wood beneath the figure, the trophy declared Bruce the number one player in the league. The trophies looked as if they weighed a ton. But once, when I was home alone and snooping around his room, I picked one up. The gold was spray-painted, the figure was hollow plastic, and the solid wood was Formica. The engraver had even spelled Bruce's name wrong—"Bruce Allan." None of that mattered. I still wanted one of my own to hold above everyone's heads. I just couldn't think what would be engraved on my trophy, or why I would ever win one.

"Time for dinner!" Mom called.

The boys ran upstairs to Mom while Dad went to brush his teeth and gargle. Dad always brushed his teeth before and after dinner.

"What's for dinner, Mrs. Allen?!" they screamed.

Mom invited all twenty of them to stay for a spaghetti dinner. But the group knew that after dinner they would be expected to go back down into the basement with Dad for several hours of postdinner game films, capped by *The Impossible Dream,* so they all politely said, "No thanks, Mrs. Allen," and headed home. Except for Clark and Bragg. Clark's parents were in the midst of a raging, alcoholic, multimillionaire divorce. Bragg's parents were strict religious types who forbade him everything. Clark and Bragg headed for the swimming pool. I tossed the *Punt, Pass, and Kick* handbook aside and ran after them, and Clark and Bragg picked me up, one held my wrists, the other my ankles. They swung me back and forth and my brothers shouted, "One, two, three!"

When I climbed out of the pool, I was not embarrassed by my see-through polka-dot dress clinging to me. I was embarrassed that Clark and Bragg may have seen the one fine hair sprouting in my underarm. Boys had armpits. Girls had underarms. I was still only eight, and the one fine hair was my most personal, intimate, biological mystery. Dripping wet, I ran into the house, past Mom yelling at me for running dripping wet onto the carpet, past Dad's gargling coming down the stairs, and straight up to my bedroom. I closed the door and ran into my walk-in closet, turned on the light, and slammed the door shut. The closet was my only quiet and private place in the house.

There was a wall of shelves and drawers for my ballet tights, leotards, and tutus—and body parts of the Barbie dolls I dismembered myself. Behind the closed door, I would rip off the Barbies' heads, their legs, their arms, and ration the pieces fairly to every shelf and drawer. On the floor, behind the piles of stuffed carnival animals my brothers had won for me, I stashed a couple of stolen tubs of Kramergesic, and all the red offense and blue defense pencils I pilfered from my father's desk.

That night, after getting out of my wet dress and putting on one of my brothers' football jerseys, I tore the head off another Barbie, tossed it in a bottom drawer, and took out a red offensive pencil. I pushed aside my hanging clothes—French, frilly dresses my mother's mother had made for me, lacy, multilayered, pink velvet-bowed necklines I would never be caught dead in. I tried to throw them out but my mother caught me, saying, "Someday you'll want your daughter to wear these." Mom didn't seem to know I had already decided I was never getting married and never having children.

Red pencil in hand, I shoved the dresses aside to find a clear space to continue my commentary on the people around me. Once, when driving into our driveway and seeing his sons play football on the lawn, Dad predicted their future careers. Years later, my father told Bruce that he saw George's leadership leading to a career as a statesman; that he saw Gregory's gentleness leading to a career as a doctor; and that he saw Bruce's quick-witted footing leading to a career as an entrepreneur. Seeing me, his only daughter, sitting on the basketball intently watching, Dad correctly foresaw that I would someday become a writer. Dad always said writers never played football, and never wore jockstraps.

I didn't see myself as a writer then, wearing lace underpants and a football jersey, preparing to write on the wall. This is what I wrote in red on the wall:

WHO I LOVE—NO ONE!

WHO I HATE—EVERYONE!

Someday I would have to own up to being a girl. Until then, I survived in that perfect age when my mother's frequent lectures about the changing female body seemed as far off as my someday playing professional football. An age when I wanted to be a boy so I could play football and at the same time wanted to be all my brothers' friends' girlfriend. An age when none of these contradictions gave me any sense of sexual confusion. An age that passed before I even realized I was in it.

Having finished tallying the daily score, I tucked my jersey into my panties, pulled on a pair of tights, slipped on some ballet slippers, and leapt downstairs, ready for another family dinner.

George and Jack, Part I

DAD HADN'T KEPT HIS rehiring promise to meet with Dan Reeves weekly. He said he couldn't, because Reeves went to a clinic in New York City to receive cobalt treatments for Hodgkin's disease. Dad didn't meet with Dan Reeves's front-office "flunkies," as Mom called them, either, because when Dad first arrived in Los Angeles he moved the Rams coaches' offices out of the executive suites in Beverly Hills down to Long Beach. Dad's Long Beach offices were several musty rooms in a private clubhouse perched above a golf course. When reporters visited Dad, they always remarked on the bag of golf clubs gathering dust in a corner of the office. One Christmas, in one of his usual "let's try this sport now" enthusiasms, Dad had bought us all golf clubs. Sometimes my brother George would use his to kill rattlesnakes with Hilda down in our canyon. "Golf?" my father would say to the reporters. "Who has time for golf? It's what you do in the off-season that dictates how you'll perform during the season!" That 1969 off-season, Dad continued to work his seventy-hour weeks. He was busy trying to win the Championship, he kept reminding reporters.

Dad was also secretly busy nurturing a relationship with another NFL owner: Jack Kent Cooke. Cooke, a resident of Los Angeles, was a major stockholder of the Washington Redskins. He shared the team's decision-making with well-known criminal trial lawyer Edward Bennett Williams, who had once defended Teamster Jimmy Hoffa, gangster Frank Costello, and, years later, *The Washington Post* and the Democratic National Committee. Cooke had immediately contacted Dad after the initial Dan Reeves firing. After Reeves fired Dad, Cooke sent several handwritten, hand-delivered notes to our house, soliciting my father to come to the Redskins. Dad declined the offers, which he said were some of the most lucrative in the history of professional football, but kept the door open. Dad made weekly visits to see Jack Kent Cooke while Cooke watched two other teams that he owned play, the Los Angeles Kings and the Los Angeles Lakers. Cooke insisted that we be his guests at the games, and so on weekends we went to the Fabulous Forum to join him.

Dad liked to drive around the empty pregame parking lot of the Forum so we could look at the impressively lit, steep alabaster columns that loomed above the surrounding dismal landscape of iron-barred liquor stores and one-pump gas stations. Inside, employees looked like they had just stepped off the movie set of *Ben Hur*. Male ushers wore orange, togalike Caesarean shifts with braided gold trim along the hem. Female ushers wore miniskirts and suede sandals with laces that wove and tied around their calves. Handmade tiles depicting the Forum's fabulous design covered the floors throughout the entire arena, exuding a sense of wealth and power to all who could afford to sit in the goldenrod plastic seats. The architect of the Forum was the same man who had designed Broadway Plaza and the Manned Spacecraft Center in Houston, but everyone, including us, called Jack Kent Cooke's creation "The House That Jack Built."

Cooke wore a lot of plaid, and he had the glowing complexion of a man who received several massages a day. Cooke referred to my father as "George dear" and "my dear George." Dad liked Cooke. He liked that Cooke didn't smoke and rarely, if ever, drank. Dad was also impressed with Cooke's rise to fame: from door-to-door encyclopedia salesman to one of the richest sports entrepreneurs in the world. Cooke was fulfilling some of my father's own dreams. As a kid, my father used to sleep on the downtown Detroit sidewalks for the chance to purchase, at sunrise, a five-cent outfield bleacher seat only to watch the Detroit Tigers lose. Now Cooke sat my father and his children in the best seats in the house. For Kings hockey, we even had two choices: the Plexiglas-shielded owners' booth directly behind the goal, or the seats directly behind the players' bench, where we could see Kings team members spit out broken teeth. Once, when we were seated in Cooke's booth, my brother Bruce dived under Cooke's feet to retrieve a wild puck, knocking a cup of hot coffee all over Cooke's lap. When Bruce resurfaced, puck in hand, Cooke barked, "Did you get your puck?" Bruce said, "Yes!" and showed the puck to Cooke. "I could have gotten you one of those if you wanted it so badly," Cooke told Bruce. "I know, but it wouldn't have been the same," Bruce said. "You're right," Cooke replied, and then he yelled to some of his lackeys, "Get me some goddamn towels!"

For Lakers basketball, we sat directly behind the players' bench, so close I could count the hairs on Wilt Chamberlain's legs. My brothers explained the rules of the game to me. I studied the players, studied my brothers, and studied the sport of men competing with other men. I watched men cry when Jerry West sank a final-second sixty-foot shot to win a game; I watched them cry and give Wilt Chamberlain a standing ovation as he jogged painfully onto the court after it had been predicted his damaged knees were ending his career. I studied my father as he leaned into Cooke during games and Cooke leaned whispering into Dad. I knew they had secrets. A photograph of the two of them together at the Forum once appeared on the sports page, with a caption that read, "Cooke teaches Allen the rules of the game." My father and Cooke talked hockey, basketball, and even the rich flavor of the Fabulous Forum hot dogs. But our family knew what the real talk was about—questions and answers: How much control do you think you'll need, George, dear? My dear George, when do you see yourself leaving the Rams? What do you think your future looks like with the Redskins, George?

Cooke was the second owner my father ever befriended. His mentor, boss, and role model had been Chicago Bears owner and head coach George Halas. Halas had given my father his first professional coaching break—a position as an assistant defensive coach and the director of Bears personnel. My father adored Halas. Yet their eight-year relationship ended when Halas stunned my father by suing him for tampering. Tampering is when a man talks to one team about coaching while still under contract with another team. In court, Dad denied calling a Rams executive (the one who later was supposed to repossess our Toronado) and asking about the likelihood of a Rams job. Years earlier, after eight years coaching at Whittier College, Dad had worked as an assistant coach for the Rams and had been fired after one season, along with the rest of the staff. After that firing, Dad had bought a car wash and named it "Rams Car Wash—Best Car Wash in the World." But the car wash was failing, and he had a wife and my three toddler brothers in a crummy house in Encino to support.

One night, on his walk home from the car wash, Dad stopped at a Catholic church. The doors were locked. Through a window, he could see candles burning inside. Dad knelt on the steps of the church and prayed that, God willing, God would find him a coaching job. A few days later, George Halas called my father. His director of personnel had just had a heart attack; would my father be interested in a job?

Dad shut down the car wash, packed a bag, and hitched a ride to Phoenix, where Halas was attending an owners' meeting. Leaving the car wash, my father left behind him the same kind of blue-collar, assembly-line work his father had performed at the Ford auto plant. My father always feared working at a faceless job with his Christian name sewn on his chest pocket, all his education in vain, his potential wasted.

Halas hired my father, and Dad learned much from the great man, including his need to control, his desire to win at all costs, and his famous paranoia. Halas kept my father at the Bears for so long partly by promising to retire and make room at the top. Halas often retired, but he always came back to work. After eight years at the Bears, my father made the kind of telephone call every coach makes every year. In court, my father admitted that even though he had made the call to the Rams, he didn't know it had been a violation of his contract. Fact is, Dad said, "I didn't read my contract." Dad not reading his contracts would always plague our family.

Dad was further crushed when Halas won the court case. Then Halas dropped the lawsuit—he'd made his point. At a subsequent league meeting, Halas called my father "a scheming, cheating, low-down, lying opportunist who will do anything to win!" A comment to which Vince Lombardi replied, "Sounds like a helluva coach!"

At the time Jack Kent Cooke and my dad sat leaning into each other sharing secrets, Cooke had just hired Vince Lombardi as head coach and vice president. Cooke even allowed Lombardi a part-ownership title. Lombardi had won five Championships for the Green Bay Packers. Cooke wanted to be a champion. One night we watched the Lakers play for the NBA Championship. At the half, they trailed the Boston Celtics by seventeen points and came back only to lose by two on the final buzzer. Some fans booed; some threw their souvenir programs onto the court. "Boy," I heard my father say to Cooke, "I thought you guys had that game."

Cooke just shook his head, sitting alone with his blank-staring wife, Jeanie, as we quietly left the owner's box.

Several days later we drove out to Cooke's sixteen-thousand-acre ranch to watch two swans mate. Dad had sent the swans to Cooke after the Lakers' loss. In a handwritten note, Dad suggested that the swans might populate Cooke's enormous man-made lake. After we drove through hours of fire-prone prairie to his ranch, Cooke informed us that both swans were male, but they seemed to get along just grand. In honor of the swans' friendship, Cooke named them George and Jack. My mother and I sat by the swimming pool with Jeanie watching Cooke and my father take a long walk along the lake, where the swans swam, each man walking with his hands behind his back, deep in discussion.

"Jack and George," Jeanie said, "they're brothers under the same skin."

"Soul mates," my mother added.

Later, in our rental car on the way home, Mom told Dad, "You'd better stay on good terms with Jack Kent Cooke." Dad silently nodded his head. The sun was setting in our eyes and a wind had picked up, blowing tumbleweed all across the road. The road was part of a public-access highway that cut across Cooke's ranch. Dad pulled down the visor to shield his eyes from the setting sun, and the whole thing broke off in his hand. The car began to weave a little as he tried to hook the thing back on, but Mom just tore it out of his hand and threw it out the window. "Drive!" she commanded.

Dad was driving the flimsy two-door rental car the Rams had given us while the Toronado was in the shop. Mum-mum, Mom's barely English-speaking Tunisian French mother, had been teaching herself to drive and had driven the Toronado into the wall at the top of our driveway, smashing the front end, fenders, and grille, and throwing the alignment out of whack. Now our two-door, no-wheel-drive rental shifted every which way across the road with the slightest wind. Dad had one hand on the steering wheel and with the other tried to tune in a sports station. When we veered into oncoming eighteen-wheeler traffic, Dad jerked the wheel so quick and hard that we skidded a dusty couple hundred yards almost sideways on the shoulder of the road until Mom grabbed the wheel and straightened us out.

"Boy!" said Dad. "Did you see that?" Then he put one hand on the steering wheel again and with the other tried to tune in a faint Dodgers broadcast as I watched our car drift across the yellow lines on the long windy road. Dad knew he was a bad driver. Once, when Double O was sick, Dad had Bruce drive him to a Rams game. Bruce was twelve years old at the time. Dad wanted Bruce to drive so that he could study his playbook. When a California Highway Patrol officer pulled them over on the freeway, Dad reprimanded the officer, "Don't you realize who we're playing today?" The officer replied, "The Eagles, Coach Allen. Now I suggest you drive and let your son read the plays out loud to you."

Now Dad suggested maybe Mom should drive, but she said, "No, this was your idea. You wanted to see Cooke and those goddamn swans. You drive." Mom had braced herself with her feet on the dashboard when Dad first drove off the road, and now I saw she kept them there.

Mom lit a cigarette and tossed the match out into the wind that blew over the miles and miles of Jack Kent Cooke's parched, tinderbox landscape. We passed by several hundred tumbleweeds, several thousand head of cattle, and what seemed like several million NO TRESPASSING signs. When Dad couldn't tune in the Dodgers broadcast, he left the dial on a religious station.

"Please," Mom said, and turned the radio off.

Dad said, "I liked that," and tuned the station in as the car drifted. Mom grabbed the wheel just in time to miss a small herd of cattle trying to cross the road.

Dad liked listening to religious broadcasts. He said it helped him with his locker-room sermons. The only other profession he had once considered was the priesthood, but it required too much time indoors. This off-season, Dad had been trying to rewrite the Ten Commandments. He was having a hard time. So far all he had was:

GEORGE ALLEN'S TEN COMMANDMENTS

1. Football comes first. During the off-season, family and church should come one, two, with football third. But during the season, the competition in the NFL is so tough that we have to put football ahead of everything else.

As Dad leaned into the darkening dusk to see because he had not thought to turn on the headlights, he said, "Heck, you know what I'd like? I'd like us all to go to church someday, that's what I'd like. I'd like to take our whole family to church."

"Church?" Mom said, and then over the seat to me, she asked, "Do you know why your father's saying that?"

I shook my head.

"I'll tell you why. Your father feels guilty, that's why. He's afraid he might have been relaxing today. He's afraid if he relaxes and doesn't go to confession, the good Lord will not forgive him for enjoying himself for a goddamn change."

Suddenly the car dropped into a steep turn and we were heading down a mountain pass. On either side of us the shoulders fell off into dark bouldered canyons.

Mom said, "Are you sure we're headed the right way? Are you sure we took the right turn out of Cooke's ranch?"

"I just think it would be nice to go to church, that's all," Dad said.

Mom flicked her cigarette out the window, and I turned around to watch it spinning on the road behind us as we sped ahead.

"The last time we went to church was in Chicago," Mom said, "and a lot of good that did, praying, getting sued, going to court. Boy, go to church some more and who knows what will happen next!"

Mom thought going to church brought bad luck. Educated by Catholic nuns in a Muslim country, she believed in a complicated system of superstitions. She had more faith in Arabic hand gestures to ward off evil than she did in the recitation of the Lord's Prayer. Dad was superstitious, too. He thought not going to church brought bad luck. I didn't know what to believe. I'd only been to church once. Throughout the service, Mom gave a continual play-by-play.

The procession of the priest: "Here comes the hypocrite."

The collection plate: "Here come the vultures."

The forgiveness of sins: "Here comes the guilt."

All the while beside us, Dad had bowed his head, had knelt in prayer, and had made the sign of the cross. He was the only one of us who took the body of Christ. When the service was over, he looked changed, less worried, less wrinkled, less Dad. "I feel so fine when I am close to God and in a state of grace," my father said as he drove us home from church that day. He didn't even sound like Dad.

Now Dad said, "I just think we have a lot to be thankful for, that's all."

"Am I not thankful?" Mom asked and lit another cigarette. "Boy, you should be married to another wife for one day, just one day. See if she puts up with what I put up with day after day after day. Maybe you'd be really thankful."

"Gee, I wish you wouldn't smoke so much, sweetie," Dad said.

"Gee, I wish I didn't smoke so much either," she said, and she took a deep drag on her cigarette. My mother had been smoking for over thirty years, a habit she learned, she said, from American GIs she visited in the hospitals for the Red Cross. She smoked to keep them company, she said. During one football game, I counted that she smoked almost fifty cigarettes, about one cigarette every five and a half minutes, I told her. "That's not much, is it?" she asked after the game, her voice rough, raw, and husky like a man's.

A sign in the road ahead indicated we were three miles from Fresno— RAISIN CAPITAL OF THE WORLD.

"I knew we'd gone the wrong way," Mom said.

Dad pulled over so far we almost plunged down a cliff. Ever since my brother George held me over the railing at Niagara Falls, I've had a fear of heights. I couldn't bear to look down into the dark abyss. A convoy of tractor-trailers rounded a curve and rocked our car, teetering on the edge of the road. His neck stiff from watching game films, Dad couldn't turn to watch for approaching traffic. Instead, he stared into the rearview mirror and asked, "Is it safe?"

"Go!" Mom would say.

"Stop!" I'd scream just as another tractor-trailer came barreling around the curve.

I thought we were going to die. It was a feeling I'd felt before.

Dad pulled slowly onto the road, taking several tries at a U-turn on the blind double-yellow curve before he had us headed in the right direction.

"When do we get that gosh-darn Toronado back?" Dad asked.

"Don't ask me. Ask your friend Dan Reeves."

"Isn't he dead yet?" I joked, giddy that we, at least, were not.

"Jennifer!" my father shouted. "If it weren't for Dan Reeves we wouldn't even have a glass of milk on our table!"

"Unfortunately, your father's right," Mom said calmly, "though I'm counting the days until that bastard is dead."

Dad tuned in to the fading radio station.

The sky grew dark around us as Dad got a crackling, far-off preacher preaching about the Peace of God which passeth all understanding. My father had found the headlights, and the green dashboard lights brightly lit his face. My mom eased up on her cigarette smoking. The winds stopped shaking our car as we approached the lights of Los Angeles. I began thinking of Jack Kent Cooke, and I wondered if he and my dad were really friends. I had met several famous men who had really impressed me—Joe Namath, Dean Martin, Don Ho. They were men with swinging style. Namath once signed my program, "Peace and love, Joe"; Dean Martin danced and sang, not spilling a drop of drink or flicking ash; Don Ho had a harem of hula girls. The only styling thing I could see Cooke had so far was an enormous shower stall with several billion oscillating shower heads at his ranch. Driving home that night, I thought maybe there was something about Jack Kent Cooke. Maybe he really was, as my mother said, "grand." All I knew was that something about Cooke made Dad think about God. We all listened now to the preacher Dad wanted to listen to, a thin faraway voice talking about being able to enter the kingdom of God. For a while, I think, Dad was considering a heaven that could be entered into without having to win a Championship, another kind of immortality that wasn't won or lost on the football field.

An Also-Ran

FOR THE SPRING recital, the part of Gigi could have been played by anyone in the class. The role required no physical skill whatsoever. All I had to do was hold on to the ballet teacher's fat grandson's thick hand while he sang to me, "Gigi, why, you've been growing up before my very eyes." He had braces. Tiny white pimples. A fuzzy mustache. The skin of his neck rolled over his tight shirt collar. His hand was so sweaty that it kept slipping out of mine. I had to act impressed and shy and coy. Made bashful by his words of affection. He had to act bold and daring and dashing. Charmed by my charms. We were the biggest phonies in the show. The stage lights were blinding. The audience was a black pit beyond. A gaping hole of judgment. After our three-minute staged romance, we received the biggest applause of the evening.

My mother waited for me outside the stage doors.

She was so proud of me!

She had always wanted a girl, she confessed.

My brothers waited in the parking lot, tossing around a football, practicing pass patterns: the flare, the fan curl, the sky. But my mother cried and sobbed into my ribbons and bows, telling me that my brothers watched me with tears in their eyes! They cried, she claimed, seeing their baby sister so grown up!

That was more than hard to imagine. My brothers never cried. Gregory cried only once, when Dad hit him and broke his nose. Bruce cried only once, when a referee made a bad call that cost the Rams a game. George never cried; I didn't think he even knew how. Even that night, just as I stepped out of the auditorium doors and into the parking lot, I saw George get blindsided by a car, roll over its hood, and land shoulder-first onto the pavement to make a diving catch without shedding a tear. Mom also told me that Dad was so proud of me. She said he was sorry he had to return to the office to make plans for Rams summer-training camp. To this day, I have never even believed my father was in the auditorium that night.

After the recital, my ballet teacher elevated me to pointe: the equivalent of a boy receiving his first jockstrap. I thought the shoes would help me become a prima ballerina. But the pretty satin shoes the teacher made such a big deal over were two sizes too small. "That way, you're more comfortable on your toes than on your flat feet," she explained. A pinch of lambswool was the only thing between my big toe and the hard wooden floor. I couldn't walk in the shoes. My calves cramped; my toes bent. Attempting a series of turns on tiptoe across the dance-class floor, I caught a horrifying, spinning glimpse of my contorted self in the mirror.

"Straighten your legs!"

"Lift your arms!"

"Smile!"

When I took off my new shoes, my toes were bleeding, stuck to my tights, and my lambswool was crusty. Dad always said it's not how you play that matters—it's whether you win, it's whether you're Number One. I could tell by watching the other girls in the class that I was far from becoming Number One. The other girls leapt over my head, did *chaîné* turns so quick and easy that I couldn't count them fast enough. My brother George had predicted that I would never be a ballerina, that I would grow up to be a six-foot-five-inch, 225-pound lady wrestler. I wanted to quit ballet. All I had to do was take one look at my pathetic bleeding toe and I knew I didn't have the character required to become a champion on the dance floor, or on the football field, or even in the wrestling ring.

I had read the inside cover of Dad's hardbound, ten-pound, three-hundred-page playbook more than once. It defined the two types of people in the world—Champions and Also-Rans.

First, a Champion:

Ambition: Desire for high goals. Hates to lose. Can't stand failure. Has goals above ability.

That was me. I had goals above my ability.

But I failed the rest:

Coachability: Takes advice. Eager to learn. Easy to approach.

Aggression: A tiger. Asserts himself.

Leadership: Sets a good example.

Take-Charge Guy: Under pressure, does something about the problem. Often a hero.

Hard Worker: One of the first to practice—last to leave.

Physical Toughness: Develops toughness by hard work. Trains all year round.

Mental Toughness: Never gives in to feelings. Has never-give-up attitude. Ignores heat, cold, and pain.

Psychological Endurance: Stays with job until the end. Reliable.

Below this, in equally bold print, was the profile of an Also-Ran:

No Drive: Goes with the tide.

Know-It-All: Rebel, griper, loner.

Mouse: High in self-abasement. Always kicking himself. Introvert.

Follower: Will go with the crowd.

Watcher: Joe Milquetoast. If there's an accident, he watches or runs away.

Corner Cutter: Ducks practice. Always has an excuse.

Hypochondriac: A muscle grabber—always has an injury.

Complainer: Always has a problem. Points fingers. Never blames self for loss.

Quitter: Can't stick to the end. Easily distracted. Starts many jobs, finishes few. Unreliable.

Quitters were either traded or cut. I did not want to be traded to another family; I did not want to be slashed with a knife. So I stuck with ballet. I smiled. I pranced. I attempted to dance. Reprimanded for wearing one of my brothers' football jerseys to ballet class, I conformed. I wore the black leotard, the pink tights, the satin slippers.

When my mother saw that I was not happy with ballet, she told me about an awkward Detroit Lions lineman who had once studied ballet to help him with fancy footwork in muddy grass.

Really? I said.

There was no more demeaning position than that of lineman. He waits at the line of scrimmage, like a horse at a starting gate, waiting to hear the quarterback's cue, Hike! Hike! He charges head-on into the opposing lineman, an elbow to the neck, a forearm to the chest, while the quarterback does something spectacular—scrambles, fakes, fades, passes, throws a bomb! *Touchdown!* All the while the lineman has been treading in a gully of mud. He's done his job: he's protected the star quarterback. He doesn't even know a touchdown was scored until he looks around and sees the whole team running to greet and congratulate everyone else on the field except him, the lineman. He takes off his helmet and walks off the field. Even the water boy ignores him. It's a dead-end thankless job.

Okay, I'll take it!

I stayed in ballet, thinking I was training to be a lineman. I still somehow thought I would grow up to be a boy. I imagined it to be an overnight metamorphosis—one day I'd wake up and *zap*, the transformation would be done. I did not imagine organ changes or growing a beard or hairy armpits. I only imagined the things I would be allowed to do once I was a boy—burp, spit, curse, play football, go to training camp, be with my father, know my father, win the respect of my father.

There was a story going around ballet class that retarded people didn't know they were; that's what made them retarded. I started thinking that maybe I was retarded and didn't know it; I was a girl who wanted to be a boy.

The Invasion

I WAS SO HAPPY during the summer of 1969; my brother George was leaving home. For some reason, I had not foreseen that graduating from high school meant going off to college. George had full football scholar-ships to UCLA and Princeton. I was disappointed only when George chose to attend UCLA to be near the family rather than going to school on the East Coast.

Mom was sad to see Georgie go; sometimes I saw her crying in the driveway watching George drive away, even though he was just going to the beach. But her mood would change when George's car leaving passed another car turning in: football season was approaching, and re-porters were beginning to drop by our house. They'd come with their notepads and their pencils and their glasses with dandruff salted along the tops of the frames. They'd come in the morning, at lunch, in the after-noon, and they'd call at dinner. They came on weekends and on holidays, and they always came without warning.

One day I answered the door, and there was a local TV reporter staring me straight in the eye. On TV, the guy looked six-foot-plus tall. In person, he looked like a Disneyland character in his shoulder-padded blue blazer, pancake makeup, heavy eyeliner, and tennis shorts. Behind him loomed an entire film crew carrying cameras, lights, and suitcases full of microphones.

"Is the coach in?" the guy asked. Is the coach in? What did this guy think? When was the coach ever in? The coach was where he always was, where he belonged, at work, working to prepare the assistant coaches to prepare the team to win the Championship. The guy said they had sched-uled an interview with the coach at 5 P.M. It was four-forty.

Mom appeared behind me, tan, barefoot, wearing a faded Hawaiian-print bikini. Years before, Mom had won a belly-button contest on the shores of the French Riviera. Now the bikini barely hid her cesarean scar as she stood sucking down a raw clam straight from the shell. She had dug up an entire towelful down at the beach earlier that day. When the re-porter asked if this was a bad time, she said, "When's a good time?" She then waved the reporter and his crew into the foyer and into the den be-side the kitchen. Mom returned to stirring her clam chowder, one eye on the pot, the other eye on the television crew that had begun to dismantle her house.

Mom called reporters coming into our house "the invasion of Nor-mandy." They dragged thick long electrical cables in through the front door. They turned back rugs, knocked over plants, and broke little porce-lain figurines Mum-mum had sent us from Paris. They duct-taped cables onto our handmade Italian tiles; they shoved us with their elbows and butts, shouting "Make room!" as they wheeled in carts of tall light stands. They bent the blinds when they drew them, and they disconnected the telephone. They peed on the rim of the toilet and left the seat up. They asked us if we had a muzzle for Hilda when she growled at them stepping over her in the laundry room, and when we said no, they gave us one. They scraped the floor rearranging the furniture in the den so Dad's chair could be beneath his Wall of Fame photographs. When they took down the photo of Dad with Nixon, Mom said, "You can leave those as they are, thank you," and they obliged. But when she turned her back, they took the photo down again. They banged us in the head swinging their boom mikes, and when Mom coughed lighting a cigarette, they all shouted, "Quiet on the set, please!" When they were finished with the den, it looked like an operating room, all the lights focused on Dad's chair, where the reporter would open and dissect my father.

Except my father wasn't home yet. There was nothing to do except wait. The reporter sauntered into the kitchen and asked Mom "What's for dinner?" while the rest of the crew went out into the front yard to grumble and smoke cigarettes. Mom asked me to get the gentleman something to drink. I poured the gentleman a warm, cloudy, overly chlorinated drink of tap water into a 1967 COACH OF THE YEAR glass. The kitchen was a mess; broken clamshells covered the counter, and one of my brothers had shot a jockstrap that still dangled above the dinner table from a ceiling light fixture. Dad's playbooks were stacked in unsteady piles along the walls. A fine layer of black ash covered everything. A couple of days before, a canyon wildfire had raced all the way up to within a few feet of our house; our whole house still smelled like smoke. When the reporter picked up one of Dad's playbooks, it blackened his fingers and hands with ash.

"There was a fire," my mother explained. "The whole canyon burned down."

"The canyon burned down?" the reporter said, sounding as if he didn't believe it.

"You can't see it with the blinds drawn," my mother said simply.

Dad prided himself on the fact that he had been home on the night the house almost burned down. I prided myself on the fact that I was the one who detected the fire. Mom prided herself on the fact that the night before the night the canyon burned, she had had a dream that our house burned down. Once, she dreamed that a neighbor's house burned down in Chicago, and the next day the house burned to the ground. Another time, she dreamed that a friend suddenly died, and the next day the friend did die. Mom had many accurate premonitions and prophecies, but she could never predict when a reporter might drop by.

The TV reporter began snooping around Mom's bulletin board. The bulletin board was an open journal to our lives, the handwritten notes Mom wrote to Dad and us kids and to herself: "Remember, Rain or Shine, Win or Lose, We're Behind You, Daddy-Pie!" and "Keep Smiling! Nobody Likes A Grouch!" and "Never Let Down Your Guard! Never Let Them Know You're Scared!" The guy reached into his blazer pocket, set down his water, took out a notepad, and began jotting down some notes.

I had been on this guy's TV show a couple of years earlier, sitting on my father's lap as he asked him questions like "Do you ever get nervous before a game?" and "What do you like to do to relax?" He never asked me a question. When I complained to my mom later, she said, "What could a five-year-old girl possibly know about football?" I knew more than this guy. This guy thought football was just a game, a sport, a play-time for adults. When Dan Reeves fired my dad, this guy said Dad had not played nicely on Dan Reeves's playground, that Dad had taken Dan Reeves's toys, the Rams players, and turned the toys against him when the players protested Dad's firing. This guy didn't know football was life. This guy didn't even know my name. He called me Jeffie all that day at the TV studio and this day at my own house. Jeffie, what an interesting name, he would say.

While the reporter took notes on our bulletin board, I crept slowly up behind him, so close I could smell the VO-5 in his hair. I stood so close behind him that I breathed on his neck when I said, "My name is Jennifer."

The guy spun around, putting his notebook down, and picking up his glass. "Say, that's good water," he said, and he drank some more. I stared him straight in the eye until he finished it all.

Dad came storming in with Double O lurching behind, back bent, arms loaded with game films and playbooks. Carrying Dad's playbooks was literally more backbreaking work for Double O than all the murder cases he had solved as a police detective. His shoulders were becoming permanently curved from the effort. Even after he dropped the new load of playbooks and films onto the kitchen floor, he could barely straighten up. He started to back out of the house, bent over, his hands massaging his lower spine.

"Okay, now!" said Double O, backing out. "Everything's under control! Everything's under control!" When Double O said "Everything's under control," what he really meant was "Duck! Take cover! Everything's *out* of control! Everything's about to *blow*!" I thought Double O meant this TV interview, which was an hour late already, was about to blow.

Dad was trying to mend his relationship with the TV reporter. Dad had locked the guy out of the locker room after the previous season's games. The guy shouldn't have taken offense; Dad had locked Dan Reeves out of the locker room after the games as well. This reporter supposedly pulled a lot of weight at CBS as a sports anchor, and CBS aired most of the NFL broadcasts. There were rumors that the guy might be headed to ABC, the network that was talking about starting a new football program called *Monday Night Football*. Adding Monday night to the football schedule was like changing Sunday Mass to Monday. *Monday Night Football*—it just didn't sound right. But if someday the reporter would end up in the *Monday Night Football* booth, Dad wanted him on his side. Dad was going to try to be nice. I could see it pained him. Dad hated being nice. He hated interviews. He hated questions. He often referred to the interview seat as the "electric chair."

"Nice jacket, Bob," Dad said, sitting in the chair.

Bob was not the reporter's name. No one corrected Dad. Dad was always confusing people's names, especially people he didn't like. He acted like it was unintentional. Like, Oh, absentminded me. He once had a boss he continually called by the wrong name until the entire organization picked up on it and began calling the owner by the wrong name as well. Finally the man fired Dad.

The reporter wanted to talk to Coach Allen about his last firing, the Dan Reeves firing.

Dad cut him off. "That's behind us now. All we care about now is getting the team into shape at training camp and preparing ourselves for the season ahead. This is the best team I've had at the Rams. I think we have a chance at the Championship."

Dad's eyebrows shifted. He sucked in his dry lips. His jaw muscles tensed and pulsed.

The reporter took a generous tack. He said, "This is the era of Allen in the NFL." He said the Vince Lombardi era had ended eighteen months previously when Lombardi resigned as Green Bay head coach after leading the team to several Championships. He said that even though Lombardi was with the Washington Redskins now, he had had his day. "This is the era of Allen," the reporter repeated.

"I hope you're right," Dad said, loosening up a little. "You know, we thought we could win the title in 1967 and then again in 1968. But I have a philosophy of coaching and it boils down to this: this is the only year that counts! I'm never concerned with seasons after this one. If I had a twenty-five-year contract, it would be the same way."

The reporter went on to talk about training camp. Dad's training camp was a brutal, eight-week get-in-shape session held at a local college campus. Dad loved training camp. He said it was his favorite time of the year: everything was organized, structured, disciplined. He made his team practice three times a day in full pads at full speed under the full California summer sun. He fined players twenty-five cents a day for every pound they were overweight. He forbade drinking water on the field. He forbade drinking milk at lunch because he believed milk clogged a player's windpipe. He forbade players from driving between the practice field and the dorms and the meeting rooms and the cafeteria; they had to ride bicycles instead. Players called Dad's training camp "concentration camp," and they nicknamed Dad "Hitler." The players who couldn't handle camp were cut or traded or put on waivers.

"Some of them called my camp a torture chamber last summer," Dad told the reporter. "Maybe it was because they weren't in shape and couldn't even run a lap without getting winded."

Dad was getting worked up now. He sat on the edge of his chair. His lips began to moisten with saliva. He licked his thumb and wiped the drip of his nose with the back of his hand.

"But isn't it tough to say good-bye to your family for eight weeks every year for the last eighteen years?" the reporter wanted to know.

"I think about the family," Dad said, "but I'd be away from them one way or the other."

What did that mean? I wondered. Did that mean that even if Dad weren't a football coach, he'd find some way to get away from us for eight weeks every year? I looked at my father and realized he had already left us.

He had that far-off look that another reporter had once described as a man "constantly searching the horizon for some stray homily."

Mom coughed, and the sound people wanted to kill her.

Dad snapped out of his gaze, then said, "I have a wonderful wife. She knows I eat, sleep, and dream football. She is very understanding. I couldn't do the job without her."

The show wrapped up. We would watch it the next night during dinner on *CBS Sports.*

As the crew packed up their gear, Mom followed them out to their truck and van. I followed her. The sun was setting, and cold summer fog off the ocean was rolling up the canyons. Mom was still in her bikini. She had something to give the reporter.

"You forgot this," she said, and she handed him his notebook from which she had quietly torn his bulletin board–snooping pages.

"Do you ever miss your husband when he's away at training camp?" the man now asked my mother.

"Not especially," she said.

Mom led me back into the house, and I closed the door behind us. I could hear Dad down in the basement trying to set up his projector to watch the new stack of films. Mom was in the kitchen, staring into the clam chowder she stirred with an old wooden spoon.

Love Story

EVERY SUMMER, Dad took the boys with him to training camp. He wanted to teach them discipline (paying the price for your father's body-breaking practices by having the players bind and gag you inside a laundry hamper left under a cold-running shower, and having the discipline not to rat them out to your old man), and hard work (making secretive, after-midnight runs to the liquor store for the curfew-bound dorm-bored players), and responsibility (turning on the practice field's end-zone sprinkler system and covering the sprinkler heads with towels so the players could sneak sips of water behind the coach's back). My brothers loved going to training camp and stuffed their summer bags with jockstraps, bubble gum, and Kramergesic. I helped Mom pack Dad's bag: a jumbo jar of peanut butter, extra bulbs for the 16-millimeter projector, extra boxes of white chalk, and a whistle. As she zipped up the duffel bag, Mom tried to suppress her ecstasy, her relief. Later she'd wipe a fake tear from her eye as we watched Dad and the boys board Double O's Rambler. Waving good-bye in the driveway, we'd wave and wave until they turned the driveway corner, out of sight. Then Mom dropped the phony sadness, rubbed her palms together, and said to me, "Free! Free at last!"

Summers, our house turned into a women-only camp—no men allowed. We opened the boys' bedroom windows to let that smelly, spermy, stuffy air out! Then we shut their doors and tried to forget about them— they were gone! I didn't miss my brothers. I didn't miss them reminding me what I wasn't going to amount to. I walked around in my ballet tights and leotard and tutu and no one said, "Where'd you get that getup?" I walked around in my bikini and no one called me "bread butt." I walked around naked without having to worry about anyone staring at my breasts and hear anyone say anything about the way I was "growing up."

Days, Mom and I spent down at the beach, digging clams with our feet in the sand. Nights, she made clam chowder while I'd take out my crayons and draw menus for the fancy French dinners we would share alone together at our restaurant we called the Villa Balina Bistro. Clam chowder, artichokes, salmon, watermelon. We ate everything my brothers hated. We ate the things that made my father shiver. We dimmed the lights, we drank wine. Mom smoked her cigarettes and I chewed my chocolate imitations. Above all, we refused to watch sports during dinner. Instead we chatted in French. I threw out the few words I knew, flipping back my long hair, saying emphatically, waving my arms, *"Mais oui! N'est-ce pas? C'est vrai!"* This was the life I envisioned if only my mother had married the Parisian lawyer she was once engaged to, not really taking into account the biological impossibility of it all. I always felt I would have been born my mother's daughter regardless of whom she married. Often I didn't even feel as if I was my father's daughter. I wished my mother would have married her Frenchman, the wealthy, intelligent Pierre. Pierre had been killed falling off the back of a motorcycle on his way to a wedding in Paris. My mother had been seventeen at the time. She learned of his death by telegram. She was so shocked, she said, she laughed for days, weeks,

months, years afterward, whenever she thought about it. Every summer evening would wind itself down through the wine, the talk of Pierre in Paris, France, and into my mother remembering the telegram informing her that her fiancé was dead.

"Can you believe it?" she'd ask me. "A telegram! That's how I learned that the love of my life was dead."

I'd seen Western Union telegrams: hand-cut strips of letters pasted on thin yellow paper like a ransom note. A telegram from Nixon was pinned to our bulletin board in the kitchen. Dad sent Mom a telegram in 1950 that my mother framed on their bedroom wall: AS THE 1951 FOOTBALL SEASON APPROACHES I WOULD LIKE TO HAVE YOU AS MY TEAMMATE. It was my father's marriage proposal. That was the closest my father would ever come to kneeling on one knee, taking Mom's hand in his, and asking, "Will you marry me?"

My father had to fly from Sioux City, Iowa, to Tunis, Tunisia, to hear her answer to his proposal. He had flown on an airplane only once before. After earning his master's degree at Michigan, he sent out 849 applications for a coaching job, and he received two replies. One was from Morning-side College in Sioux City, Iowa. He got so airsick flying from Detroit to Sioux City that he overslept and missed the interview. The administration gave him a second chance and ultimately his first coaching job, though the president of the Methodist college said they were taking a chance on hir-ing a Catholic. Then, a few years later, my father spent two days on air-planes flying from Sioux City to New York to Paris to Tunis. All during the trip, he wasn't worried whether my mother would accept his proposal or whether he would arrive in Tunis airsick. His main worry, according to one of the letters he wrote to my mother, was the escalation of the con-flict in Korea. In his letters, my father always referred to himself in the third person. "What if war breaks out and George gets stranded in Africa?" my father wrote. "Is there football in Africa for George?"

By the summer of 1969, my parents had been married seventeen years. Mom said if it weren't for training camp, the marriage would never have lasted, that she would have divorced my father long ago. She said if Dad and the boys were around the house twelve months a year, she'd go mad. I did not want to see my parents get a divorce because I was sure my mother would get custody of me and my father would automatically get my brothers. I was afraid that my father would think having George, Gregory, and Bruce was enough of a victory that he wouldn't put up a fight to get me, too. That would have broken my heart.

"Anyway," Mom would say, tossing back the last of her wine, filing away her memory of Pierre's death, "that's all in the past now. You can't go back, can you?" Then she'd say, *"C'est la vie!"*

I hated when she said *"C'est la vie!"* I felt as if she had already given up on her life, her fate, her marriage, her husband, us, me.

After doing the dishes, we'd step out on the balcony and look at the view. The lights of Los Angeles shimmered in the smog. The ocean was blacker than the sky and looked to me even deeper, like a bottomless hole the whole city was on the edge of falling into. A gambling barge covered in year-round Christmas lights was the sole indication that the ocean was only the ocean. My mother claimed the barge for herself. "That's my barge," she'd say as if she were announcing that she was still alive. She told me she made similar claims during the war, while standing in the hills of Carthage. One night watching battleships at sea shell the village below her, she told herself, "If Carthage is still standing at the end of this, I will be still standing, too." Most nights, looking out at the lights, we didn't talk too much, we just looked out at the view. Sometimes we'd hold hands.

Then the telephone would ring.

Dad called every night at exactly the same time, 9:05 P.M. He'd call to tell us practice was "so-so," that he had a good "meal-o," and that he was going "beddy-bye." Dad talked like a child to Mom when he was away at camp, and Mom treated him like one. "Okay, now," I'd hear her say, "you have sweet dreams." Sometimes she'd sing him a little French lullaby over the phone. It didn't matter that he didn't know what the words meant. He only knew that it was the same song Mom sang to me when she put me to bed. *Vole, vole, petite mouche. . . .* It was a song sung to a little fly, asking it to bug off and fly away, the French equivalent of "Shoo fly, don't bother me." *"Vole, vole,"* my mother would sing to my father, *"vole, vole."* Fly away, fly away.

While Mom talked to Dad, I gathered up all our bedtime supplies for the long night ahead: one box of frozen Reese's peanut-butter cups, one baguette, two packs of cigarettes (chocolate and tobacco), a Fabulous Forum Club ashtray, a bottle of water, and two cognac glasses. I placed them all on a rusty Cinzano cocktail tray that had come from my mother's father, whom we called Pup-pup. He was once the main importer of wines and liquors in Tunis. Pup-pup and Mum-mum loved my father, and he loved them. Years before they had had a young son named George who had died of leukemia. They often viewed my father as a son, calling him their "son-in-love." They used to visit us from Paris during every football season. They knew all the rules of the game—celebrations *only* after victories; after defeats, no talking, no toasts, no fun. When they left to return home to France, my mother had to console not only her crying parents but also her weeping husband.

Now I held the Cinzano tray engraved with my mother's family name, Lumbroso, and waited for my mother to finish singing my father to sleep.

After she hung up, we'd lock the doors, disconnect the telephone, and head upstairs—Mom to her bed, me to Dad's. We turned on the TV and set ourselves up for the late movie, the late-night movie, and then the late-late-late-night movie. Mom's recollections and feelings toward my father matched the tone of the movies. We'd start with a romance, a *Casablanca*-like black-and-white film during which my mother would tell me she had fallen in love with my father because he was "so American." Mom had been in Sioux City, Iowa, visiting an officer and his wife she'd met during the war, when she first laid eyes on my father. She said it had been love at first sight during a dress rehearsal for a play at Morningside College, where my father had his first coaching job. At the precise moment that she and my father met, the theater lights went off. She and my father spent the rest of the evening together, holding one enormous spotlight for the actors to complete the rehearsal. "You think I'm making this up, but it's true," she'd say. In the months to come, their dates involved milk shakes, picnics, milk shakes, golf, and milk shakes. Mom said she had never met anyone so straight. My father would diagram football plays on picnic napkins, writing, "George laterals to Etty," and diagram Xs and Os and arrows on tablecloths and menus, and Mom thought, "How sweet, he's really trying to tell me something about his feelings." After she realized that he wasn't telling her anything, that he was simply doodling football plays during their dates, Mom left Sioux City for Tunis, telling him, "It was nice while it lasted."

The late-night movie would be something like *Hush Hush, Sweet Charlotte* with Bette Davis starring as "Charlotte," a southern spinster cruelly shunned by her community for the unsolved grisly murder of her boyfriend. Now, Mom's memories would darken as well. Mom remembered that after she accepted Dad's marriage proposal and returned to Sioux City, Dad wanted them to be married in a Catholic church. The priest said he would marry them only if Mom agreed to raise as Catholic any children the marriage might produce. As a young woman, my mother had had an "incident" with a priest in Tunis, so Mom said "Over my dead body" to the priest in Sioux City. The priest answered, "Then the marriage will not last." My mother and father were married by a justice of the peace in a Jewish friend's home with two witnesses. Dad's parents could not afford to travel to Sioux City for the wedding; Mom's parents were nursing her sister through a serious illness in Tunis. For her wedding, Mom wore a silvery blue dress she later ruined trying to make into a skirt. Mom said that on her wedding day in Sioux City, she was thinking of Tunis, Pierre, and an uncertain future with a coach of a sport she did not understand. Mom said her wedding day was the saddest day of her life.

After Bette Davis crossed the threshold of insanity, it was time for the late-late-late-night movie, nearing 2 A.M., and we would be watching something like *Night of the Living Dead,* and Mom would start complaining about the upcoming season. Dad often spent night after night sleeping on the sofa in his office. Mom talked about the trust she had in him not to have affairs. His only mistress is football, she'd say, and not very happily. On the TV screen a zombie would be falling out of the trunk of a car. I'd close my eyes not to watch. Smelling Mom's cigarettes, and hearing screams and dying whimpers, I'd fall asleep. Mom said the horror films helped her insomnia. She'd developed insomnia since marrying my father, waiting up for him to come home from work. When they were first married, Dad worked so late that Mom called the Sioux City police to go look for her husband. The police told her they knew where he was, in his office. Mom just didn't understand football back then. Back then, she thought a team losing 52 to 0 could certainly come back in the fourth quarter. She thought there were eight men on a football squad. She thought a tight end's hamstring was a select cut of meat from the butcher. Her ignorance seemed to endear her to my father. Weeks after their wedding, he mailed her a typed postcard, which Mom still kept on her bedside table. On the front was a photo of a Chinese restaurant in Miami where they had dined during their honeymoon:

Dear Mrs. Allen,

This is to inform you that your husband, George, is very much in love with you in spite of the fact that you don't know how many men there are on a football team. I wanted you to know this because you might be able to sleep better at nights.

Most sincerely,
(unsigned)

I'd wake up in the morning, and the TV would still be on, broadcasting a morning show, the weather forecasting more sun, the news covering another Apollo launch, the sports running a clip of the Rams training camp. I'd go down and fill my bottle with milk and wait to smell the morning's first cigarette of the day coming down the stairs preceding my mom in her bikini, ready to begin another long summer day.

"I had fun last night, didn't you?" she'd ask, a little hung over from the movies, memories, and cigarettes. She'd pick up the paper I'd already brought in and turn to the TV listings. "*Return of the Living Dead* tonight," she'd say, raising her eyebrows. Then I'd toss the sports page to her that I'd scanned for news of my father, and she'd grab her cheap drugstore reading glasses and read to me the news from the Rams training camp. She'd save that section in particular for our clam digs at the end of the day.

"Voilà!" she'd say. "That's what I think of football!" A photo of Dad at his Rams training camp with his players would soon be covered with raw clams, broken shells, and wet sand. Then she'd laugh a laugh that would take me a long time to ever completely understand.

"I'm only kidding," she'd say. "I hope you marry a man as nice as your father."

Mind Over Body

DAD HAD A HISTORY of pulling muscles and breaking bones at training camp. The summer before, Dad raced a player in the forty-yard dash and tore a hamstring. Another summer, he broke his wrist and required a cast. In the following weeks, the Rams won three preseason games in a row. Dad thought the cast was bringing the team good luck. When the Rams team doctor, Dr. Jules Rasinski, told Dad it was time to remove the cast, Dad was afraid that taking it off would change their luck from good to bad. The doctor told Dad that the cast had to go; his hand was healed. Dad then asked Dr. Rasinski to recast his hand before every game. The good doctor obliged. When the Rams winning streak ended, Dad said, "Get this goofy cast off of me. It's bad luck!" Dr. Rasinski cut it off immediately.

This summer, toward the end of training camp, Dad was blindsided during practice and knocked off his feet. He came down hard on the turf and broke three ribs. Elated, Dad predicted the broken ribs would win the Rams at least ten games. Dr. Rasinski agreed with the prediction, then telephoned my mother and warned her of her husband's latest injury. When the coach came home, the doctor said, he shouldn't be allowed to do too much housework.

My mother said, "You're kidding, right? You think George even knows how to pour his own milk?"

Dr. Rasinski was kidding. He was a big kidder. He was also one of our few real friends. Dr. Rasinski was the main man responsible for convincing Dan Reeves to hire Dad back at the Rams. The players' strike had been influential in making Dad's firing a national sports headline. But it was Dr. Rasinski who convinced Reeves to take my father back. A few days after the firing, Dr. Rasinski drove up to Dan Reeves's Bel Air estate to try to talk him into hiring George Allen back. That little talk turned into Dr. Rasinski spending the entire night hopping from bar to bar all over Los Angeles with Reeves, matching him drink for drink, trying to convince him that Allen was the most devoted coach he would ever find in the National Football League. Reeves wanted the recently retired Vince Lombardi to replace Allen. Dr. Rasinski convinced Reeves that Allen was his man. The night ended, near dawn, where it began: Reeves's home lounge for one last drink. Later that day, Reeves telephoned Dr. Rasinski and said he'd meet with Allen, but only if Dr. Rasinski came.

All the way there, Dr. Rasinski coached Dad. "Listen, when Reeves asks you, 'What do you want to drink?' say a double."

Dad nodded his head.

Reeves greeted the men at the door. When Reeves asked, "What do you want to drink?" Dad said, "A double."

"Double what?"

"Double blackberry brandy."

Reeves and Dr. Rasinski had to laugh. No man drinks a double black-berry brandy. Reeves had to admit, the coach was a sincere square.

Years later, when I asked Dr. Rasinski why he so wanted to help my father get his job back, he told me, "I liked your father. I wanted your father to live a long life. Coaching football kept him alive."

Dr. Rasinski was always saving our lives. When Dad lost weight, Dr. Rasinski gave him vitamin shots. When Dad's ulcers acted up, he gave him ulcer pills. Once, at a Rams banquet party, when he found my mother crying into a glass of wine, he asked her what the matter was. She cried to the doctor, "Will we make the play-offs?" Dr. Rasinski took her behind a tall velvet curtain and gave her a shot of B-12 in the rear end, helping her face the rest of the banquet.

On a camping trip to Alaska with Dad and my brother George, Rasin-ski again would save a life. Flying to a deserted island, one of the seaplane's pontoons broke as they were landing on a strip of ice. Their Alaskan guide left them there and flew off for help. The guide was gone for two days. Just up the beach from where the guide left them, Dr. Rasinski discovered a freshly killed caribou carcass surrounded by bear prints the size of dinner plates. The men settled into their makeshift shelter—an overturned canoe the guide had left. The guide had also left them a .45 pistol with two bul-lets. Later, my father called the misadventure the most relaxing vacation of his life. "Relaxing for him," said Dr. Rasinski. "He slept while George and I kept watch all night!" A reporter once asked my father, "If you were stranded on a deserted island, what five things or people would you want with you?" My father replied, "Sioux Indian Chief Red Cloud, Bob Hope, the Bible, a set of weights, and Dr. Jules Rasinski."

Dr. Rasinski always made sure my father had an end-of-the-season physical. He said my father was in fine health for a man forty-six years old. But my father lied about his age—he was actually fifty-two—and he dyed his hair with Grecian Formula to keep it jet black. Fans guessed my father's age to be somewhere in his mid-thirties. He did look young, and he kept in shape. He maintained his collegiate stamina. Dad had been a member of the Sigma Delta Pi fraternity—a national honorary athletic fraternity that required boys to maintain a B average. Dad could still run the hundred-yard dash in a little over ten seconds flat, high-jump five feet, long-jump seventeen feet, run the 120-yard high hurdles in sixteen flat, do a twenty-foot rope climb in twelve flat. At training camp, after practice, he'd test himself: could he keep up with the boy he once was? In one of the hundred notebooks in which he wrote to and about himself, he commended his efforts:

"Standing 6'1", weighing 169 lbs., George Allen maintains his college weight."

Actually, I later learned that my father's college weight was 145 pounds and could only earn him a slot on the college B-team. He lied about his age because he didn't want his fellow players to know that it had taken him seven years to finish college. His studies were constantly interrupted by his having to double up on full-time jobs to help his sister support their parents and also to pay his college tuition.

Dad valued youthful appearances, but when it came to selecting talent, he sought age over youth. During that 1969 training camp, my father made seven trades for aging veterans. Dad wanted men who willingly overtaxed themselves, men who barfed on the field, passed out, woke up, and then asked for more. He said these were men with "character," men who gave the club some polish, men with experience. These were men just like him, men who worked mind over body, men with scars. One recent trade was for running back Tommy Mason, a small, compact, balding man who once played with several broken ribs. Another team had tossed Mason off as a has-been. But Dad saw in Mason, and in these other older players, their ability, and most important, their yearning, to make that last extra catch, that last extra tackle, that last extra interception that could win the game and lead the team to the Championship.

Dan Reeves did not agree with Dad's philosophy, nor did he share Dad's vision of what he saw in these veterans. Often, to acquire these players, Dad traded away future draft choices. Dan Reeves was one of the original inventors of the draft, a system that ensures that every year each team has a chance to select fresh young college men to add to their rosters. Reeves saw Dad's methods as a slap to his main contribution to professional football. This summer Reeves had not yet been to Rams training camp. He'd been released as an outpatient from a New York City clinic, but he still didn't have the energy to return to his home in Los Angeles.

On the last day of training camp, Dr. Rasinski telephoned my mother to tell her about a special TV program on George Allen to be aired that evening. That evening, I saw my father for the first time in months, tan, lean, and limping around the field. Another pulled muscle, I thought. He was blowing his whistle, sweating, looking exhausted even before the season began. A couple of his players slumped off the field.

"Is the team overloaded with veterans who often play well but can't seem to win the big one?" one reporter asked.

Dad's response: "Age is all in your mind."

Then he jogged, hiding his pain, off the practice field for the last time that summer.

"There are few who work quite like Allen," the reporter observed, "and none who enjoy punishing themselves as much."

I was attracted to Dad's self-punishment, his masochistic air, and his martyrdom. I started to think that maybe if I broke a few bones somebody besides Mom would pay attention to me. Later that night, I walked to the top of the driveway and tried to break my ankle. I put my ankle up against the driveway post in a position similar to that of an advanced ballerina—twisting, rotating my ankle and knee outward, while wedging it between the massive driveway stones. My self-absorbed little game paused when Double O's headlights shined on me.

Someone honked the horn. I jumped out of the road. A real hero would have allowed herself to be driven down dead, would have stood up and begged to be run over some more! Call me a champion!

I heard my brother George scream, "Sports!"

My father and brothers went running into the house. Double O greeted me, "Is everything under control?"

When I ran inside, my brothers were watching the late-night sports on the big color TV in the den. I flipped on the little kitchen TV and saw that some famous people in a Beverly Hills home had been found tortured, slaughtered, and murdered, followed by the newscaster announcing another chilling fact: the Rams 1969 football season was about to begin.

"Everything's under control," I told Double O when he came in the house to see if everything was.

"Everything's under control."

The Almost Undefeated 1969 Season

THE LOS ANGELES MEMORIAL Coliseum was a modern replica of the Roman Colosseum where the upper classes watched members of the lower classes fight each other to the death and where people of the wrong faith were destroyed by wild animals. Rams games were not much different. Inside the massive ellipse-shaped arena, the rich and the famous came to witness a weekly Sunday bloodbath while laughing back fistfuls of peanuts and gulping down cupfuls of ice-cold Coke. On the eastern end of the field, a twenty-foot-high cast-iron Olympic torch stood in the keystone-marble arch set along a series of arches that formed a peristyle. To the west, a constant flock of lost seagulls hovered, awaiting the game's end, when they would swoop into the stands to scavenge for scraps of leftover trash.

Since 1924, the Coliseum had hosted one Olympiad, one World Series, and the first Super Bowl. General George Patton marched his troops through the stadium in a victorious World War II celebration. President John Kennedy gave his Democratic convention acceptance speech on the fifty-yard line. When my father led his Rams onto the field for the first time that season, he expected a standing ovation from the otherwise lukewarm, seen-it-all, Hollywood Rams fans. "If I don't get a standing ovation, I've failed," my father told reporters. "Standing ovations, they're reserved for generals, presidents, and kings," my father reminded his team at the first game of the season.

Heading up the freeway, on the way to Rams games, I was always the first to spot the Coliseum's unlit torch looming high above the urbanscape: higher than the nearby neon Felix the Cat car-dealership sign, higher than the nearby Egyptian-like Shrine Auditorium, and even higher than the several hundred tall Royal palm trees that had been planted fifty years before in an Olympian effort to bring some grace to the city of Los Angeles. I knew that the torch burned only during the Olympics, but some nights, after games, I would stand on our balcony looking down over Los Angeles and think I could see the flickering flame burning twenty miles away. It was my brother George who pointed out that I was looking at a refinery chimney burning off a tall flame of gas.

If the traffic backed up on the freeway, Mom got off a couple of exits early. Dad had already arrived at the stadium hours before with the boys and Double O. In our auspicious, newly refabricated, Rams-horned mock chariot, Mom cut down one-way streets the wrong way in a rush to get to the Coliseum two hours before kickoff. We drove through neighborhoods fronted with chain-link fences and collapsed porches. Rows of the houses had been burned through to the roof. Many of the players were born in communities like the one surrounding the Coliseum. Just as football delivered young men from the coal mines of West Virginia and the steel mills of Pittsburgh, it delivered young men from L.A.'s broken squalor of Watts, Compton, and Inglewood. People who couldn't afford a three-dollar ticket for a nosebleed seat in the Coliseum lived in its shadow. From the front seat of the Toronado I saw kids half my age holding handmade signs pleading for us to park in their driveway for fifteen cents. Mom pointed to the free season-ticket VIP-parking pass stuck to the inside of our windshield and drove on.

As soon as Dad was hired by the Rams in 1966, he visited these neighborhoods on his welcome-to-L.A. self-guided tour. He would direct Double O to drop him off anywhere in Watts, and Dad would get out of the car, walk up, shake the hand of the first person he'd meet, and say, "Hi, I'm George Allen, head coach of the Los Angeles Rams. I think we're going to bring your town a winner." People looked at him incredulously. Who was this nut? Was he running for political office? Dad's visits coincided with the first anniversary of the Watts riots. Dad knew that. He told people that he believed that football could heal the city's riot-torn wounds. He believed that only sports could mend people's lives. "Take a look at my own life," he told them. "My father once lived on the streets, drinking, gambling, looking for a job, just like this, in Detroit during the Depression." Dad told them that his childhood hero was the boxer Joe Louis. Joe Louis symbolized the risen black man victorious over the white man. Dad respected that. So did some of the men Dad met. The Rams' front office thought Dad was naïve, making a fool of himself and his team, going around town like a traveling salesman. Dad wasn't afraid of the front office's opinion. He wanted more Rams fans. He passed out Rams T-shirts like the ones my brothers wore to his sidewalk-converted Rams fans. Dad said it never hurt to see a white kid and a black kid both wearing T-shirts that read, LA RAMS!

Arriving at the Coliseum, Mom would park our Toronado alongside the many other official team Toronados. She'd comb her hair in the mirror, get out of the car, and then head to the tunnel leading down into the locker rooms and wait for David "Deacon" Jones.

I was terrified of David "Deacon" Jones. Standing almost six feet six inches tall, weighing in at 250 pounds, Deacon was the black defensive end who invented the deadly "head slap." At the snap of the football, Deacon charged ahead with fast legs, with quick hands that slapped heads this way and that, knocking some off balance, knocking others unconscious, as he made his way to reach his prey—the quarterback—whom he'd trounce to the ground in one perfect sack. Combined with the fact that Deacon could run the 40 faster than guys half his size, quarterbacks and opposing linemen alike feared him. Deacon's head slap was so lethally effective that the league eventually officially had the slap outlawed. After that, Deacon changed his tactics. He created a vast arsenal of moves. And, in time, he came to rely on his breathtaking speed and quick agility to get through the offensive line even faster and with a deadlier precision to execute his quarterback sacks.

The networks liked to replay Deacon's sacks in slow motion; they reminded me of the fast leopard taking down the pathetic gazelle on *Animal Kingdom*. Even up against scrambling quarterbacks such as Johnny Unitas and Fran Tarkenton, Deacon was on them, sacking them into a heap of stretched-out jersey and sticking-out shoulder pads. Then Deacon would extend one of his massive hands to help the guy up. There was something less than friendly about the way he did it. It was more like, "Get up, I want to knock you down again." Deacon once said, "There were some quarterbacks I liked to sack, and some I wanted to kill." Although sacks were not officially recorded until seven years after Deacon retired, statisticians have tallied up Deacon's total to be 180 sacks. "That's one hundred and eighty quarterbacks shitting in their pants," my brother Bruce explained to me.

Game days, there would be Deacon in his street clothes at the entrance of the locker-room tunnel, looking for someone in the crowd.

"Deacon!" Mom would yell. "Hey! Deacon!"

Deacon would turn and see us and smile. "Hey, Mrs. 'Sock it to 'em'!" he'd always say to my mother. "What's happening, little girl?" he'd ask me, his hands reaching out to slap me ten. His knuckles were swollen; his fingers seemed as long as my hands. Terrified, I'd hide behind my mother's burning cigarette.

"Are you going to sock it to 'em, Deacon?" Mom would ask, borrowing the familiar line from the TV show *Rowan & Martin's Laugh-In*. "You going to sock it to 'em, sock it to 'em, sock it to 'em?"

Deacon would laugh and squeeze my mom in a massive hug and answer, "You ain't seen nothin' yet!" Deacon would pat my head and tell me to be a good girl, and then he'd head into the locker room. Years later, Deacon told me that his affection for my mother was based on his deep respect for my father. Deacon said he had once heard my father reprimand my brothers for avoiding their many duties at summer training camp. "You don't see Deacon shirking his responsibilities," Deacon heard my father say. "How do you boys expect to grow up to be like Deacon if you keep goofing off?" Deacon said it was the first time he'd ever heard a white man view him, a black man, as a role model. After that, Deacon looked to my father for guidance on the field. But off the field, before games, it was my mom he was looking for in the crowd before each game; the "sock it to 'em" exchange was part of his superstitious ritual to guarantee a good game. Once, when he missed her, he was late to the game because he had waited so long for her; Double O had to lead the shaken Deacon down the tunnel wondering if he could play without hearing my mother's "sock it to 'em" chant.

With that ritual finished, Mom grabbed my hand, her big diamond rings digging into my fingers, and dragged me through the turnstile and straight into the women's room. There we lingered, waiting to greet the usual wives: the one with hair perfectly pitched high on top of her head, her clothes perfectly coordinated royal blue and golden gold, her terrified silence as perfectly audible as my mother's as they greeted each other with nervous, shaking head nods. In a slow whisper that she seemed barely able to get out, my mother would lean into the wife's ear and say, "We better beat those goddamn bastards." The woman nodded a sober, all-knowing nod. If we didn't beat the goddamn bastards—who knew? Who knew where we would be in a year, a new team, a new town, a new owner? Who knew if there'd be any team at all? Who knew what the smaller personal consequences would be if we didn't beat those goddamn bastards? Even as a child I knew the history of some of the wives in that ladies' room: the woman who married a football coach mainly because her father had been a football coach; the expensively disheveled woman we believed was quietly drunk all the time; the wife who drank and was addicted to pills, who seemed the happiest of them all, chatting chatting chatting at the mirror and retying her Rams gold-and-blue JCPenney scarf fifty times. Then there was the unlucky wife the other wives for some reason stayed away from, whose husband had changed jobs seven times in seven years, making a joke that seven was lucky, no one able to bear it if it wasn't. The league called these women "the wives," and I had a sense that my mother did not number herself as one of them. She was the head coach's wife, and secretly, she later told me, she was afraid to befriend the other coaches' wives in case my father had to fire their husbands at the end of the season. Plus she was French and she had naturally curly hair. She strutted out of the women's room, her nostrils flared, her nose held high above the perfume, the cigarette smoke, the hair spray, and the fear.

Once out of the women's room, we'd spot Henry Fonda with his binoculars tucked under his arm, heading through the turnstile. We'd see Elizabeth Montgomery with her bag of peanuts, heading into the women's room. We'd see Michael Landon, laughing with the Dixieland-band members who stood at the stadium gates, blowing trumpets and beating drums, welcoming fans into another great season of the Los Angeles Rams. We'd see the same program sales boy from last year—this year with a little more facial hair, his voice a little deeper, yelling, "Programs, here, get your programs!"

Then we would head down the long, unlit, cinder-block tunnel to our seats. Our tunnel was Tunnel 8, and it led to fifty-yard-line seats. It was so dark the only light was the light beyond the tunnel leading us all out into the sunny stands. The tunnel was so long, I could barely hear Jim Nabors singing the "Star-Spangled Banner." My mother never stopped walking when she heard the national anthem. She walked faster, pulling me along, my kneesocks falling to my ankles. Several fans would be stopped, holding hands to hearts in the dark. One never failed to yell, "Hey, lady, there's a war in Vietnam! Slow down, what's your hurry, show some respect!" She never slowed down. If we were hearing the national anthem, we knew we were late. We'd come running out of the tunnel, and then, and only then, would we stop, stunned every time by the size of the stadium that averaged some eighty thousand fans belting out,

"And the home,
  of the,
    braaaaave!"

Air horns blew. Programs flew. Pom-poms shook. We'd take our seats
side by side and give a wave to Gregory, who chose to sit in a seat several
rows away, alone in the stands. Gregory didn't like the sidelines. He said he
preferred the stands because the view was better. Mom said he preferred
the stands because he didn't like the violence on the field. Now Gregory
waved at us. We'd wave back, deliriously happy to be at the game at
last. All the firings, and rehirings, and lawsuits, and highlight films, and
front-yard pile-ons—it all came down to this: the moment the coin is
tossed and the call is made: heads or tails? Now our family could coach,
scream, smoke, cry, and pray that somehow we'd remain united, married,
and alive in one place under one roof for one more year if we could only
do one thing that day, beat those goddamn bastards.

I felt I had a purpose then. I wasn't a grade-school girl in a white lace
blouse and a fake leather miniskirt, chain-gnawing down my chocolate cigarettes. I wasn't a superstitious child rubbing her miniature gold football
locket on her skirt's belt loop in hopes of bringing her team good luck. I
wasn't the daughter of the head coach, the kid at school who knew more
than most kids about football and a little less than most kids about the other
wars going on in the world—Vietnam, civil rights, Charles Manson. I was
a fan. I could intuit what play would be called next. I could call penalties
before the referee. I believed I could psychically disrupt the opposing quarterback's audible calls, making them incomprehensible to his offensive linemen, throwing linemen off-sides. And I was never happier than I was then,
just another fan in the Coliseum, rooting for the 1969 Rams.

The Rams won in 1969.

By the eleventh week of a fourteen-week season, the Rams had won
eleven games in a row. We were the only undefeated team in the league.
My father's prediction that the Rams would go undefeated seemed about
to come true. We had clinched the NFC Western berth in the play-offs.
And my father's wish for standing ovations was granted. At every opening
kickoff, and at the end of every home game as the team jogged off the
torn-up turf, the Rams fans stood and cheered.

From victories on the road, Dad brought me snow globes of each con-
quered city: Baltimore, Atlanta, Chicago, Green Bay, and Philadelphia. I set

the snow globes together as a sort of shrine on my night table: snow globes, Rams pom-poms, and a black-and-white photograph of the handsome, part-Filipino Rams quarterback Roman Gabriel, starring as a Native American in the recently released western *The Undefeated*. Gabriel had become my favorite player, a man I thought maybe someday, if I had to, I would marry. On the field, he was my father's kind of hero—a born leader who would be named the NFL's Most Valuable Player in 1969. Off the field—in the film, anyway—he played the very image of the kind of man my father despised: a disobedient, long-haired, poncho-covered drunk, tossing a shot of tequila over his shoulder in a fit of boredom while a cigarette stub singed his dirt-filled fingernails. That season I counted each victory for the Rams and Gabriel and Dad as a victory for me.

At school, no one called me a loser.

"Have you met Deacon Jones?" the bully in the class would ask. "Did he really cremate that guy's head?" Yes, yes, and yes, I'd answer. Then the bully would let me in on a game of all-boy kickball.

The girls were more interested in my postgame rendezvous at Matteo's bar. There, after home victories, Dean Martin would greet us with cigarette and martini in hand. Dean had been to the game earlier that day. He'd beaten us to the bar. He'd tell my father, "Great game, George," then want to discuss Dad's reason for calling a draw play on third-and-long. For the girls, I'd continue my own version of what happened next: Dean asking me what I wanted to drink. "A Shirley Temple?" the bartender would suggest. "Give the girl a Martin," the tall, dark Dean would say. "Give the girl a virgin Dean Martin!" And then, as I sipped my sweet drink, he'd sing, "Everybody loves somebody sometime." That's what I told the girls on the playground. The Brownies enclosed me in their circle of secret friends.

At Matteo's, after many cheers, and many handshakes, and many rounds of milk "on the house," my father would drive us down the desolate Sunday freeway home. Double O would have gone his separate way hours before in his Rambler, our whole family now in the Rams Toronado. My three brothers would fall asleep in the back. I'd slump up against Dad, using his shoulder as my pillow. He'd say, "Why don't you stretch out, relax," and I'd kick off my game-day shoes, collapse my head onto Mom's lap, and put my feet across Dad's lap. I'd feel the steering wheel skim my ankles. I'd try not to sleep because I never wanted this moment to end: this feeling that Dad was safely in control of our lives, that everyone was content, and that Mom was at peace. But I could never stay awake. I'd fall asleep, wishing, dreaming that our victories would never come to an end.

A Meaningless Game

THE TWELFTH GAME of the season was to be played in Los Angeles against the Minnesota Vikings. The Vikings, like the Rams, had already earned a berth in the play-offs. A win or a loss would not affect either team's chance to advance nearer to the Championship. Reporters called the game a "meaningless game," a "nothing game," a "pointless contest." My father scoffed at their ignorance. "There is no such thing as a meaningless game," my father said. "Every game is the biggest game of your life." In turn, reporters noted that Allen was putting unneeded "emotional strain" on the players. Shouldn't Allen allow veterans like Deacon Jones to take the game off? Shouldn't the coach be thinking about resting Gabriel's arm? Remember the start of last season, the reporters said, when Allen revved emotions so high that by the end of the season the team was emotionally strung-out and physically spent? That was the thing I had to learn about reporters: even when you were feeling a little bit better about your place in the world, they always pointed out some little flaw that could put an end to your short-term happiness. Even if you had failed to notice the problem, a sportswriter was always there, like a hovering conscience, to remind you of your troubled past and all your worst possible failings in the future. For the upcoming game against the Vikings, the reporters predicted a disastrous yet meaningless loss for the Rams.

At the game, fans such as Senator Hubert H. Humphrey and California governor Ronald Reagan sat cramped in the stands, while reporters sat, where they always sat, in the best seats in the house—in the press box, a Plexiglas-enclosed booth situated at the highest point in the stands. I once climbed the several hundred steps up to the box and stood outside its security-locked door just to see what the world looked like from above. It was miraculous—a view second only to that from the Goodyear blimp—and I decided right then that if there were a God, he had only to peek over the shoulders of the sky-high reporters in the Coliseum press box to check our tallies of Win, Loss, and Tie to figure out when we might be in need of one of His miracles that Deacon, Roman, and my father could not always provide.

Dan Reeves sat in the press box along with the other front-office executives. He would arrive at the game unnoticed and take his seat in the box, as the rest of the front office toured the pregame sidelines, shaking players' hands, before making their drunken, foot-slipping way up the steps to the press booth. After the game, Reeves would leave the stadium as unnoticed as he had arrived. He was a mysterious creature that 1969 season. We would hear that he had attended a game. We would hear about him going out with some reporters and throwing back a few drinks after a game. We would read about it all in the sports pages. But Dad never saw the man. Only reporters confirmed sightings. Reeves had a lot of reporter friends in Los Angeles. Reporters wrote that Reeves was in recovery, with an energetic spirit and a quick wit. Still, by the end of the season, before the game against the Vikings, Reeves had returned to the New York clinic where he would remain, too sick to attend any more games.

After the so-called meaningless Vikings game, it was my father whose health appeared to wane. Reporters described my father as "white with pain," and "as if he had been shot in the stomach," and with the look of an "undertaker." The Rams had lost to the Vikings, 10 to 7. In the postgame locker room a reporter tried to look on the bright side. Perhaps now the pressure to have a perfect, 14-0, undefeated season had been lifted. "Pressure?" my father replied. "Pressure? We *like* pressure, we *want* pressure, people who don't like pressure ought to be *dead*!" Another reporter suggested maybe the coach could take an evening off from football, go out and enjoy himself for a change. "Enjoy myself?!" my father shrieked. "Nobody should go out and enjoy himself after a loss. This is no time to enjoy yourself."

My mother and I listened to the interview broadcast from a fan's transistor radio in the locker-room tunnel.

"I have no words of wisdom," my father said. "Go to the Vikings' locker room. You can get your words of wisdom there."

My mother and I waited for what seemed like several hours for my father to appear. We waited standing beside the woman who had her transistor radio positioned on the child's seat of a shopping cart filled with homemade brownies. We called her the Brownie Lady for all the brownies she made for every Rams player and every Rams coach, each one individually wrapped in a paper towel, each one individually marked with the man's name. She was a short, stocky woman with an eye patch that she constantly readjusted with thick stubby fingers. My father once offered her free tickets to the games, but she declined. She believed that her listening to the games on her transistor radio was bringing the Rams good luck. Dad thought her brownies were bringing the Rams good luck. When my father exited the locker room, he never failed to stop to talk to her before greeting anyone. When I watched him, so at ease with her, I thought, she must be like his mother, my grandmother, whom I only met once. Hours after the Vikings game had ended, the Brownie Lady stood, loyally waiting along with us. In her shopping cart, only one brownie remained, marked COACH ALLEN.

I had wanted to go home with my brothers George and Gregory, who caught a ride with Double O, but my mother told me, "No, your father will be glad to see you." The longer we waited, the more I feared the long drive home with my father. When the stadium lights shut off, the tunnel went completely dark, and I could not even see my mother beside me. I reached for her hand, and the Brownie Lady took mine in hers. Her palms were rough as tree bark. She told me, "Hold still. Your eyes will get used to the dark." A rat ran up the ivy-covered walls, and I could hear haunting sounds of the last tall rusted Coliseum gate creaking shut, and the lonesome sound of a siren shrilling through a nearby neighborhood. Fog was coming in around us. I was cold and hungry. I eyed the brownie marked COACH ALLEN.

"There he is!" the Brownie Lady whispered, and there, through the weak light breaking through the fog, I could make out the faint impression of my father's hunched walk through the locker-room doors and up the tunnel's ramp.

My brother Bruce followed close behind.

I stepped up to greet my father, and he walked right past me.

When the Brownie Lady offered him his brownie, he said, "I don't deserve it."

My mother followed my father, and the Brownie Lady handed the brownie to me, saying, "Tell him, next week, I'll make his with walnuts, maybe that will bring us good luck." I took the brownie and followed my parents and my brother to our car. Once we were all in the car, with Mom and Dad up front, and Bruce and me in the back, I blurted out, "We're still in first place! We still have the best record in the National Football League!" I was about to add, "It's only your fifth loss in forty games!" when my brother Bruce elbowed me in the head. Dad put the key in the ignition. He started the car. He sighed. He said, "Jennifer . . ." As soon as he said "Jennifer," I knew I had made a big mistake. "Jennifer," he said, "after a loss like this, those other games don't mean a damn thing."

Dad started the car again. The engine made an awful screeching sound. Mom lit a cigarette.

Bruce began to read the play-by-play aloud. "Coin toss, Vikings versus Rams . . ."

Bruce's voice was hoarse and tired from screaming at the referees. All the long way home I listened to Bruce replay every play of the longest night of my life. The seemingly abstract words—"clipping," "off-sides," "face mask"—took on a gravity I had never heard before. Each word was ripping a limb off my Dad; each word was tearing an organ from his gut. "Every time I lose," Dad often said, "I die a little." That night, I saw a bit of my father die. I had misunderstood the importance of this game. Dad had talked to me like I was just another reporter. I felt like one. An outsider, a betrayer, a dunce.

Then I noticed that I had absentmindedly eaten Dad's entire brownie, without offering him a single bite.

Joy to the World

CHRISTMAS EVE, Mom was sitting at the kitchen table, writing Christmas cards to "hypocritical sons of bitches" who sent us the same. Our kitchen windows were draped in Christmas cards from teams around the league—colorful team photos of every coach who had, at one time or another, knocked us out of the play-offs, or out of the Championship, or even out of a job. There were also cards from coaches' families, expensive portraits of families dressed all alike in reds and greens and golds. Most of

the cards had not a handwritten word on them, only an expensive em-
bossed greeting that read "Happy Holidays" or "Joy to the World."
"Happy Holidays from the Minnesota Vikings," Mom would read aloud.
"Happy Holidays, my ass, they hope we rot in hell."

After the Vikings defeat, the Rams lost the next two games. One reporter wrote, "The emotional system of the team has broken down." Another one predicted, "George Allen's Rams seem to be on an emotional
crash course headed for destruction." In a couple of days, on December
27, we were scheduled to play the Vikings again, this time in Minnesota
for the NFC Western Conference Championship. Dad had left for Minnesota with the Rams several days before. He wanted his Southern California team to become acclimated to playing in a blizzard.

Now Mom sat at the kitchen table, writing out Christmas greetings on
our Thrifty Drug Store card: a photograph of our dog Hilda with a bone
in her mouth. "Happiness is . . ." the message read, "the George Allen
Family." Mom had wanted to have a family picture gathered around the
Christmas tree, but we had waited until that Christmas Eve morning to get
one. There were only a handful of picked-over spruces and pines remaining in the Boy Scout tree lot. The best of the worst leftover trees was pathetic; its weak limbs couldn't hold up even the cheapest of Christmas
ornaments. Mom made sure to decorate the tree with things we kids had
made years before in kindergarten—torn egg-cartons, broken pine cones,
faded photos. She dragged the ornaments out every year, held them to her
breast, asked, "Do you remember making this?" and then would begin to
cry. Mom cried a lot around Christmas. She said Christmas always brought
some kind of tragedy. Christmas of 1939, her fiancé died. Christmas of
1943, her father was taken away by the Nazis. Christmas of 1949, she
broke up with my father. Christmas of 1950, the coach proposed marriage. Christmas of 1965, George Halas sued us. Christmas of 1966, we
lost to the Green Bay Packers in Los Angeles. Christmas of 1967, we lost
to the Green Bay Packers in Green Bay. Last year, Christmas of 1968, Dan
Reeves fired my father. "Christmas," she said this Christmas. "Do you see
why I hate goddamn Christmas?"

Still, she went through the Yuletide motions. She hand-signed each
Christmas card. She decorated the house with plastic mistletoe, dusty velvet toy reindeers, and moth-eaten homemade felt stockings. She wanted
to like Christmas—I could see her straining to enjoy the holiday as she

pounded out holiday song after holiday song on the baby grand piano, "Joy to the World," "Silver Bells," "Holy Night"—but she chain-smoked through each melody, and I could see that she no more believed that a virgin could give birth than she did that Christ died for sins we had not had a chance to commit yet. "And why would God have his only son killed?" she asked me while I addressed a card to the Dan Reeves family.

Mom said she did not believe Jesus was the son of God. But I could tell she still wanted me to believe in Santa Claus. I was a couple of weeks away from my ninth birthday, and I still liked to believe I believed in Santa Claus. But that Christmas, all the mystery and wonder of Santa was replaced by a blank scoreboard: would we win, or would we lose? If we won in Minnesota, we were headed to the Super Bowl in New Orleans. If we lost, we would have Dad home, two days late, after Christmas. Then, we would have to watch Dad coach another runner-up, better-luck-next-year-coach Pro Bowl.

"Hey, you boys," she screamed, finishing her last card for the evening, "you all better go to bed soon if you want Santa to come!"

George and Bruce were stretched out across our two new leather couches waiting for sports to come on the TV. George chewed tobacco. Bruce ate uncooked ravioli out of the can. Gregory was outside, sneaking cigarettes, nearly electrocuting himself decorating the house with strings of broken lights.

"Sports!" George screamed.

I sprang to the TV . . . Channel 2, Channel 4, Channel 9, Channel 7, Channel 11, Channel 5.

"It feels a lot warmer than eleven degrees!" Dad was saying cheerfully, standing on a snow-and-ice-covered field in St. Paul. Behind Dad, special machines were blowing snow off the field at the rate of ten tons a minute. A six-foot snowdrift had blocked the locker-room door earlier that day. Dad laughed it off: "A little snow never hurt anybody!" The reporter, dressed in earmuffs, a wool overcoat and scarf, and huge leather gloves, informed my father that the forecast was for five inches of snow at kickoff.

Dad turned the cotton collar of his golf shirt up around his neck. "Weather is a state of mind," he said.

The camera scanned the practice field to show the Rams cowering in a huddle, hands tucked into pants, flimsy, floppy golf caps on their heads. A couple of them stamped their feet, blowing their breath into their cupped hands. Double O passed by, smoking a cigarette, carrying a stack of snow-covered game films. Earlier that day Double O had put tall tarps up around the chain-link practice-field fence to keep the other team's spies from watching practice drills. Now the tarps were collapsing under the weight of the drifting snow, their torn ends flapping in the wind.

The sports edition ended with a shot of my father jogging across the field with a miniature Christmas tree in his arms. The reporter indicated that the tree had been given to the coach by a former Miss Minnesota, who had been born in Los Angeles and claimed to still be a Rams fan at heart. Dad looked happier than I had ever seen him look around us at Christmas.

We shut off the TV.

It was late. It was already Christmas in Minnesota.

Coach of the Year

OVER CHRISTMAS, we had scored a few more free TVs from Ram sponsors around the country. Now we had enough TV sets so that none of us had to watch the game together. We could each watch the game on our own TV in our own bedrooms. The last time we all watched a game together, George beat up Bruce, and Bruce beat up Gregory, and I bit my nails, and Mom screamed "Stop, stop, stop!" and held a knife above her head and threatened to kill herself if we didn't stop fighting. For this game, Mom pleaded with me, "Please, watch the game with me, I need you." I gave Mom her stomach pills, her cigarettes, and her ashtray. Then I sat in Dad's bed beside Mom's and held her hand and sipped my milk from my baby bottle.

Kickoff. 21 degrees. Overcast. No wind.

First quarter: Rams 7, Vikings 0.

Second quarter: Rams 17, Vikings 7.

Halftime, we all gathered in the kitchen, devouring bloody scraps of leftover Christmas roast beef. Bruce sucked the strings. Mom ate the gristle. Gregory smoked a cigarette on the balcony. I drank my bottle.

Second half: we watched our lead slowly slip away.

Final score: Rams 20, Vikings 23.

Postgame, we all fell into a deep silence, picking up our Christmas gifts, dismantling the tree, taking down the Christmas cards. We knew the last thing Dad would want to do was to have to celebrate Christmas with us.

That night I vowed never to drink from my baby milk bottle again.

That night I stopped believing in Santa Claus.

That night I heard Mom playing the piano, composing a slow, funereal, end-of-the-season dirge.

The following day, Dad was seated at the breakfast table. The sports headline read, GEORGE ALLEN VOTED NFC'S COACH OF THE YEAR. The votes were cast by sportswriters from every NFL city.

"I don't deserve this award," Dad told us kids. His voice was gravelly. He hadn't shaved. He looked about ninety years old. "My players deserve this award. Without those men, I wouldn't have had the success I've had. I owe everything I have to the Rams."

We all stared at him, there in his pajamas and robe, holding up his empty milk glass. We kept our Christmas gifts for him—a new whistle, a jar of peanut butter, a blue-and-gold striped tie—hidden behind our backs, and later we tucked them away in the attic with the rest of the Christmas decorations, saving them for what we hoped to be a merrier celebration next year.

ALL DAY LONG, the telephone rang. All day long, Dad told reporters, "The season's over. That's behind us. Now I want to get to know my family. Having a father like me has been hard on them. All season long it's football, football, football. Now I'd like to spend some time with my family." Dinnertime, Mom took the telephone off the hook so we could enjoy another leftover Christmas dinner together. When Gregory failed to read Dad's hand signal to pour him another glass of milk, Dad flicked Gregory's arm and said, "Hey, what planet are you on?"

Gregory answered honestly.

"The moon, Dad," he said. "I'm on the moon."

Dad lifted Gregory up by the shirt collar.

"Stand up," Dad said.

"Sit down," Mom said.

Gregory sat back down.

Dad picked up a dinner plate and George stood up. It was the first time I had seen anyone take a stand against Dad. George said, "If you're going to hit him, you'll have to hit me first."

Mom screamed, Hilda barked, and I ran upstairs into my bedroom and into my closet.

Still, from behind my bedroom door and my closet door, I could hear my father shouting and chairs crashing and Hilda barking.

When all the screaming stopped, I came out of my closet and out of my bedroom and heard Gregory crying in the bathroom across the hall from my room. He was crying over the sink, splashing water onto his face and his newly broken nose. I watched the blood swirl down the drain.

"That bastard," Gregory was saying, "that bastard."

Later that night, when the house was quiet, I went to look to see where everyone was. My brothers had all gone off to their own bedrooms. Their doors were closed. No sound of TVs on. No sound of Bruce whispering himself to sleep. Mom was smoking a cigarette alone in the kitchen. Dad, I thought, was down in the basement, watching the Vikings game film. I went back up into my room. I sat on the floor in the dark surrounded by my new Christmas toys: a miniature Rams helmet radio, a Suzy Home-maker Oven, a Minnesota snow globe.

Then I heard Dad ask, "Do you like your typewriter?"

I jumped. I hadn't even heard him come up the stairs.

Dad said, "Do you know how to use that typewriter?"

I shook my head.

I still hadn't tried to use the Royal typewriter Dad had given me the previous Christmas. It had sat on the floor since then, gathering lint and catching moths. Its thin ribbon was worn and torn and faded. Dad showed me how to rethread it. He showed me there was still some good ribbon remaining in the spool. Then he reached into his back pocket, pulled out a Rams notepad, and put a sheet of paper in the typewriter. He tapped on some of the keys. J-E-N-I. The typing sounded powerful. The print looked impersonal. I could type anything, and no one would know who had typed it. I could write anything, and no one would detect my hand-writing. Dad said typing was better than longhand. More legible. He tried to kiss me good night. I pushed him away. "Whiskers," I complained, "your whiskers are rough."

Dad rubbed his face. He looked tired and sad. I felt sorry for him. He told reporters he wanted to get to know his family, and I believed him. He knew little about us. But instead that day he had pushed all of us away.

"Merry Christmas, Dad," I told him, watching him walk out of my bedroom. "Merry Christmas."

1970: *A Silver Anniversary*

DAN REEVES APPEARED thin and gaunt at the 1970 preseason game to celebrate the start of the Rams' silver-anniversary season. Before kickoff, a couple of front-office executives led him gingerly out of the press box and down the long stadium steps to the field, where he received an NFL award for his contributions to professional football. Then, after the brief ceremony, Reeves was escorted off the field and presumably onto an airplane and was flown directly to New York City, where he would spend the rest of the season in a hospital. "A dying owner and a lame-duck coach," one reporter wrote. "This is what the Rams have to look forward to in their silver-anniversary season."

Dad didn't talk to Reeves all season long. Dad had other worries: Would Roman Gabriel and Deacon Jones, who were on and off the bench with injuries, make it through the season? If the Rams didn't reach the Championship, would he be fired again? All I could do was look at the game clock—first quarter, second quarter—waiting for the time to tick away to tell us it was over and our Rams years had ended. Some games, when I couldn't bear to watch the clock, I'd look through the program at the many local advertisements. One moving company ad pictured a football player carried off the field on a stretcher. The slogan read, "We'll carry you anywhere!" It was the same moving company we used when we left the Chicago Bears. For a moment I'd imagine my entire family on that stretcher, being carried away to another team, another town, another owner. For another moment I'd imagine that my entire family was being carried to the grave.

The Rams ended the season in second place, failing to reach the play-offs.

On New Year's Eve, two weeks after the season ended, Dan Reeves telephoned my father at home. Reeves told my father he couldn't talk long. He was calling from a hospital bed.

"It was a cold conversation," Dad told us kids after he hung up the telephone. "No gratitude, no appreciation, no thanks for what I've done."

My father was the most successful coach in Los Angeles Rams history. He had the third-best coaching record among active coaches in the National Football League. Still, that night, Dan Reeves fired my father.

Three months later, Dan Reeves was dead. He was fifty-nine years old. Only six years older than my own father. I had heard how football shortened players' lives, how too many head slaps made a man's speech slow and tongue-thick, how too many tackles made a man's knees wobble and collapse, how years after he played his last game, a Hall of Famer would need a steady supply of pain pills to make it through one day. That night, I saw how football could shorten a coach's life, too. Watching my father's hands fumble with the telephone to dial the number to his lawyer, I wondered how many more years would pass until my father's life was taken by football.

HALFTIME

Father's Day

SIX MONTHS AFTER LEAVING us to sign with the Washington Redskins, our dad came home. The day before Father's Day, Dad showed up at our house in Palos Verdes, fit, rested, and younger-looking than when he had left in January. He had redyed his hair jet black. He said he had changed the entire Redskins training schedule to spend a week with us. But he brought only an overnight bag. In it were Redskins T-shirts for the four of us kids.

The following night, at dinner, Mom was putting candles on the Father's Day cake. She had saved the candles from the last family celebration, her and Dad's twentieth wedding anniversary, which we had celebrated without him. The candles were waxy stubs with anniversary cake still stuck to them. She was having a hard time making them stand up straight. Dad kept wondering about us taking a vacation while he was home.

"Look," Mom said, "the only one who doesn't get a vacation when we take a vacation is *me*. So if you want to go somewhere with the kids, go, it's okay with me. I don't mind. I'd rather stay here than be somewhere else!"

"Why don't you two go somewhere together?" Gregory suggested.

"No, he doesn't want to go anywhere with me," Mom said, and Dad agreed, "No, I don't want . . . I want . . . I want . . . I want us all to go somewhere, all of us somewhere *together*."

Dad reminded us again that he had changed the starting date of Redskins training camp to be with us. We all knew that the start of training camp was the most important date of the year because it signified the official start of football season. Dad said he thought maybe we would go camping, but no one had made an effort even to pull out the free camping gear Montgomery Ward had given us when Dad was named Coach of the Year. He thought maybe we could even get some McDonald's hamburgers and head down to the beach and have a picnic at sunset, he said, but none of us wanted to have to walk down the cliffs to the beach these June days when the peninsula was stuck in a fog bank so thick you could not see across the sand to the waves even in the middle of the day.

"I don't care to go anywhere!" Mom said. "I've got too many things to do here!"

"Like what?" George asked.

"Like *everything*!" Mom said. "Besides," she added, "I'd rather be here than any other place in the whole world."

"Is this the same cake we had for my birthday?" I asked Mom. The cake looked like a leftover birthday-anniversary cake in one.

Mom said, "When you taste it you'll find out."

"No cake for me," George said.

"No cake for me, please, either, Mom," said Bruce.

"What's that?" Greg asked about the brown sauce Mom poured over the cake and ice cream, and I said, "Roast-beef gravy?" and George said, "Oh, is she spoiled!" and Mom said, "Will you all shut up?" and then Dad said, "You are all so gosh-darn rude. Everybody talks at once. One of these days I'm going to send you all up to your rooms for the whole night!"

Bruce spoon-flung some ice cream into my hair. I went to get up from the table to wipe it out, but the tablecloth was caught in my tutu. When I stood, I took the tablecloth with me, nearly dragging everything off the dinner table. It almost spilled my father's milk. "You know, Jennifer," he told me, "you're getting to be as rude as your brothers. You pulled the whole tablecloth up!"

I sat back down. I untucked the tablecloth.

My father never got mad at me. This was one of only two times I remember my father getting mad at me. The other time came when I was twenty-five years old, living in New York City, and had called home to say that I had found a roommate—a boy! My father hung up on me. I thought we had been disconnected. When I called back, my mother answered, telling me, "Your father's very disappointed in you." But I wasn't dating the guy. He was only my roommate. "So what?" my mother replied. "It's a boy, and nice girls do not live with boys." And then she hung up on me, too.

"Who didn't get any?" my mother asked now.

"Maybe Jennifer wants some," my father said.

"No, thank you."

"Did you have any, Jen?"

"No, thank you."

Gregory broke into applause for Mom for her good Father's Day cake, and all of us immediately stood to give her a standing ovation until Dad said, "You know," and the tone of his "you know" told all of us to stop clapping and sit down.

"You know," Dad said, "one of the things that disappointed me today was that I checked the sprinklers, and all five sprinklers were not working, and not one of you guys even bothered to see why they weren't working."

"Is the water off now?" Mom asked.

"I'll fix them," George said. "Which ones are broken?"

"No, I hired a guy to come," Dad said.

"You mean you hired a guy to come fix them?" George groaned.

"Yeah, he's coming tomorrow."

"I fixed all of them last summer!" George said.

"See," Mom said, "the reason Daddy says that is because he doesn't usually know or take care of or worry about sprinklers. So one afternoon he decides to do it and it becomes a big engineering project. He doesn't know how many times we've had to fix it ourselves, or call somebody, or put up with it!"

"You didn't fix it," Bruce said, "*I* fixed it!"

"Yeah," George said, "all you do is break it, playing baseball like a moron."

"Oh, I really break it playing baseball!"

"All you have to do is walk on them and they break, moron."

"The grass is all dead back there," Dad said. "It must have been broken for six months."

"You know why?" Mom screamed. "I'll tell you why! Because when I turn the sprinklers on, I'm usually too busy to just stand there!"

Dad often just stood there by the sprinkler gauge, hands on hips, staring at the sprinkler spray over the lawn, the leaves, and the flowers.

"When I have the sprinklers on," Mom went on, hacking away at the Father's Day cake, "I also have the washing machine going, or the iron burning, or a pot boiling on the stove—I don't have time to sit and stare off into the sunset—so that's why I have not noticed that for six goddamn months the goddamn sprinklers have been broken!"

"I'm not saying *you,*" Dad said. "I'm saying that the kids are at the stage where no one has a job anymore." Dad would soon be named chairman of the Summer Jobs Program for needy youth in Washington. He thought all us kids should have jobs by now. None of us did. Not even George, who was about to enter his second year in college.

"Just to empty the wastebasket is an argument," Dad said. "That's the stage they're in right now—nobody cares. Nobody has enough thought to even pull a weed out of the yard. And here we are trying to save the house."

When Dad talked about saving the house, what he was really talking about was Saving Mom. My mother once said that through all our moves and my father's changing of coaching jobs—from the Morningside Chiefs to the Whittier Poets to the Los Angeles Rams to the Chicago Bears to the Los Angeles Rams to the Washington Redskins—building family houses was how she kept her sanity. Saving the house was Dad's way of saving Mom's mental health.

"I'd, uh, I'd think maybe it would be, it's a difficult thing," Dad said, "but I think maybe it would be better if you and the kids stayed here for this season, you know? We don't have a house there, we haven't got this house rented, and we don't know what we're going to do, you know? So it might be better, even though it's inconvenient for everyone to stay here this fall, you know, that the kids go to the same schools, and they move after that, maybe, move next year."

No one said anything.

Everyone sat there for a while, not saying anything, until George said, "Stop breathing, Brucie."

Mom put down the carving knife she had been using to saw apart the birthday–anniversary–Father's Day cake. She sat down in her dinner-table chair. She didn't say anything.

"I'm just so gosh-darn busy," Dad tried to explain. "Maybe it would be better for everyone if you stay here while I coach the Redskins."

Dad didn't want any of us. Not even Bruce. He wanted to leave us behind like he had left behind Deacon Jones and Roman Gabriel and Merlin Olsen. He had left Los Angeles with all he needed: thirteen former Rams players, three former Rams assistant coaches, Double O, and Dad's personal, nerves-of-steel secretary, whom Mom had dubbed "George's other wife, Shirley." Dad didn't need us anymore. We hadn't brought him the luck he needed to win the Championship in Los Angeles. Why drag us across the country to Washington, where we'd probably bring him more bad luck and be nothing more than loud distractions he would have to come home to and have dinner with?

Then Bruce started singing "Happy Father's Day," and Gregory and George and I joined in, and we passed out the Father's Day gifts. On Father's Day we all got gifts. I got a Nerf ball. Bruce got a T-shirt. Gregory got some socks. George got something that needed batteries. Dad got a plastic photo cube of our family to take with him to Redskins summer-training camp. George took it out of Dad's hands, looked at it, and said, "God, are you people ugly! Don't ever tell me I'm ugly!"

Dad gave Mom a box and said "Happy Anniversary, I mean, Father's Day," and she opened the box and inside was an enormous diamond ring.

Mom looked at the ring.

"Over my goddamn dead body are you leaving me here alone with these kids!" she said.

Within two days, the boys were shipped to Redskins summer-training camp, my mother returned the diamond ring, and the movers came. The movers shipped half our stuff into storage in Virginia; the other half they packed, moved, and stacked into our three-car garage in Palos Verdes. My mother had decided not to sell the house, or lease the house, or even find a house sitter for the house. She decided to leave a few things there—a couch, a chair, the beds, "just in case we want to come back."

My mother's parents had recently given her the sole surviving souvenir from their bomb-rattled home in Tunisia: a crystal chandelier. On the day the movers packed up the last of our belongings, my mother asked one of the men if he could be so kind as to hang the elegant chandelier in the dining room. The rosette, in the center of the ceiling, had remained empty for the three years we had lived in the house.

"There," she said to me, regarding the hanging chandelier, "isn't that beautiful?"

We stood there staring at the chandelier hanging alone in the dining room, where, to this day, our family has never once eaten a dinner together. Mom began to cry. "Don't worry," she said, wiping her eyes, and added, as if talking to herself, "we can always come back."

THIRD QUARTER

Redskin Park, 1971 Season

REDSKIN PARK WAS a six-acre site carved out of the Virginia forest at the end of a dead-end road called Redskin Drive. About twenty-five miles from downtown D.C., the Park's nearest neighbors were a row of unmarked warehouses. The main, two-story red-brick building, with THE REDSKINS scrolled across the facade, contained over twenty thousand square feet of offices, meeting rooms, locker rooms, training rooms, weight rooms, and film rooms. There were windows only on the second floor, ensuring that no passerby could peek in on the team while at work. A ninety-car parking lot guaranteed employees ample, free, no-tow-away parking. Behind the building were two practice fields: real turf and Astro-Turf. Both fields were girded by an eight-foot chain-link fence on the street side, and on the other side by a forest of trees over fifty feet high. No one could set foot in the building or on the practice field unless given clearance by either my father or Double O. During off-hours, Double O paced the chain-link tarp-covered fence, warding off any onlookers. During practice, Double O sat with binoculars on the roof of a neighboring warehouse, keeping watch for spies by ground or by air. During team meetings, Double O zipped by on his one-speed bicycle, scanning the parking lot for trespassers. Redskin Park had the secrecy of the CIA with the aura of a mental institution. Reporters called the Park "the Bunkers," "Camp Paranoia," and "Fort Allen." Dad called it "Shangri-La."

When reporters asked Redskins president Edward Bennett Williams if he thought the $500,000 price tag of Redskin Park was exorbitant, Williams replied, "I gave George Allen an unlimited expense account and he has already exceeded it." Along with the unlimited expense account, Williams had given my father the most lucrative coaching contract in the history of the NFL—a seven-year deal with an annual salary of $125,000—and an option to purchase 5 percent of Redskins stock—and the full authority of being both head coach and general manager, which allowed him to sign players, cut players, and trade players, as well as negotiate each player's salary. Money, to my father, was not a concern. Winning was—and Washington had not had a championship winner since the Korean War. "I think it's important to have a place the players can call home," Dad had explained to Williams when he received the bill for Redskin Park. "Here we have everything under one roof. Here we have everything we need to succeed. This will be our home."

My mother and I had been living in our new home—the Dulles Airport Marriott, ordering our meals from room service—for several weeks with Hilda and a six-week-old German short-haired puppy named Dixie. When we first toured Redskin Park, the regular season had not yet begun, and Dad and his Redskins were still living at summer training camp, a couple of states away, in Carlisle, Pennsylvania. Guiding us through the double-locked doors of the building, Dad's secretary, Shirley, spoke in a whisper, as if someone might be listening. She pointed out the new oil-painted portraits of Edward Bennett Williams, First Vice President Jack Kent Cooke, and one portrait of the late Vince Lombardi, the former coach of the Redskins, who had died the year before. There was another portrait of the team founder, the late George Preston Marshall. In the center of them all was my father, Head Coach and General Manager George Allen. The paintings vaguely resembled the real men. Still, looking up at those men looking down on me, I felt slightly intimidated by their glossy, self-assured expressions. With every step up the stairs, we were coming closer to the heart of the matter at hand—my father's new home office, where, for the next seven football seasons, he would reside sixteen hours a day, six days a week during home games, sixteen hours a day, four days a week during away games.

My father's office was larger than our living room back in California. The desk was larger than our dinner table. The leather couch was longer than our foyer. On a table beside his desk, Dad had set up our old home-movie projector, stamped PROPERTY OF THE LOS ANGELES RAMS. A special daytime/nighttime movie screen had been installed across the room just beneath a framed black-and-white portrait of Sioux Indian Chief Red Cloud. Chief Red Cloud's descendants had recently named Dad an honorary chief for having helped the tribe set up a football program, scholarship fund, and gym on their South Dakota reservation. "I love the Indians," my father said with tears in his eyes when certain tribes had recently protested the "Redskin" name as racist. "Being called a Redskin is an honor," Dad said, and he even went so far as to change the Redskins helmet insignia from a feathered spear to the profile of Chief Joseph, a Native American chief of the Northwest whose pacifist approach had unified several warring tribes. With his new projector screen, my father could watch a game film without wasting any time getting up to turn off the lights. My father could efficiently study game films for hours without interruption. The office was also equipped with a private bathroom and a small refrigerator filled with milk and ice cream and peanut butter and jam and bread. This way Dad wouldn't waste any time walking down the hall to the men's room or driving anywhere for breakfast, lunch, or dinner. While my mother studied the height of the bathroom counter and the placement of tiles in the shower floor, I took a seat in my father's tall leather chair.

The chair tilted and swiveled this way and that. I tilted the chair backward and put my feet on his desktop. Then I dropped my feet and swiveled the chair backward, and there, looking out the office windows, I could eye the two practice fields encircled by a track and, positioned between them, on the fifty-yard line, the tallest filming tower I had ever seen. For an instant, I felt the power of being my father, George Allen, the guy who ran the entire Redskins enterprise on the fuel of peanut-butter-and-jelly sandwiches and the open-ended Redskins expense account of Edward Bennett Williams. I swiveled back around and put my feet up on his desk again. No distracting family portraits cluttered the desk, only one sign that read, IS WHAT I AM DOING OR ABOUT TO DO GETTING ME CLOSER TO MY OBJECTIVE—WINNING? Here I was George Allen, with two women, my wife and my secretary, at the foot of my desk, and at the tips of my fingers a complicated telephone system with so many hold buttons that I could put every owner and coach and reporter involved in the National Football League on hold, or, if I desired, disconnect each and every one at once.

"One thing about George," my mother was saying to Shirley, "he always knows what he wants, and he knows how to get it."

My mother was smoking, using her cupped hand as an ashtray as she motioned my feet off the top of my father's desk and then me out of the chair. We followed Shirley through the rest of the upstairs, through the "war room," a.k.a. the draft room, where the walls were already covered with floor-to-ceiling charts indicating every top college player's statistics, and where the tables were covered with telephones, and where there was not one single chair because sitting down was not conducive to thinking on your feet during Dad's war, known as the draft. We passed through the film rooms where canisters of film were stacked and numbered and named along tall shelves painted in Redskins colors, burgundy and gold. We passed through the secretary cubicles, the assistant coaches' offices, and even the men's room. We surveyed the brand-new white porcelain urinals. I had never seen a urinal before. When I stepped closer to study how the thing flushed, my mother yelled at me, "Don't touch that, that's filthy!" and Shirley assured my mother that the urinals were, coach's orders, sanitized twice daily. With the tip of her lit cigarette, my mother ushered me out of the men's room, and I followed Shirley down another staircase and into the weight room, the basketball court, the handball court, the saunas, the whirlpools, the players' locker room, and the coaches' private dressing room, complete with showers and toilets. My mother took a last drag off her cigarette, dropped it into a toilet along with her palm of ashes, and, using her foot, pressed the toilet handle down. We watched the cigarette swirl down the toilet while my mother said an Arabic expression: "May you use it, ruin it, and buy another one." In that instant, my mother had bestowed a blessing upon the entire Redskin Park.

Shirley then took us out to the two practice fields. We did not dare set foot on the real grass. A special scientifically grown sod had just been laid. It was dotted with Q-Tips used to mark spots where the sod did not knit properly, leaving holes and gaps in the turf that might lead to ankle, foot, and knee injuries. Shirley said the sod would have to be ripped out and redone. I asked Shirley how much that was going to cost, and Mom said, "What do you care? Are you paying the bills around here?" The Astro-Turf field appeared perfectly placed. Players would practice on this in the week leading up to away games played on AstroTurf. The league upheld artificial turf as the latest solution to the perils of mud and dirt, key elements that slowed the game down, kept scores low, and stunted ticket sales in cities burdened with bothersome weather. Players hated Astro-Turf: injuries soared on the new plastic grass. Underneath every AstroTurf field is a thick layer of cement. Players said they might as well play their games in a paved parking lot. Compared to AstroTurf, grass cushioned your fall like a pool of water. The Redskin Park endzone was not yet finished. It was still cement—unbearable to even imagine.

"We gals better get moving," Shirley said as she herded us back through the locker-room doors and down the long hall leading to the equipment manager's den. My mother eyed the massive laundry room, where washers and dryers were the size of small cars and where hampers were the size of large beds. Shirley directed us to view the bulletin board that every player had to pass by and regard on his way to throwing in his soiled jersey and pants and jockstrap. The bulletin board was called the "Motivation Board," and the "Vengeance Board," and the "Gripe Board." Here, Double O had posted newspaper clippings from around the country. Clippings degrading the Washington Redskins. Clippings claiming the Redskins would not even go 7-7 this season. Clippings to motivate the team to believe that the whole world of football was rooting against them. My father's main way of motivating was not through praise but through the basic paranoid philosophy of "It's us against them." Also posted on the board was a handwritten note from my father to his men: "We are all a bunch of cast-offs," he reminded his team. "We all have something to prove."

Alongside the clippings was the Redskins 1971 season schedule. I was stunned when I saw the thirteenth game of a fourteen-game season: Washington Redskins vs. Los Angeles Rams in Los Angeles, Memorial Coliseum, December 13, *Monday Night Football*. It did not even occur to me that we would ever have to play against our former Rams. But I now saw that those men Dad had not brought or could not bring with him to Washington—Deacon, Lamar, and Roman—were already looking forward to beating their former coach and friends. Reporters were calling the game "the George Allen Bowl" and predicting that both the Rams' and the Redskins' play-off chances would be decided at that late-season game. When I pointed this game out to my mother, my mother looked at me incredulously, and asked, "Where have you been?"

Our Rams Oldsmobile Toronado had been replaced with a Redskins Lincoln Continental chauffeured by a man named Leroy. Our blue-and-gold team-colored game-day dresses had been replaced with the burgundy and gold team colors of the Redskins. Our Palos Verdes home and Mom's cooking had been replaced with a Marriott airport hotel and Marriott room service. We had made all the adjustments necessary to move from the Rams to the Redskins. This last emotional leap was difficult for me to make.

"You mean we're supposed to hate the Rams?" I asked.

My mother looked at Shirley.

Shirley said, "You don't have to hate them."

Mom instantly corrected her. "Sure you do, I do, I hate those bastards."

A year ago these men were her "babies." Now they were "those bastards."

"Don't worry, you're young, some day you'll understand," my mother said.

I followed her through the Redskin Park doors toward the parking lot, where Leroy stood opening the doors of our air-conditioned limousine, asking, "Home, Mrs. Allen?"

"Home," my mother answered, and soon we were back in our Dulles Airport Marriott hotel room.

The New Kid

I DIDN'T WANT LEROY to drive me to my new school. Leroy would be a dead giveaway that I was the child of someone who either couldn't drive or didn't have time to drive or thought they were too important to drive. No one would ever even know George Allen had a daughter. Dad never mentioned me in interviews anymore. When Washington reporters asked about his family, Dad mentioned only his three sons and the positions they played: George, University of Virginia, quarterback; Gregory, Langley High School, place kicker; Bruce, Langley High School, punter, cornerback, holder, and quarterback.

Back at the Rams, I had often talked about Roman and Deacon, using football as a leverage to make friends. When I left Palos Verdes, they slapped my back, said, "Hope you lose, I mean, win!" I begged them to sign my autograph book, and when they did, I secretly hated every single one of them for liking me only because of my dad. Now there was no reason to talk football. I'd never show interest in any football on the playground, never show I knew how to fade back and make a perfect spiraling pass, never mention the word "Dad" at all.

My mother drove me to school the first day. She skidded our brand-new Redskins-colored Cadillac (burgundy exterior, gold interior) over the NO PARKING curb. I was late. I was late because we had spent the morning fighting over what I was going to wear—"You don't want to look like a hippie slob your first day at school!" she said. I asked, "Why not?" We compromised. I could wear my leather Tijuana sandals that laced around my ankles. But not my floppy hat or peace necklace or bell-bottoms. I had to wear daisy-printed culottes. I hated my culottes: a skirt disguised as shorts.

My mother insisted on taking me to the classroom. She made me hold her hand as we walked down the long school hallway to my fifth-grade class. The door was open. My mother stepped into the room. She wouldn't let go of my hand. "Excuse me," she said, "I'm sorry we're late." The teacher said nothing. She looked bored, then annoyed. She had thick eyeglasses in black frames, and pimples on her fat arms that poked out of a thin, see-through sleeveless blouse. I surveyed the room and had never seen a more sickly group of kids. Everyone's face was pasty white. A lot of them wore glasses, braces, and head braces. They were skinny, shriveled, and unkempt. They were the children of the nation's finest—CIA agents, U.S. senators, and U.S. congressmen—my mother had told me. That's how she had chosen this school. High academic excellence.

"I'm Mrs. George Allen," she said to the teacher, loud enough for the whole school to hear. "This is my daughter, Jennifer."

There it was, "Mrs. George Allen," my future, sealed.

"Mrs. George Allen," the teacher said, "as in *the* George Allen?"

"Yes," my mother replied, beaming.

I ran to find the only empty chair. At a table just beside the teacher's desk.

Before leaving, my mother stopped beside me. "Don't I get a kiss?" she asked loudly. The class was waiting to see if George Allen's daughter would stand and give her mother a kiss. "Or has kissing your mother gone out of style?"

A couple of kids laughed.

I refused to budge.

My mother left.

The teacher resumed roll call. "Allen," she said, "Jennifer Allen?"

I could feel the eyes of every kid in the class on me. Their eyes were measuring me up. Could I fulfill their parents' hopes? Could I, the daughter of the coach, take them to the Super Bowl? Could I make them feel like their life was worth living?

I put my head down on the desk.

"Miss Allen," the teacher said, "when I call your name, I expect an answer."

A spit wad hit the back of my neck.

I sat up.

"I'll try again," she said. "Allen, Jennifer, Allen," she said, looking beyond me, across the entire classroom. "Is she here today?"

"Here," I said, raising my head, "I'm here."

She still looked beyond me.

I raised my hand high in the air. "Allen," I said, "Here, I'm here, I'm Jennifer Allen."

Renters

PRESIDENT RICHARD NIXON dispatched his aides, John Ehrlichman and H. R. Haldeman, to help my mother find us a home in Washington. The men sat my mother down to a brief lunch at the White House at a small table with a red telephone, a direct line, they told her, to the president. Throughout the lunch, the men kept one eye on the telephone. The men spread out a map of the metropolitan area—Maryland, Virginia, and the District of Columbia. The men suggested Alexandria, Virginia; Potomac, Maryland; and the Watergate apartments as prime places to live. Then the telephone rang. The men folded up the maps. Sent my mother on her way. Mom left the White House, calling Washington a hellhole and a deathtrap and a poor re-creation of Paris, France.

"Washingtonians think their town resembles Paris," she told me. "If Paris passed gas, you'd have Washington."

The area where we finally settled was a few minutes from downtown Washington and a couple of miles from my school, in the town of McLean,

Virginia. McLean was the home of the CIA, Ted Kennedy, and Ethel Kennedy. Downtown McLean looked like something out of the TV show *Mayberry.* Stoplights hung from electrical wires nailed to wooden posts. The lights swung unsteadily in the slightest wind. No shopping malls, no strip malls, only a couple of one-story stores with hand-painted signs that read ESMERELDAS and THE HAMLET. A small supermarket named Giant Food, and a one-pump gas station where a couple of boys my age sat, shirtless, smoking cigarettes by the ice machine. There was no ocean view because there was no ocean. The horizon was a two-lane road surrounded by trees greener than any trees I had ever seen. The oxygen level made me dizzy. The humidity made me slow with the weight of the sticky gnats that hovered around my head.

Our new home was located in a community of town houses called Merrywood-on-the-Potomac. Merrywood was not merry, was not located in the woods, nor was it on the Potomac. It was a luxurious, exclusive neighborhood consisting of eight identical town houses. Each town house had four floors, seven bedrooms, five bathrooms, and one maple tree. Each cost around half a million dollars. The entire complex resembled a large castle. Windows remained shut and sealed. Doors remained closed and double-locked. On occasion, a neighbor appeared. She was an elderly woman, dressed in a silk robe with a flock of shih tzus at her velvet shoes, who came out every evening to retrieve the morning newspaper.

We lived in the "model home," a house completely furnished with expensive antiques, elaborate chandeliers, and fancy velvet window trimmings. In each room an intercom played the same song incessantly, an instrumental rendition of Roberta Flack's "Killing Me Softly." The place smelled like a brand-new car and had the intimacy of a furniture showroom. Everything was perfectly in place. My mother said the home was "good enough." She said she'd rather keep our belongings in storage until she found us a real home. Meanwhile, we tried to make the house our home. We bought an air-hockey table and put it in the living room beside the embroidered couches. We put a basketball hoop above the two-car garage, and we converted the mahogany-floored family room into a tae kwon do training room. We let our dogs, Hilda and Dixie, roam free. One day Hilda snatched the neighbor's most puny shih tzu by the neck. Hilda shook the dog until it was dead. She'd broken the dog's neck instantly, I could see when I studied the poor animal where Hilda had deposited it—in the trash can in our front yard.

Soon, before the season had even begun, we received a Merrywood-on-the-Potomac Neighborhood Association petition. We were the only renters on the property, the association reminded us. We would not have much to stand upon should the association try to evict us for our many violations: unleashed dogs, a basketball hoop, visible trash cans. The letter was signed by neighbors we had yet to meet. Their names reminded me of evil characters from children's rhymes—the Leaches, the Lynches, and the Judges.

Mom refused to take down the basketball hoop, or leash our dogs, or move our trash cans.

Then another day Dixie showed up with a neighbor's Chanel purse. Mom had always wanted a Chanel purse. This one was red alligator with a gold Chanel-insignia clasp. But Dixie had ruined it. She chewed on it under the air-hockey table, using it as a teething bone. On yet another day, a next-door neighbor's plaster cupid fountain was mysteriously stolen, and then spotted, from his top-story window, in our backyard. Still another day, my father was seen "indecently" taking a neighborhood stroll in his robe and pajamas after a long day's work. A couple of days before the season opener, a lawyer rang our doorbell. He served us our eviction papers filed by the Merrywood-on-the-Potomac Neighborhood Association.

Soon, a reporter appeared at our doorstep, asking where we would move next.

My mother invited the reporter in. He was a short man with a big nose and garlic breath. I'd seen his mug shot in the local sports pages. He had seen the coming and going of many coaches and many teams in Washington. The Redskins were the only sports team in town. The baseball team, the Senators, had left long ago. There was no hockey team. No basketball team. Only the Washington Redskins. The guy was obviously desperate for any story, even one as insignificant as where the new head coach lived. Mom showed the reporter an aerial photograph of our home in Palos Verdes.

"This is why I haven't found us a home here yet," she told the reporter. "Because nothing can replace our *real* home."

The reporter noted that Redskins president Edward Bennett Williams had mentioned his growing concern over our decision to keep our home in Palos Verdes. Were we leaving the door open to return to the Los Angeles Rams? the reporter wanted to know. After all, Dan Reeves was dead. The new Rams owner, Carroll Rosenbloom, might be someone with whom Allen could work well, the reporter observed.

"It's none of anyone's business how many homes I have," my mother informed the reporter. She then announced that she planned on leaving Merrywood as soon as possible. She told the reporter she was going to build us another home in Washington. It was news to me. I thought we were going to keep our lives simple this time, just move into something already built, not start all over from scratch.

The next day in the sports pages, the reporter quoted a Merrywood neighbor as saying, "I hope the Redskins lose. I do, then that George Allen and his family will be moving soon!"

The reporter also keenly observed, "Mrs. George Allen has enough confidence in her husband's ability to keep a job that she has decided to build a home here in Washington."

"I have enough confidence in me, *period,*" Mom said after reading the article aloud. "I have enough confidence that I can build us another goddamn pièce de résistance!"

But until Mom found the perfect piece of property on which to build her new masterpiece, we would remain at Merrywood-on-the-Potomac indefinitely.

"It's only temporary," she reminded me each time I found another Neighborhood Association warning tucked under the trash can at our front doorstep. "This is only temporary."

"Temporary" lasted four more years.

The Box

"I WANT THREE INTERCEPTIONS, two fumbles, and one cripple," Mom said to Dad.

"Did you hear me?" Mom asked.

Dad nodded his head.

"What do I want?" she screamed.

"Three interceptions," Dad mumbled.

"And?"

"Two fumbles."

"And?"

"One cripple."

"Good," she said, goosing Dad out the front door, "now beat those goddamn bastards!"

It was the day before opening day at RFK Stadium. Dad was heading off to spend the night with the Redskins at the Dulles Airport Marriott. Dad didn't like players to be with their wives having sex the night before a game. Dad didn't like players to be playing with their children the night before a game. The night before a game, Dad wanted everyone under one morose roof. "Wives and kids are fine. But it's the football season now," Dad said as he slid into the Lincoln. "No more distractions!"

We watched Leroy drive Dad away. We waved good-bye in the driveway. Then, once the Lincoln turned beyond the bend in the road, we stopped waving.

"Good riddance," Mom said. "We better win that goddamn game."

The day before game day sent a shock of panic through our house. We called it PGP, short for "pregame panic." PGP meant all rules were off. If Mom told me to do something I didn't want to do, I could tell her to shut up. She, in turn, could tell me to drop dead. My brothers, if they were even around, could be counted on to tell us to go straight to hell. No one took it personally. We went to bed without dinner. Slept, dreaming of bodily dismemberment.

Game day, if the telephone rang, we picked up the receiver and slammed it back down. What idiotic idiot was calling us? Didn't they realize today was game day, biggest-game-of-our-life day?

Game day, Hilda bounded for Dad's closet, where she'd spend the entire day cowering behind his jogging shoes. Dixie disappeared into the woods, gone until after the scores were in.

Game day, Mom made a Redskins good-luck rice-pudding brew. She had invented the idea while watching a French-cooking TV show hosted by a witchlike, crazy-haired chef. Mom cleaned out Hilda's water bowl. She put the cooked rice and the raw eggs and the fresh milk into the bowl, and then she would have me hold my hands on her hands as we stirred the brew with a broken wooden spoon she had often used to discipline my brothers. As we stirred the brew, she had me chant along with her, "Stirring and stirring and stirring the brew, Redskins, devour them! Redskins, devour them!" Then she would pour the concoction into her grandmother's tureen, an ancient piece of kitchenware adorned with faded hand-painted pictures of headless chickens and legless pigs, and slide the potion into an oven set on high. We'd hope that our hex had worked. We'd hope that hours later Dad would be seated at the kitchen table, eating his victory witches' pudding, telling us, "Boy, there's nothing like winning."

Game day, my brothers rode in separate cars to the stadium. No one wanted to ride with anyone. We might have to kill each other if anyone talked, coughed, or sighed.

Game day, Mom had two burning cigarettes, one in each ashtray in the back of Leroy's Lincoln.

Her smoke made me sick. So I'd sit up front with Leroy. He'd crack a window to let in some fresh air. Every few miles, he'd slap my back and ask, "How ya doing, buddy?"

"Fine, buddy!" I'd slap him back. "Fine!"

"Could you shut that window?" Mom would scream up at us. "It's ruining my naturally curly hair!"

Leroy obeyed. The windows went up. Then he checked all the door locks and locked us in.

Leroy was also Edward Bennett Williams's driver. My mother felt that this was a breach of the contract. Mom said Williams had informally promised us a chauffeur when we came to Washington. The contract hadn't specified a private chauffeur, I once told her, and she snapped at me, "What do you know about contracts? When have you ever had a goddamn job that required reading and signing a goddamn contract?"

I wondered if Leroy knew that my mother didn't want him driving us anywhere.

I felt sorry for Leroy. A thankless job, having to be quiet and subservient while driving around "important" men like my dad and Williams. His full name was Leroy Washington, and he'd sometimes joke to me that he was related to the D.C. mayor, Mayor Washington. But when I called him Mr. Washington, he'd always protest. He'd say, "No, no, no, my name's Leroy, Leroy's my name," and then he gave off his loud laugh. He could always laugh. Even if we lost, he managed to sneak a smile at me, or a wink, or a slap on the back. When we discovered that we shared the same birthday, he said we were brother Aquarians. With a laugh and a big hand slap, he said we'd be brotherly friends forever.

My mother thought Leroy was a spy for Edward Bennett Williams. She was certain that anything we said, Leroy would repeat to Williams. She made me promise never to talk to Leroy about anything. Like anything what? I asked. Like *anything,* she said. But then, on the way to games, she would be reeling off uncensored babble in the back of the Lincoln. As we passed by Washington's monuments, she'd scream, "Paris, my ass!" As we headed through the poorer neighborhoods that circled the downtown stadium, she would recite an Arabic expression to thwart the "evil eye." Then, as Leroy veered the Lincoln off the four-lane avenue and down a one-way, one-lane street, she'd shut up. Leroy would tell us he was trying to avoid stadium traffic, but there wasn't any stadium traffic at that time because we always arrived over an hour before kickoff. He would drive the Lincoln down a street lined with seemingly deserted homes. Some had boarded-up windows. Some had broken windows. Some had barred windows. Some had been entirely burned down, only the remains of a brick chimney standing in an empty lot filled with broken bottles and plastic bags. Then suddenly a ghost of a child would appear, tossing a football up into the air. Leroy was trying to show us something, I felt. He never said a word. He remained unflinching behind the wheel as the kid tossed the ball at the back of the Lincoln, knocking the fender as we sped ahead to the waving flags of the stadium, there in the distance, beyond. All along the stadium's uppermost brim, Redskins flags and the American flags waved, side by side, in the high swirling winds.

"Who've you got there?" barked the stadium's gate guard.

The Lincoln idled at the end of a steep ramp, inches in front of a massive steel gate doorway, large enough to fit a sixteen-wheeler truck. The gate guard wore a Redskins windbreaker. The few teeth he had were trimmed with gold.

"Mrs. George Allen, here," Leroy told the guard. The guard peered through Leroy's window into the back of the Lincoln. My mother let out a lungful of her cigarette. Then she asked, "Are we going to beat those goddamn bastards or are we going to beat those goddamn dirty bastards?"

The guard straightened his cap.

"Yes, ma'am," the guard said, "right away, ma'am," and he whistled and another guard appeared, a dwarf-sized man, who helped pull the steel chains that rolled up the massive gates.

We were on field level. I could see the turf, and smell its fresh dirt. I rolled the windows down to get a full sense of this underworld gearing up for the game ahead. A tide of Redskinette cheerleaders gathered around our car. Dressed in white go-go boots and burgundy ice skater–like dresses, hems trimmed with fuzzy fake boas, the Redskinettes linked arms and broke into a frenzied, leg-kicking cancan. A boot hit the side mirror, and I thought it cracked, but the Redskins band engulfed us before I could check. I had read about the history of the Redskins marching band; how it was the first marching band in the NFL, how this group of bartenders and taxi drivers and shoe salesmen volunteered every Sunday to play in the league's last remaining marching band, all for a free ticket into a Redskins game. The band members were dressed in what looked like modified, left-over Santa Claus suits. The brass players wore Indian headdresses; the rest wore simple Redskins baseball caps.

Leroy parked the car beside the Redskins' locker-room doors.

He said he'd meet us when the game was over.

He then led us to the elevator and introduced us to the elevator guard: "This is Mrs. George Allen."

The elevator was empty. We stepped in. Just before the elevator doors closed, I saw Leroy getting into the Lincoln to listen to the game on the radio.

Along the way, the elevator stopped and the doors opened to collect men from various enemy camps: the St. Louis Cardinals coaches, all dressed alike, Cardinals-red wool ball caps, Cardinals birds stitched into the chest pocket of T-shirts, and Cardinals-red polyester bell-bottom coaching slacks. The coaches eyed my mother briefly, then set their gaze on the floor numbers, their faces bearing the common mark of men ready and willing to face their own death. Along the way, referees stepped aboard. Chewing gum and popping breath mints, the referees were a sorry-looking group, dressed in geeky zebralike costumes that fit too tight around the gut and too loose around the neck. The referee's only power resided in the small, bright yellow flag that hung from his back pants pocket, a powerful reminder that this man could, by the mere flick of a wrist, turn a win into a loss or a loss into a win. Along the way, reporters stepped aboard, too. Reporters' eyes always looked as if they had stayed up the entire night before sharpening pencils and threading typewriter ribbons and oiling typewriter keys, all the while second-guessing what they had written in yesterday's sports column, wondering, Had I, could I, did I predict the unpredictable?

Then, a priest stepped aboard. His serene expression made him appear lost, confused, unaware of those who surrounded him. This was the only man who seemed to have nothing at stake in the game. This was Sunday, game day, after all, not Sunday, Mass day. I wondered why he was even here. Then I thought maybe he had come to read the last rites to a dying player or a heartbroken coach on the field.

The elevator was now filled to maximum capacity. A reporter elbowed my head. A referee's flag tickled my neck. A coach stood on my toe.

There would have been more room had my mother not taken up so much space. The men had stepped away from her—sealing her into her own private cloud of Chanel No. 5. With seven gold bangles along her arms, her Hermès scarf tied loosely around the handle of her purse, her skirt to her knees, her legs standing strong in French high heels, my mother gave off a message. "Danger: keep away." My mother was the most confident woman I had ever known. Confidence, she said, was all about standing up straight and believing in yourself. She credited her father with giving her such strength. She said she knew her father loved her, and that was what gave her so much belief in herself. It wasn't that my father didn't love me, it was just that he didn't have the time to consider the question: do I love my daughter? Maybe that was why I had no confidence even to speak up now, crammed in the back of the elevator.

My toe was broken. My neck had a rash. My head ached. I waited until everyone else piled out of the elevator, and then I stepped out last.

"Your shoes are untied!" my mother yelled at me as I hopped on my one good foot out of the elevator. "Comb your hair! Straighten your skirt!"

Then she spotted a reporter trying to sneak past us undetected.

"Excuse me," she yelled out to the waiflike man. "Are you the gentleman who criticized my husband's tactics in the draft?"

Before the waif could fumble an answer, Edward Bennett Williams scooped us into the hook of his arms and escorted us down the long corridor lined with photographs of Vince Lombardi. Lombardi on the sidelines, Lombardi in the locker room, Lombardi at his desk. The photographs stopped at Williams's office doors, where a butler, dressed in a white dinner jacket, asked if we cared for a cocktail, a coffee, a soda. There was a pregame party going on. By the looks of everyone there, tipping back drinks and laughing deep-throated laughs, you'd have thought the game was over and the Redskins had already won. The place was packed wall-to-wall with Williams's friends. I recognized a few—Art Buchwald, Senator Ted Kennedy, Mrs. Vince Lombardi—there were more friends here than we would ever have. Williams had friends with cocktail tumblers, friends patting each other on the back, friends who obediently stopped all drinking and patting and laughing when Williams interrupted them to say, "Excuse me, I'd like you to meet Mrs. George Allen."

For months leading up to this first game of the season, Williams had called my father "the greatest football coach in the league" and even "the greatest football coach in the world." Williams's words pulled a lot of weight in Washington, and when Williams introduced my mother to his many friends, they all appeared sincere when they took her hand in theirs and said, "I am honored." One man quieted down quickly and became daintily polite when Williams introduced Mrs. George Allen. The man took my mother's hand in both of his hands. I was afraid to watch what came next. He kissed her hand. His lips smacked her fingers. Big mistake. I knew she was disgusted. She always said you could tell a cultured man from an uncultured man by the way in which he kissed a woman's hand. She'd tell me, "A cultured man's lips only graze the skin." This guy left a huge wet spot on her hand. He said to her, "I am honored, Mrs. Allen," and my mother nodded her head in an abbreviated royal nod. She then wiped her hand on her scarf, turned to me with a vague smile, and asked, "Should we go to our seats?"

We visited Williams's stadium office only that one time. Even as the season progressed and the temperatures dropped, my mother refused to go again. I begged, just once, could I go to warm my feet? My mother forbade me. "These Washingtonians," she said. "What do they know about football? They think this is just another political game?" She'd shake her head. "This is a war, a goddamn holy war!"

In time, Williams understood; he stopped inviting us entirely.

SEASON TICKETS WERE sold out, year in, year out, whether the Redskins won, lost, or tied. In the early 1970s, a waiting list for season tickets stretched over three thousand names long. The list of season-ticket holders read like a guest list to a bipartisan gathering: Senators Edward M. Kennedy, Robert Packwood, and Strom Thurmond; Mayor Walter Washington; U.N. Ambassador George Bush; *Washington Post* president and publisher Katharine Graham; and Congressman Morris Udall. Most season-ticket holders sat with the general public—in extra-wide twenty-one-inch seats. Some sat in private, forty-two-dollar mezzanine box seats with floorboard heaters and red-blazered ushers serving hot dogs, peanuts, and beer. We sat in box seats. A Plexiglas partition separated our twenty-eight-seat box from the boxes on either side of it—on one side, Edward Bennett Williams, on the other, the press.

My mother sat in the front-row center of our box. She surrounded herself with a weekly cycle of friends—friends visiting from Chicago, friends visiting from Los Angeles, friends visiting from Paris. She invited people who otherwise wouldn't have a chance to go to a Redskins game: the milkman, the high school football coach, Double O's girlfriend, Marge. Williams filled his box with Joe DiMaggio, Nancy Dickerson, and an array of Kennedys. After a couple of games, Williams telephoned my father at Redskin Park. "Your wife's not inviting the right kind of people to the games," he told the coach. My father told Williams, "Ed, that's the least of my worries. Right now I'm trying to get our team to the Championship!" When Dad told Mom what Williams said, she offered to relinquish her twenty-eight-seat box. Who needed it? Williams could have it, she said. She'd sit in the stands. But then, when Williams asked if he could borrow a couple of her seats for some of his friends, she replied, "Over my dead body. This is *my* box!"

During games, my mother spent nearly as much time looking at Williams as she did watching the real game at hand. She began inviting people into our box who would especially turn the blood of Williams, a known Democrat. Over the years, she invited Henry Kissinger, John Ehrlichman, and the ambassador from Iran. Williams pegged his new coach as a Republican sympathizer when in fact my father had no political preference. He never even voted. Elections fell during the football season. My mother was not registered to vote. She said she resented the fact that someone would tell her when to vote and when to serve on jury duty. Plus, she was ashamed that she had given up her French citizenship to become a citizen of a country she deemed infantile.

Once the Redskins started winning, Washington partisanship was tossed out of the stadium. When the team was introduced, everyone, from Henry Kissinger to Ted Kennedy, rose for a standing ovation.

Even my mother stood. Seeing Coach Allen run out onto the field, leading his entire band of Redskins, my mother said, she forgave her husband entirely. She forgave him for all he had put her through: the broken sprinklers, and the missed concussions, and the lame wedding-proposal telegram. I didn't forgive him. I simply understood him better. I saw his ego emptying out onto the field in one loud, cheering rush. I saw his intense preparation adding up to this: to rise out of some bottomless void that he must have felt inside so that he might have a momentary chance to become a winner.

After the Redskins won, one, two, three games in a row, our postgame exit out of RFK Stadium became treacherous. Once, when Leroy didn't park the car under the stadium, we had to make our way out of the stadium gates and into the public parking lot. Then fans charged at us—floating, bobbing, disembodied heads screamed, "We love you, George!" Fan fingers pawed at me as I tried to hold on to my father's coattails, leading us through the crowd and to the Lincoln. I lost my grip and was sucked into a vortex of fans spitting, "George, George, George!"

"Make room for the coach!" someone screamed, and a wall of fans shoved me back. Someone else lifted a fist to the air and shouted, "Hail to the Redskins!" and a chorus broke out into an impromptu song, "Hail to George Allen!" Somebody stepped on my foot, and someone elbowed my neck, and someone else shook his jowls at me, telling me, "We love you, honey, we love you!"

As I watched my father climb into the Lincoln, I made a push through the crowd. I couldn't get through. I saw fans rushing toward my father, grabbing for his hands, his arms, his head. For a moment I felt sorry for them all: what was missing in their lives that they needed to look to my father, and football, for strength? For another moment, I felt panicked—my father was about to leave without me! I started to crawl out, on hands and knees, to make it through the tangle of legs and spilled beers and torn programs. Finally Leroy saw me, pushed a few fans aside, and pulled me close. He helped me into the Lincoln, shut the door after me, and made his way behind the wheel, just in time to lock the doors and start the engine.

As the car slowly pulled away, a fan hurled himself onto the windshield.

A cop pulled the guy off, and as the car left the stadium I saw the cop lift his billy club to curb the fan's enthusiasm.

These people, these fans, these absolute nuts, I thought, what lives would they have without the Redskins?

It hadn't occurred to me yet to ask myself this same question: what life did I have without the Redskins?

A Weekly Contest

AT SCHOOL, weekly popularity contests were held during lunch. A group of popular girls listed the name of nearly every girl in the class, followed by a series of questions: Love? Like? Hate? The girls then sent the questionnaire to the popular boys, and the boys rated each girl accordingly. After lunch I would rummage through everyone's sticky banana peels and leftover bread crusts in the cafeteria trash, saying I had accidentally thrown my retainer away again. The Redskins dentist had recently fitted me with one the wrong size. At least it was free. Once, he left me in the dentist chair so long with the gas mask on my face that I began to hallucinate. After lunch I'd say I was looking for the retainer, when really I was looking for those notes to see how the boys graded me. I wasn't even listed. For weeks I sat alone at lunch and watched the girls pass their notes to the boys, and I wondered, When would I be rated? Loved? Liked? Hated?

At lunch I had volunteered to help the handicapped kids who could not eat by themselves. There were only two of them, a girl and a boy. I would meet them both outside their closetlike classroom and lead them to the lone cafeteria table pushed up against the auditorium stage. I fed the girl, whose fingers couldn't manage a fork, and I poured the boy his castor oil and helped him so he wouldn't swallow his tongue when he took it. We would eat in silence while in the rest of the cafeteria kids screamed and ate and laughed. When the bell rang, I helped them clean up their hands and faces with the special cloths their mothers put in their lunch boxes, and then I led them back to their private class, where they seemed to remain hidden until the next day's lunch bell rang. I never saw these kids out on the playground. I never saw them on any school bus. Often I wondered if they sometimes spent the night there. After I stopped volunteering to help them, I could never look over at them at their separate cafeteria table, managing an awkward, lonely lunch with some other volunteer who had used the kids as a humanitarian excuse to not be seen eating lunch alone.

Once the Redskins earned a first-place slot in the Eastern Division, I stopped volunteering. By then, I was invited to sit with the popular girls, who wore makeup and stockings and identical velvet butterfly chokers as a symbol of popular unity. All the girls had gone to first base, some to second base, and a couple had even gone to third. Except for those sweaty moments during *Gigi*, I hadn't even held a boy's hand yet. The most intimate I had been with a boy was kicking one in the nuts in fourth grade. But I didn't tell the other kids that. I told them I had a boyfriend back in California who was in high school, a surfer–football star named Jake whom I'd gone all the way with—look, here's his ID bracelet to prove it. They eyed the fake silver ID bracelet I'd gotten in the mail from Bazooka Joe Comics after sending in a hundred strips and two dollars.

"Jennifer Allen," they read. "That's your name."

"Don't wear it out," I said.

"Well, why would—what's his name, Jake?—give you an ID bracelet with your name on it?" the most popular girl wanted to know. She was a Marcia Brady clone. Same straight hair, same perfect teeth, same sass. Her boyfriend was a future basketball star. He already stood a gangly, awkward five feet ten. He, along with a crowd of boys, waited for my answer.

"I said," she said, "why is *your* name on *your boyfriend's* bracelet?"

The others leaned in to hear my lame answer.

"It was a gift," I said. "He wanted me to have a bracelet that reminded him of me."

My story didn't even make sense to me. She shook her head in disbelief. The boys adjusted their silver and copper bracelets bearing the names of soldiers missing in action and of prisoners of war in Vietnam. That was the real bracelet I wanted, an MIA or a POW bracelet, but my mother forbade me to wear one.

"Why? To look like everyone else?" she asked.

"Yes!" I said.

"Well, that's the wrong reason," she said. "If you really knew what 'missing in action' and 'prisoner of war' meant, you wouldn't be able to bear wearing a reminder of those men."

One day after lunch, when everybody was throwing away their trash, the future basketball star asked me if I wanted to go steady.

I didn't know what "going steady" entailed. I didn't even wonder what would be required of me as a steady. I simply answered, yes.

He'd dumped the most popular girl for *me*!

He walked away, satisfied, a noticeable added bounce in his Converse high-tops.

Seconds later, the most popular girl tugged at my long hair. "Hey, Allen," she said. "Hear you're going steady with my ex-boyfriend."

She then informed me that the only reason he wanted to go steady with me was to cop a couple of free Redskins season tickets.

"Season tickets!" I shrieked. "Season tickets are sold out!"

She bit a hangnail off her finger.

"Season tickets?" I moaned. "The waiting list for season tickets extends into the next century!"

"Oh, well," she said, spitting the hangnail at my feet, "guess you'll have to tell him."

I wasn't going to tell him. You tell him, I told her.

Before leaving me, she said, "By the way, nobody believed your story about Jake."

They hadn't fallen for my story about Jake? Too late. I had already fallen for the dreamed-up Jake with the blond hair and the blue eyes. He was my idealized boy-man who had yet to grow up, a boy-man who would sit for long hours with me, holding my hand, listening to me talk on and on about nothing and everything and say nothing back to me. Ours was a perfect relationship. I now see that my idea of Jake was my exact relationship with my father: distant, absent, mythic. But at the time I simply thought, well, until I find my perfect man, I'll console myself with Jake.

I told the most popular girl to tell the future basketball star that I was breaking up with me. I mean, I said, tell him that I'm breaking up with him. She eagerly charged out of the cafeteria to tell him the good news. They got back together immediately.

Now I peeled the stuck paper napkin off my wet retainer. I wedged the ill-fitting appliance back in my mouth and tried not to cry. I never approached the basketball star to ask if it was true that he only wanted season tickets. I just figured, why had I thought anyone would be interested in me, and me alone, without my dad?

Walking out of the cafeteria and onto the playground for PE class, I told myself, look, the guy's a loser, a slow long-distance runner. That day in PE, I beat him in the fifty-yard dash by a tenth of a second. I'd clocked 7.2, he clocked 7.3. For weeks I held my score above him as my medal of honor. "7.2," I'd tell him, "7.2. 7.2. 7.2. 7.2.!" I could tell it got to him. When he took an easy shot on the basketball court, I would yell, "7.2!" and he would miss the hoop by a mile. When he ran in the fifty-yard dash for the President's Council on Physical Fitness and Sports Award, I would yell out "7.2!" It was hard to yell "7.2" with my retainer in my mouth. I would have to take it out to yell clearly and loudly across the school's big grass field. I probably looked like an idiot doing this, but it was worth it. I didn't have a boyfriend. At least I was still the fastest kid in the fifth grade.

Over-the-Hill Gang

THE ANNUAL POSTSEASON draft is a system designed to ensure that each team has a chance at acquiring new, vital college blood. Teams draft in the inverse order of their combined standings, meaning the team with the worst record picks first; the team with the best record picks last. There are seventeen rounds, and each team gets to choose one player in each round. The team can also trade the choice for an active player, or for several other choices in different rounds. The draft is similar to the stock exchange, except that in football, humans are the currency and coaches trade. In the "war room," where the draft is conducted, coaches chain-smoke and talk on telephones and perform a series of frantic hand gestures. Each college player's potential has been studied and analyzed, his season statistics printed on a chart that hangs on the war-room wall. Each coach must decide his team's weakest spot and then try to fill that spot with a fresh young soldier. Many see a draft choice as a magic, lucky playing card. How a coach plays his picks says a lot about how he feels about young players versus old players, about the present versus the future.

When my father arrived at the Redskins, the Redskins' draft bank was full, and the Rams' bank was empty—because my father had traded away the Rams' picks for older, "character-driven" men. My father knew the Rams were desperate to fill their bank, so he offered the Rams twelve future Redskins draft picks for eight veteran Rams players—causing reporters to rename the Redskins the "Ramskins." My father traded Redskins draft picks into future years when he was not under contract with the Redskins—1978 and 1979. In 1971, he reconstructed the squad, fueling the Redskins with some of the oldest players in the league. Sure, maybe these Redskins geezers might win a few this season, but what about next season, and the season after that? Trading future draft choices was mortgaging the future for the present, reporters said. Why not rebuild the squad with young talent for a secure future? My father replied, "The future? I don't care about the future. The only thing I care about is now. I want to win now, not in the future."

"The future is now," Dad said several times after D-day, draft day.

"The Future Is Now" soon became the Redskins' motto for success.

A couple of *Washington Post* reporters used the expression for the title of a book they were writing about my father. When my mother learned that the writers were borrowing her husband's words, she screamed, "Plagiarism! How dare they make money off your ideas!" At a cocktail party hosted by *Washington Post* executive editor Ben Bradlee, my mother introduced herself to the two writers. "It's nice to meet you," she told the men. The men nodded their heads. It was nice to finally meet the wife of the man they had been writing about for the past year. Then my mother informed them, "It's nice to meet you because I'm suing you." Edward Bennett Williams was the *Washington Post*'s legal counsel and counted Ben Bradlee as one of his best friends. Mom did not know that when she threatened to sue the *Post*'s writers she would be facing Edward Bennett Williams in court.

Dad persuaded her not to sue.

Dad said, "We need the *Post* on our side, sweetie."

The *Post* seldom seemed to be on the Redskins' side. Reporters criticized Dad's conservative, dull offense and joked about his use of Double O as a Redskin Park security guard with his bicycle and his binoculars. Reporters said that if my father could have designed a retractable roof to cover the practice fields, he would have. Reporters often referred to Dad as

"Nixon with a whistle," a man who was constantly looking over his shoulder for the next enemy attack. One reporter wrote, "Every time I approach Redskin Park, my stomach turns at the thought of having to face the General, George Allen." Dad telephoned Ben Bradlee and said, "Gee whiz, Ben, your guys are supposed to support us, not destroy us." Bradlee explained that the sportswriter's job was not to be the local team cheerleader.

Dad told Bradlee, "When your guys come to practice, they write down every play we practice. They print it in the paper. They're telling our enemy our plan of attack!" Dad did not think he was being overly paranoid. He thought he was being perfectly pragmatic. Reporters citing practiced plays was akin to announcing where we'd bomb next in Vietnam, Dad told Bradlee. Dad feared that the Cowboys and the Giants and the Eagles were reading the *Post*'s sports pages to determine what the Redskins would do next. Every morning Dad read the local sports pages of his upcoming opponent, trying to decipher a game-day strategy in what reporters wrote in the distant cities. Every night, working long past midnight, he would telephone Cowboys and Giants and Eagles headquarters to see if anyone answered. Were they working as late as he was, he wanted to know. My father never wanted anyone to outwork him and he never wanted any reporter to undermine his secret plans. When Ben Bradlee could not promise the coach that his reporters would not report on what they had seen, Dad locked the reporters out of practices and limited interviews to five minutes.

Dad would have preferred that reporters never set foot in Redskin Park. Most teams offered the media special heated and air-conditioned rooms, complete with a private bathroom, telephones and desks, hot coffee and fresh doughnuts, a hospitable place where reporters could comfortably gather and type out their daily notes. Dad gave reporters an abandoned, unheated camper-trailer, parked on the shoulder of the road alongside the twelve-foot-high tarp-covered Redskin Park fence.

"Here's your press office," Dad told them. "Write your hearts out."

Double O bicycled by the trailer several times a day. He kept track of the reporters who carried their typewriters into and out of the camper. Double O never caught on to what a couple of *Washington Post* reporters discovered—that the narrow window in the top bunk of the trailer gave the reporters a perfect, if slight, view of the practice field. Reporters lay propped on their elbows in the top bunk of the bed. As fall turned to winter, their frozen fingers typed out each and every play the coach called and each and every play the team ran. At the time there were two newspapers in Washington, the *Post* and the *Star*. Both papers struggled to find a different slant to the same story: what defensive maneuver were the Redskins plotting next? What quarterback was Allen starting next? Who was injured and who was healthy?

Once the whistle was blown and practice was over, reporters were allowed their five minutes of questions. Dad refused to even answer the simple question "How was practice, Coach?" "Oh, so-so," he'd tell the reporters before disappearing into the locker room. Reporters around the league complained to NFL commissioner Pete Rozelle. Pete Rozelle was the former Los Angeles Rams public relations director and general manager who had once worked closely with Dan Reeves. Rozelle was at the Rams during my father's brief 1957 stint as an assistant coach. Rozelle knew that without media support the league would fail. George Allen was the most difficult coach in the league, reporters cried. Something must be done to force him to show us some respect! Rozelle sent my father a couple of letters, telling him, in essence, "Now, George, you have to conform to NFL media policies."

My father conformed. He extended postpractice interviews from five minutes to eight minutes.

One day a man in a three-piece suit hand-delivered a letter to our home. I thought it was another Merrywood eviction notice. I took the liberty of opening it myself.

"Dear Coach," the letter began:

> *You are the one who has the responsibility for the Washington Redskins, not a few "cry-baby" reporters. Run your team as you see fit. You will be held accountable for the success or failure of the team. Those writers with the sharp pencils will judge you, in the final analysis, by your won/lost record. They will go with a winner and against a loser—just like the fans and owners do.*
>
> *Tell them all to go to hell—you're the coach and they live off what you make in the way of news.*
>
> *Good luck.*
> *Sincerely,*
> *Ted Agnew*

Reporters had it in for Vice President Agnew. Lately they'd even been criticizing his golf swing after he drove a golf ball into a fan's head.

Dad had Agnew's letter framed and hung in his office at Redskin Park. I had been to Redskin Park only that one time. Whenever any kid asked me, I could not even recite the address, or Dad's telephone number, or how to get there from the Dulles Airport Marriott, where we met Dad every Friday night for dinner. Redskin Park didn't matter much to me now. The Redskins were winning and that was all that mattered.

Once the Redskins went 5-0, making them the only undefeated team in the league, a *Washington Star* reporter gave Dad a break. The reporter renamed the team the "Over-the-Hill Gang." "Hail to the Over-the-Hill Gang," the reporter wrote. "Perhaps Allen has mortgaged the future, but at least for now, we're number one." This particular reporter wore braces on his teeth, and he had the narrow shoulders of a man who had once carried the coach's playbooks. He had played high school football long ago. But he had dislocated his shoulder reaching for a wayward pass. That ended his football career. His name was Steve. For a few days, Steve became the only reporter in Washington Dad would call "a friend."

Dad showed Steve his appreciation by offering to let him into a Redskins practice.

"But first," Dad said, "you have to promise you won't report what you'll see."

Steve couldn't promise.

The coach locked Steve out of practice.

The friendship quickly ended.

Game Day

THURSDAYS WERE BRUCE'S junior varsity high school games. Fridays were Gregory's varsity high school games. Saturdays were George's varsity college games. Sundays were Dad's Redskins games. I went to football games four days a week. My brother George never even played. We knew, driving two hours each way to his games, that he wouldn't be called into play. He was red-shirted, meaning he was a recent transfer student;

he could dress up in a uniform yet had to sit on the sidelines the whole game. We went anyway. For support, my mother explained. I went to every one of my brothers' games. I watched each brother sit on the sidelines, waiting to make that one single pass, that one single kick, that one single punt. And then I would give each one a standing ovation. Dad never went to their games. He was busy with his own game. Some day, I imagined, someone would come watch me play my game.

One night, waiting in the parking lot for Bruce to exit the locker room, I asked Mom, what game did she think I could play?

"Soccer?"

"Bruise your shins."

"Softball?"

"No grace."

"Basketball?"

"For behemoths."

"Swimming?"

"Big shoulders."

"Track?"

"Thick thighs."

"Tennis?"

"Boring."

"Field hockey?"

"Too violent."

"Golf?"

"Not a sport."

"Listen," she finally asked, "why don't you stick with ballet? Why don't you stick with ballet and perfect it?"

I liked the idea of perfecting something, so I said, "Okay. I'll go back to my ballet."

My mother found me a ballet teacher, a retired second-string ballerina who told me, "All my dancers are striving to be professionals. Are you?"

I told her I was.

I was willing to study ballet six days a week.

She let me into her class held in the living room of an enormous old house with splintered wooden floors and yellowed cracked mirrors. The place looked haunted and so did the dancers, their eyes sunken in their heads, their expressions bearing the mark of born losers. One look at these girls and I could tell none of them would ever make the pros. They all had wide thighs, broad hips, and squat necks. The teacher was built just like them. Her exercises were shaping them into a clone of herself. She had dyed red hair pulled into a bun so tight at the base of her neck that it stretched the skin of her face. She wore a black leotard that was cut low down her broad back and faded pink tights that hugged her legs hard as rocks. A sheer shirt was tied around her hips in an attempt to cover up hips wider than her shoulders. She strode around the room, cane in hand, whacking at each girl she passed. She tapped her long cane at slow feet, at sunken shoulders, at a lazy elbow. She snapped her fingers to shut off the pianist, and shouted, "Silence!" She stopped to demonstrate. Her image was horrifying, her limbs appearing disjointed in the fun-house mirrors. She lifted her chin, took a deep nostril breath, and began to show us how the exercise was done. I watched her watching herself perform to see if she still had it in her, if she could still outperform these mere amateur teenage dancers with aspirations beyond their talents. Of course she could. She had once been better than all of us. Yet she was still just another second-rate dancer taking out her aggressions on a group of hopeless hopefuls. After class, all the girls sat slumped on the dressing-room benches, peeling dead skin off their blistered toes, talking about how lousy they were in class.

I quit after the first class.

I told myself I did not have time for ballet, going to football four days a week.

Besides, at Bruce's games I had seen my future in a girl who knelt at the sideline bench, wrapping up a player's kneecap. Her name was Peggy Jackson. She was black, a teenager, and good-looking. She wore a football jersey tucked into her tight hip-hugging pants. In her back pocket she carried an Afro pick, a screwdriver, and a roll of trainer's tape. To me she was a vision. Ponytailed, miniskirted cheerleaders couldn't compete with her. She wielded more power than those rah-rahs ever could. And while my brother Bruce performed death-defying feats that left him unconscious, lying motionless on the field, I preferred to watch Peggy, the high school football-team manager, instead. After the games, I watched Peggy pick up pieces of broken equipment—a cracked helmet, a torn jersey, a ripped chin strap—drop them all into a big laundry sack, and head, with the rest of the team, into the boys' locker room.

My mother blew my cover.

Once, while waiting for Bruce to stagger out of the locker room after another spectacular, concussion-producing victory, my mother told Peggy, "Jennifer idolizes you."

It was true. I did idolize Peggy. Peggy shrugged her sharp shoulders and told me there was nothing to idolize. She said, "All I did was ask for the job, that's all." She then asked me, "What grade are you in?"

"Fifth."

"Well," she said, "by the time you're in high school, you'll be able to play on this team. You won't have to just stand on the sidelines like me, you'll be calling the shots." She patted my head, got into her Camaro, and sped off.

My mother said, "When men start having babies, then girls can play football."

Just then, Bruce stumbled off the curb, tripped over an empty Coke can, and asked, "What's for dinner?"

"Look at you!" Mom cried. "You were the only one with a beautiful face!"

Before this, Bruce had been the Muhammad Ali of my brothers, the only one who had somehow survived without a broken bone, without a scar, and without a clue as to what it meant to be sick. Now, looking at Bruce, well, I could barely look. His forehead was bleeding, had been bleeding, and would bleed some more. He handed me his helmet in a gesture that meant: I lost a part of my brain today, can you find it in there?

Dad had specially ordered Bruce's helmet. The latest example of 1971 professional football technology, the helmet's shell was lined with gel-filled capsules intended to soften the skull-shaking impact of an average tackle. I had once read that getting hit by a six-foot-five, 245-pound tackle was the equivalent of being in a forty-miles-per-hour, head-on car crash. As a punter, Bruce experienced an average of five to ten head-on collisions per game. I peered into Bruce's helmet and found a clump of hair, a splatter of blood, and a dirty jockstrap. No signs of human brain, I told him, and tried to hand him back his helmet. He reached out to take it, but his wrist went limp.

I kept the helmet as we got into the car, me in the back, Mom and Bruce up front. Bruce slid in, shut the door, then opened the door and barfed out onto the high school parking lot. He wiped his mouth clean with the back of his sleeve, and announced, "I never get sick."

My mother eyed me in the rearview mirror.

"You see how easy it is to be a boy?" she said. "Someday you'll see how good you have it, being a girl."

Until then, I held my brother's helmet on my lap and leaned out of the way of his poor projectile aim. All the way home, his game-winning barf shot out the car window and into the wind, splashing the backseat with his guts and his shouts of "I never get sick!"

George Allen for President

"IT'S NOT A PLEASANT thing to have to see George Allen lose," Edward Bennett Williams was saying. "George reminds me of one of those German generals who, after he lost a battle, feels compelled to commit suicide."

The Redskins had lost their first game. It was an away game, in Kansas City, and by the time the game was over, it was nighttime here at home. I watched the late-night sports and the postgame news conference where Williams analyzed my father's behavior.

"No one takes losing more personally than George," Williams was telling reporters. "Fortunately, George does not lose often."

I said good night to Mom, deep into her carton of cigarettes, and went to bed, thinking of what Williams had said. I tried to picture my father committing suicide. I could see a gun, but I couldn't see my father knowing how to work it, how to hold it, or even how to pull the trigger. I could only picture my father calling on his son Gregory to come help him.

"Gregory, how do you work this goofy thing?" I could hear Dad say, and in trying to demonstrate, Gregory would shoot himself.

Later, my mother shook me awake.

I could smell a fire. She dragged me to her bedroom. Mom's polyester blanket had a cigarette burn in it the size of a football. Hilda snored nearby on Dad's bed. The TV was blasting a news flash: REDSKINS LOSE.

A helicopter gave an aerial view of a ten-mile-long traffic jam on the Dulles Airport access road. The Redskins were scheduled to arrive at Dulles any minute. For the last few hours over twelve thousand fans had raced to welcome the team home. A couple of drivers had tried to drive on the shoulder to beat the traffic and were now stranded in a deep gully that ran on either side of the desolate road. One man's car flipped over, the TV reporter said. The man died, trapped in his car, while an ambulance tried to break through the delirious fans yelling, "We're still number one!" Over 150 police and patrolmen worked overtime. Over 500 people missed their flights. Inside the terminal, a couple of women felt faint and had to be carried off on stretchers. Two men suffered heart attacks. Waiting beside the designated Redskins gate, the TV reporter stood, visibly shaken, trying to recite the exact, estimated time of arrival of the Redskins. He held his finger to his ear and spoke, but his words were drowned out by the drunken fans dancing around him. The terminal's usually polished granite floor resembled a postconcert parking lot, littered with beer cans and broken bottles, while fans chugged back beers and bottles of whiskey, singing "Hail to the Redskins." At one point, the airport's public-address broadcaster joined in the chant, and finally the reporter gave up and sang the song himself: "Hail to the Redskins! Hail victory! Braves on the warpath! *Fight!* For old D.C.!"

What if the Redskins had won? I wondered.

Then how many would have been dead?

"Mass hysteria," my mother said. "You'd think the war was over!"

The camera shifted to the tarmac where the entire 150-man Redskins band, dressed in full costume, stood on the roof of an army trailer, while Redskinettes circled around them, shaking pom-poms and kicking go-go boots high. A banner below them read: GEORGE ALLEN FOR PRESIDENT.

"Can you believe these people?" my mother said. "Don't they have anything better to do?"

I also found the celebration unsettling. Fans had often told me, "Your father has made me a winner!" I never knew what to say to those fans. Was I supposed to reply, "Glad you finally feel like a winner," when really the fans were not winners, the Redskins were winners? I never understood how a fan could become as involved as, if not more involved than, we were in the game of football. That night, my spirits were not lifted by these fans. If anything, I felt worse seeing their desperate hope for a coach who would take them to the Super Bowl. The nation's capital's mental health seemed to be riding on the Redskins' record.

As the team lumbered down the steps of their chartered jet, I spotted my brother Bruce carrying Dad's playbooks. Bruce led Dad through the crowd of fans. Someone put a plastic Redskins beret on Dad's head. It looked ridiculous. He couldn't get his arms free to remove it. So many fans were grabbing at him. One pulled him up onto a ladder and handed him an air horn. He was expected to give a speech on this makeshift podium. The cheers were still so deafening, I could barely hear what he said.

It sounded like my father was saying, "It's unbearable, it's absolutely unbearable."

What he probably said was, "It's unbelievable, it's absolutely unbelievable."

The camera was knocked to the ground. A brief blackout. Then another camera picked up the slack and gave us a view of the back of my father, talking to the crowd, waving his politicianlike hand. The angle reminded me of the famous photograph of Robert F. Kennedy, taken from behind, on his presidential campaign that abruptly ended with a bullet in his head. I now feared for my father's life. Stepping down off the ladder and into the mass of fans, my father disappeared like a fish in a whirlpool drain. Bruce, too, was nowhere to be seen.

Early the next morning, a man in a dark suit and dark sunglasses knocked on our front door. He looked like a mortician.

"White House," the man said.

I thought my father was dead and the president was already sending us a letter of condolence.

Instead, it was a handwritten note from the president.

"Dear George," the note read, "I saw the game on TV yesterday. A truly great team must prove it is great in defeat as well as in victory. The Redskins showed they were a great team yesterday."

It was signed, "RMN."

THE WASHINGTON POST called Nixon the Redskins' number one fan. Reporters said my father and Nixon came out of the same chip-on-the-shoulder mold. They had first met in the early 1950s in Whittier, when my father was the coach of the Whittier College Poets, and then Congressman Nixon was visiting his family. Back then, the two men shared an interest in rhubarb pies, football, and ambition. A *New York Times* reporter saw it differently. The reporter called my father, a winner of two Coach of the Year awards, "a loser just like Richard Nixon." But I did not see Nixon as a loser. I saw Nixon as a loyal, compassionate fan, especially after Redskins defeats. I knew little about Nixon's political history, his loss to John F. Kennedy, his kitchen debate with Khrushchev. I knew only what I read in the many handwritten notes that arrived at our home after every Redskins game.

No one could lift Dad out of a losing slump like President Nixon. Nixon often telephoned our home after a defeat. "The White House calling for Coach George Allen" became a familiar voice I heard on the other end of the telephone line. I once listened to a telephone conversation between my father and the president. The president spoke to my father like a son. "Now, George," he would say, "you have a lot to be proud of. . . ." My father's response was: "Gosh sakes," "Gee," or "Boy, oh, boy." My father called Nixon "Mr. President." "Call me 'Dick,' " the president said, but my father could not bring himself to call the president "Dick." "Thank you for calling," my father would say, "Mr. President."

That season, Nixon invited my parents to White House dinners; my father declined because they fell during football season. Nixon even offered to host a White House dinner in my father's honor; my father declined because it was during football season. Nixon asked my father if he wanted to light the White House Christmas tree; still my father declined, saying he hoped to be in the play-offs by Christmas. My mother then invited President Nixon and his wife to sit in our box. Nixon declined. The president said he did not want to take up all our seats with Secret Service agents. Most likely, he feared being booed out of the stadium. Nixon had been promising to withdraw troops from Vietnam. So far, our troops were still at war. Plus there was a presidential election coming in the year ahead. Nixon and Democratic hopeful Senator George McGovern had one thing in common: they both were solid Washington Redskins fans.

When the Redskins entered a mid-season two-game losing streak, Dad telephoned the president and asked him if he could please visit the team at Redskin Park. My father notified the local press. Players were skeptical when reporters arrived at practice with cameras and notepads. Moments later, the president arrived by helicopter. He shook players', coaches', trainers' hands. Dad then let him call an offensive play, a reverse, that would later trouble the Redskins. He posed for photographs. Even a couple of players, staunch Democrats who had partied with Hunter S. Thompson, and another who had golfed with the Kennedys, mugged for press shots with the Republican president. My father gave Nixon a tour of the two practice fields, noting the fine hem, the perfectly laid yard lines, the unique, accurate drainage system. The president nodded in appreciation, and then the two men stepped aside, away from the cameras and the reporters and the troops. The men looked off to the horizon, as if into a sunset in broad daylight. All around them, cameras flashed. A photograph appeared the following day in national papers, showing two men, one in a windbreaker and baseball cap, the other in a wool winter overcoat, the two bonded in a seemingly common vision—to take over the free world. The visit was a shot of vitamin B-12 to the team now struggling to maintain second place in its division.

After the president left, Redskin Park resumed its secretive air. Reporters and photographers were shooed off the grounds. Gates were locked. Blinds were drawn.

The Redskins won the following week, and the president was deemed the Redskins' good-luck token.

When reporters asked Edward Bennett Williams why he had not been at Redskin Park to meet the president of the United States, the Redskins president had no comment.

Jockstraps

DO YOU TUCK the straps into the cup, or do you wrap the straps around the cup? Do you fold the cup? Is a cup even foldable? Are jockstraps foldable? I had a laundry basket full of jockstraps. Somehow, for some reason, the morning after a Redskins banquet, this simple act of folding jockstraps had become a biological puzzle, and I began to wonder, how did a guy even put a jockstrap on? I knew the cup went over the dick, but where did the straps go? Up the butt? Between the legs? Around the hips? I had once seen my brother Bruce dress our dog Dixie in a jockstrap, but Dixie was a girl and the cup just hung there between her legs like an empty sock. How could a thing like this protect the entire male species from getting their dicks and balls smashed? It should have been made of steel. A steel cup could protect anyone. This, this cotton macramé cup, this couldn't save anyone's anything.

I analyzed each one. They reminded me of one of Mom's feminine, sanitary, harnesslike contraptions she had been talking about for the past year, telling me, "One day you'll have to wear one of these!" Yeah, right. The thought of me wearing one of those things was as far from my mind as the Redskins-versus-Rams game at the end of the season. That's to say, very far. I never thought more than one game ahead. Mom was always thinking ahead, whether it was planning her own unexpected death or telling her own daughter about her eventual bodily dysfunction. Mom often led me to the cabinet under her bathroom sink and explained to me for the zillionth time what I had to look forward to in this long female life. I had the same attitude toward this as I did her telling me where the safety-deposit key was—"In case something happens," she would say, "this is where everything is!"—total disbelief. I would think, no one's ever going to die. I would think, I am never going to have to wear one of those sanitary feminine harnesses. I will never be caught dead wearing one of those ugly things. I would rather be found dead wearing a jockstrap.

Any jockstrap.

If only I could figure out how to put one on.

I had my choice between twenty, thirty, maybe even forty clean, bleached, and unstarched jockstraps. Each one had ALLEN written along the elastic band. I found a special one, Magic-Markered COACH ALLEN. I had seen my father naked once, when I was a child, and it was enough to answer any questions I would ever have about the male body. My mother, the uninhibited European, thought it would be a good idea if my father and I took a shower together. I must have been about six years old. My father and I obliged. We spent the entire one-second shower with our backs to one another, and when Dad turned off the water, we both ran our naked, separate, shivering ways. My father was a very modest man. I cannot imagine him walking around naked even in front of his own football players or assistant coaches in a locker room, or even in front of his own wife in his dressing room. My mother wasn't shy. She would mop floors in her bra and underwear and ask, "What? What are you looking at? Do you want to mop the goddamn floors?"

I had seen my mother naked more times than I wanted. The female body was strange enough without my having to question how the male body worked. In the male body, Mom said, there was a lot going on under the surface.

The night before, at a Redskins gathering, a herd of beer-drinking former Rams players called me over to their table. They had all known me since I was little girl, waiting in the Coliseum tunnel, sucking on my baby bottle of milk. Back then, they would give me a pat on the head and tell me, "Drink your milk if you want to grow up to be big and strong." Now they shot me looks that made me blush. "Jennifer, Juniper," one of them sang, "whatcha doing, Jennifer, my love?" I was wearing my first training bra, a lace blouse, a miniskirt, nude stockings, and shoes with two-inch heels. "You've become," another one said, "a young woman." Just his words, "a young woman," completely undressed me. Then he asked me, "Come sit on my lap. Come sit on Uncle Diron's lap."

Uncle Diron was a six-foot-five, 245-pound defensive tackle from Texas with muttonchop sideburns, wide teeth, and thick arms that had dismembered numerous quarterbacks. Now he was stretching one of those arms toward me. I stepped back. "That's a pretty skirt," he said. Diron's biggest rival was Dallas Cowboys quarterback Roger Staubach. "Roger Staubach wears skirts," Talbert often told reporters. Skirts? I thought then, I bet Uncle Diron never asked Roger Staubach to sit on his lap in a skirt. "Come on, girl, sit on Uncle Diron's lap," he said again. He stretched both arms out toward me. One of his hands alone was the size of my head. "No, thank you," I said. The rest of the players tossed back their beers, burped, and laughed. "She don't want to sit on your lap, Uncle Diron," one of them said, and another said, "She knows you're just a dirty old bastard," and one other said, "She'd rather sit on mine! Come on, Jenny!" I backed away from the table and directly into another player, Roy Jefferson, the lean, tall, swift wide receiver who always wore the most current '70s fashions—crushed velvet bell-bottoms, a paisley polyester shirt, a colorful knit beret, and a leather shoulder bag that resembled a purse.

"Now who do we have here?" Jefferson asked me.

I put out my hand. I introduced myself as Jennifer Allen, Head Coach George Allen's daughter.

Roy Jefferson shook my hand.

"Nice to meet you, Ms. Allen," he said and led me over to my parents standing at the buffet table. At that moment, Roy Jefferson became my hero at the Redskins. He not only saved me from those other guys, he treated me like I was somebody other than the coach's only daughter. Plus, Jefferson could always be counted on to make a perfect, game-winning catch. After that night, after every game, outside the locker-room doors, he would greet me. Win or lose, Jefferson would say, "Hey, Ms. Allen, how're you doing today?"

The day after the Redskins banquet, I wanted to ask my mother what was with these jockstraps? I wanted to ask my mother if it was okay that I had refused to sit on Uncle Diron's lap. I knew that my mother's answer would be to drag me to the cabinet under her bathroom sink and begin her dissertation on the merits of hygiene, Midol, and Clorox. So I put the jockstraps down and searched for an answer in the few books we had. One book titled *Boy Behavior* described the psychological results of studies done at a Men's Christian Association summer school. There I read about the influence fathers have on a boy's life, from early childhood visions of a year-round Santa Claus, to early adolescence, when fathers are seen as heroes, to late adolescence, when fathers are viewed as saviors, counselors, and guides. There was another book titled *Today's Boys Today.* The entire fifty-page text was devoted to the growing pressures young men face when making the decision of a lifetime—do I enter an individual sport or a team sport? There was also the *Illustrated History of Professional Football,* with black-and-white photographs of squat men wearing baseball-like pants and leather-cap-like helmets and high-top sneakers on dirt gridiron fields. There was a book on the history of the National Football League titled *Their Deeds and Dogged Faith,* and there was a biography of the late Vince Lombardi, titled *Lombardi.* But there were no books on how to raise a girl, or why girls should not sit on men's laps, or how a girl could fold her family's arsenal of jockstraps.

I closed the books and tossed the jockstraps back into the laundry basket.

In the coming weeks, the school nurse passed out parent-consent forms, indicating that she was about to embark on a series of sex-education classes. I looked forward to the class, hoping it would answer some of my questions. The nurse wheeled in an overhead projector, pulled down the film screen, and turned off the lights. She first showed us male sexual organs, pointing out each part with a long stick. "Testicles, penis, scrotum" sounded to me like playing positions—half-back, quarterback, center. When the nurse showed us a slide of the female sexual organs, I, along with all the boys in our class, sat up straight in my chair. Vagina, uterus, fallopian—I had never heard these words before. The female design was everything the male was not. The male reproductive body was so simple, so direct—stand, shoot, *score!* With the female body, who knew what might happen? There was one egg, two tubes, and an array of hormones that could screw things up. An egg could travel down either tube, could stop along the way, get caught, stuck, trapped. Or an egg could not drop one month. The next month, who knows what an egg might do? It all depended on hormones, the nurse explained, and female hormones, who could control those? The entire female system resembled a pinball machine—you never knew which way things were going to go—but at least with a pinball machine, flashing lights would tell you when the game was over, off tilt.

"We were born out of a rib of Adam!" a Christian girl shouted out in the middle of the nurse's lecture.

Several other girls silently nodded their heads, confirming all our beliefs in the impossibility of women achieving equality just by burning bras in bonfires.

Fucking, screwing, balling, those things boys talked about on the playground, the nurse now called "procreation." When the nurse explained "how babies were made," one sheepish girl asked, "Do you have to take your underwear off to make a baby?" These were mechanical questions. A front line of sperm charging at the one egg was merely a metaphor for an age-old football question, "When a defensive blitz occurs, how must the quarterback react?" None of these explanations answered my question, Why didn't I want to sit on Uncle Diron's lap?

Soon everything became clear to me.

In fact, the very next day.

"You're a woman!" my mother screamed when she saw my underwear in the laundry basket. She immediately got on the telephone and informed all the secretaries at Redskin Park, "My little baby's not a baby anymore!" After that, everyone approached me differently. I could tell who my mother had told by the way they approached me after Redskins games, asking me in a singsong tone reserved for lunatics, "How are *you* today?"

I was certain she had even told Leroy, who now slapped me a little more gently on the back. My brothers stopped tossing me the football. If I tried to run toward them, yelling, "Sack!" they'd stiff-arm me, push me down, say, "No more games for you." I'd crumble into a pile of tears. They'd stand above me, looking down at me, "What's wrong with you?" and Mom would remind them, "She's at *that* age." Even my brothers' friends now fled from me. After a while, I didn't blame them. I felt like Hilda must have felt after she rolled in some animal's carcass and couldn't understand why no one wanted to embrace her.

When I told my mother this, she handed me a bottle of Midol and a case of Kotex. She then told me, "All of this is part of being a girl. You get sensitive, you cry, you can't play with boys anymore."

At eleven years of age, my playing days were over. I was already washed up. My father and my brothers now looked at me like they looked at men they met who didn't play sports, couldn't talk sports, would never understand sports: weaklings, wanna-bes, and, the worst, writers.

"You mean," I cried to my mother, "I've become everything we despise!"

"I'm afraid so," I thought I heard her say.

But what she really said was this: "Isn't it wonderful to be a girl?"

Liberation

THE REDSKINS HAD WON. We were now one victory away from reaching the play-offs. The following week, we would head to Los Angeles to play the Rams. The Rams were one victory away from reaching the play-offs, too. The winner of the game would enter the play-offs; the loser would stay home for Christmas. While waiting for Dad and my brothers to come out of the Redskins locker room, I read a psychologist's article on the feminization of males in *PRO!*, the official program of the National Football League. "Women can never be more than second place in sports," the psychologist wrote. "They can cheer their men on, but a quick review of the record books, comparing achievements in sports of men and women, confirms the distinctness of the sexes here." The psychologist then cited one particular factor impinging upon the masculine identity of males: women.

"Sports are the only place where a male can know his biology is not obsolete," the psychologist reasoned. I didn't realize that American masculinity was threatened by the women's liberation movement. I only saw how the movement threatened my mother. She recently appeared on a local D.C. talk show denouncing women's lib, telling the newswoman, "I am proud to be called a housewife, the wife of, and the mother of. I don't need a separate identity to let me know who I am." My mother despised anything with the word "women" in it. She encouraged me to feel the same way. "Don't trust women," she'd often tell me. "They'll stab you in the back."

My mother believed that a woman's place was patting a man on the back after his big game. Just as she did after every single Redskins game.

Late that afternoon, we watched players exit the locker room. Mom ran to greet each one. "Let's beat those goddamn Rams next week!" she shrieked, punching a guy in the arm. She zeroed in on those who would hold a grudge against their former teammates.

I read my article.

"I've known women who thought football was worthless and brutal," one NFL coach said. "But women don't understand the nature of the male."

Football wasn't worthless and brutal! A girl's monthly cycle was worthless and brutal!

The psychologist continued, "Athletics help assure the male of his difference from the female in a world where his functions have come to resemble theirs."

What world was this guy talking about? Not my world. My world had clearly defined functions: girls fold jockstraps, serve dinner, clear the table. Boys wear jockstraps, eat dinner, leave the table.

The shrink then defended the homoeroticism of football, the slapping each other on the butt, the physical intimacy of players piling onto each other, the end-zone bear hugs, the need for male bonding not otherwise accepted in society. Next to this article I saw a Vitalis hair-balm ad, along with the Vitalis ballot for fans to nominate and vote for the NFL Man of the Year. One of the nominated Redskins was tight end Jerry Smith. Smith was an exceptionally reliable player, a part-time surfer, and also a full-time homosexual. No one seemed to know this about Jerry Smith until several years later, when he died of AIDS. Even after Smith's death, my father still did not understand his former star end. When a reporter asked my father, "Did you know Smith was gay?," my father replied, "Heck yeah, he was one of the happiest guys on the team!"

The shrink ended his essay with a quote from a book titled *The First 50 Years: The Story of the National Football League.* I had seen this book in my brother Bruce's room, on his shelf beside his trophies and his collection of cracked football helmets. I read it aloud to my mother.

"In football, men's own self-image is continually tested: their pride, their courage, the meaning of their pain, the reality of their hostility, their need for group affection, the level of their ability, their worth to other people. In football," the shrink wrote, "a man receives a supreme test every Sunday."

My supreme test every Sunday?

Trying to not run into the locker room after the game.

More than going on the field, I wanted to go into the locker room.

Locker rooms, where men can be men. Locker rooms, where the floor was flooded with inches of blood, spit, and phlegm. Locker rooms, where men cried. Locker rooms, where men laughed. Locker rooms, where men knelt in prayer. Locker rooms, a place I visited only when watching high-light films—Dad cheering, "Hip, hip, hooray"; Dad receiving a game ball; Dad dancing a jiglike victory dance, while all his men circled him, clapping their hands, go, coach, go, be happy, be jubilant, be blessed.

"That's not your test," my mother reminded me. "Your test is standing here patiently, waiting to greet your father."

I looked up and saw that we were the last ones waiting. All the other wives and daughters had gone home with their men.

"You think you're not important, standing here, waiting to greet your father?" Mom asked me. Then she began reciting poetry she attributed to Milton. " 'They also serve, who only stand and wait,' " she said. She let the words sink in before asking me, "Do you know what that means? That means you're serving—just by standing and waiting, you're providing a great service to men. How many American women can do that?"

Just then my three brothers appeared, along with Dad, showered and refreshed and reeking of mouthwash and aftershave and deodorant. They wore blazers and button-down shirts and ties. They were spotless. We, my mother and I, were a mess. Our hair was windblown, our dresses stained with ketchup, and our hose holed. Peanut shells, gum, and worse were stuck to our shoes. We both had bad, anxious, game-day breath.

I went to kiss Dad and tell him, "Good game."

He went to shake my hand.

"You can kiss your daughter," Mom told him.

Dad dropped his hand. He gave out an uncomfortable laugh. He seemed to have forgotten who I was.

I rolled up my *PRO!* program and slid into the Lincoln beside Leroy.

"How ya doin', buddy?" Leroy asked me, softly tapping my back. "How you doin'?"

"Fine," I said. "Good," I said. "We won."

Vengeance

CHRISTMAS TREES TOPPED the marble peristyle. Lights draped the scoreboard. Santa rode a sleigh, yelling, "Go Rams!" Banners hung all along the concrete wall girding the Los Angeles Coliseum's field.

RAM THE RAMSKINS!

GO HOME GEORGE!

But we *were* home.

Seeing Roman and Deacon storm the field under the roaring din of some eighty thousand cheering fans, I felt I was home. Earlier that week, Roman Gabriel had told reporters, "George Allen is liable to leave the Coliseum with a football in his mouth." Deacon Jones added, "George Allen taught me how to be a winner, but game day, I'm going to shove it right down his throat."

Roman and Deacon, the same guys Dad had once told us we kids should aspire to, were now degrading Dad. Now, heading into the Monday night game, I was supposed to pray for their deaths.

On the Redskins' first drive, when the Rams intercepted a Redskins pass, I jumped up and cheered. I had forgotten who we were. We were the Redskins, not the Rams.

My mother yanked me down to my seat.

"Are you out of your mind?" she screamed.

How could I root against Roman Gabriel? How could I pray against Deacon Jones? How could I not still love the royal blue Rams, the Coliseum lights lighting up the smoggy orange nighttime sky, and the foot-long hot dogs, always burnt and tasteless and dry?

Then, behind me, I heard some guy yell, "George Allen is going to walk off the field with a football shoved up his ass!"

I turned to look at the guy. He was a former Dan Reeves flunky. Sitting beside him were a woman and another man. They knew who we were. From a Rams Thermos the woman poured tall drinks into Rams cups she shared with her companions. The other man lit a cigarette, and during the remainder of the game, he flicked ashes into my hair. "Screw Allen!" he yelled at the start of every drive.

"Ignore them," my mother told me. "Don't even look at them. Ignore them."

I had to remind myself that we were seated on the visitors' side.

"This is it," my father kept saying on the sidelines of this same game. "Goddamn, all it is is guts down here."

I had to gather up my guts to find the hate in me to love the Redskins more than the Rams.

Even now, when I watch the film of this game, I still have a hard time rooting against the Rams. The game was an important breakthrough for *Monday Night Football,* bringing in several million television viewers. The game was also important for the league, a display of outright revenge, with eight Redskins playing against former teammates and friends on the Rams. And the game was important for my father; a win would vindicate him in the eyes of reporters—George Allen's new team has exceeded his former team's strength, they would write. But I did not see any of that when I watched the game in the stands. All I saw was that I could not stand and applaud Roman and Deacon's defeat, even as the Redskins won, 38 to 24. We had knocked the Rams out of the play-offs. The Redskins were going to the play-offs for the first time in twenty-six years.

I watched big, bad Deacon walk, head hung, helmet in hand, off the field.

I said to my mother, "Don't you feel sorry for them?"

"Sorry for goddamn who?" she asked. She stood. She lit a cigarette and then turned to the three mournful fans seated behind us. They all sat, looking down into their empty Rams cups held in their shaking hands.

"Was Dan Reeves your friend?" my mother asked.

The three slowly lifted their heads. They looked up at my mother.

"I'm sorry Dan Reeves is dead," she told them. "I'm sorry Reeves isn't alive to see this."

My father was awarded a game ball. He later gave the ball to my mother and had it inscribed, "To my wife, Etty, for all your love and support, love, George Allen."

"That game was the greatest game of my life," my mother maintains to this day.

To me, the game was the saddest game of my life. That game I learned that loyalty and love and friendship lasted only as long as a coaching contract.

Saint George

A HANDFUL OF PRETTY HOTEL CLERKS, dressed like Santa's elves, were gathered around the Redskins palming handfuls of candy canes off the receptionist's desk. One player asked, "What's for Christmas dinner?" Another asked, "What's your number?" Yet another asked, "Were you a good girl or a bad girl this year?" The girls took out a menu that listed the night's Christmas dinner, made specially for the visiting Redskins. That's when my father stepped in, ripped the menu from the elves' manicured hands, and said, "You know, what really worries me is guys getting off track here. Guys worrying, well, what are we going to eat for Christmas dinner? Roast beef or turkey? Dumplings or gravy? Heck, the only important thing right now is to win!"

The elves disappeared. The players dispersed.

My mother butted in. "It's Christmas, George," she reminded him. "It's Christmas."

"Christmas?" Dad said. "Well, so what, you have Christmases all your life."

A couple of Redskins fans, dressed in full Redskins regalia—the hats, the jerseys, the sweatpants—passed by and said, "Merry Christmas, Saint George!"

Dad waved, signed a few autographs, and then led us to our hotel suite. A fan had left a poem titled "A Visit from Saint George" under our door. The poem began, "'Twas the night before Sunday, and throughout the room, the air was quite cheerless and laden with gloom, for the Redskins were dreading the 'morrow to come, when to their opponents the team might succumb . . . when what to their wondering eyes should appear but a man who had chosen to coach his career, who promised a Championship team he would forge, all knew in a moment it must be Saint George."

"Cute, isn't it?" Dad asked, after I read it. There was nothing cute about what we faced tomorrow: the San Francisco 49ers with John Brodie at quarterback and Gene Washington at receiver and Bing Crosby singing the national anthem. The forecast called for rain. The field was AstroTurf. Playing in the rain on AstroTurf, players resembled children running and diving in a front-yard game of Slip and Slide. Dad showed us this, making us watch 49ers game films the entire Christmas night, studying the hazards ahead of us. That night I dreamed of fumbles and missed field goals and dropped interceptions.

Game time, my mother and I had second-row seats on the ten-yard line on the 49ers side. There was a steady rain. We had to buy and wear 49ers ponchos while rooting for the Redskins. We watched the Redskins take a quick lead, 10 to 3. Then, on the 49ers' eight-yard line, about to score again, my father called a reverse. A reverse is when a quarterback fakes to the back, and the wide receiver runs behind the quarterback to take the hand-off. It's a trick play. A gimmicky play. The kind of play my father would never call. It was the exact play President Nixon had called at Redskin Park. The 49ers defense didn't fall for it. The defense read it at the snap of the ball, and knocked us for a thirteen-yard loss. The subsequent field goal was blocked. Our drive was stalled. At halftime, the Redskins were ahead, 10 to 3.

Second half, the game clock moved too fast, too slow, and sometimes seemingly not at all. The Redskins went on to lose, 24 to 20.

The season was over.

FAKE SNOW HAD BEEN SPRAYED along the passenger windows of the Redskins' chartered bus. My mother and I took the first seats on the bus. Through fake snow and rain-steamed windows I saw my brothers, one by one, stepping onto the other Redskins bus, the one reserved for assistant coaches, trainers, and second-stringers. For years I had wanted to go to an away game with my father and his team and my brothers. Now, waiting for the team, I wished I was home eating candy canes, watching TV. The bus driver sat in his seat, rearranging a strand of Christmas bulbs draped across the dashboard beside a Polaroid picture of his family. The bus driver had two sons and a wife. They were all dressed in 49ers gear and gathered around a Christmas tree.

Diron Talbert was the first man on the bus. There he was, the biggest, meanest, scariest man alive. He looked as if he had been crying, was now crying, and was going to cry some more. I didn't know what to do. Should I smile? Should I cry? Should I say, "Good game, there's always next season"? He walked on past me. I watched the rest of the team slowly march onto the bus. With each player's step, the entire bus rocked, Christmas bulbs swayed, and my heart sank. I looked up at one player, and then another and another. Each one was noticing me, the coach's daughter, sitting there in the first seat. "What is she doing here?" I thought each one thought. I thought the same. What was I doing here? I was seeing something that girls should not see. For all the times I had seen my father defeated, I had never seen his men as defeated as this. I had always thought his players were stronger than he was. I now saw that they, too, were just men, broken by the score on the board. I looked down. I sank into my seat. I watched each labored step forward into the long off-season ahead.

I heard one man sniffle.

I heard another man blow his nose.

One seat remained empty. The seat directly across from us. It was my father's seat.

The windows were steamed.

The bus driver turned on his radio—Bing Crosby was singing "White Christmas."

Someone coughed.

Just then, Double O stepped onto the bus. He shut off the radio.

My father stepped aboard.

"Okay, then," Double O said, and the bus driver shut the bus doors, locking us into our shared defeat. Throughout the long ride to the airport and the long flight home, I regretted having come to the game. Now I knew what it was like to be a part of the team. And I didn't want to be a part of any of it.

When we returned to Dulles Airport in an icy-cold dawn, a reporter stopped our family on our way to the Lincoln.

The reporter asked my father if he was sorry he had dragged his family across the country on Christmas only to witness such a dismal defeat. My father put his arm around my shoulder. He pulled me close.

"I think it's good for kids to go through experiences like this," my father told the reporter. "Before the game, it's torture, you don't want to eat, you can't sleep. But this is what you need to succeed. Overcoming obstacles, getting torn up inside—that's what life is all about."

Two weeks later, my father was named National Football League Coach of the Year. The year before, the formerly competing National Football League and American Football League joined to become the twenty-six-team National Football League: two conferences composed of thirteen teams each, competing as the National Football Conference and American Football Conference for a chance to play in the Super Bowl. When my father won the award in both his conference and the league, he won the highest praise of sportswriters across the country. A celebration was scheduled at a black-tie Washington banquet. The event fell on my twelfth birthday. I asked my father, "Dad, can I go too?" He didn't say yes. He didn't say no. He simply asked me, "Is my tie straight?" I helped my father with his shirt studs, my brothers with their cuff links, their cummerbunds, and their fake bow ties.

Waving good-bye to them as they headed out the door, I asked my mother again why I couldn't go.

She gave her usual answer.

"Girls are not allowed to do these things," she said.

"I'll remember that," I said, heading to bed, understanding that these things were what life was all about.

Double-Dealer

IN THE 1972 off-season, my father traded away a future draft choice that he didn't even possess to two separate teams. He traded the choice to head coach Tommy Prothro of the Los Angeles Rams, and to Harland Svare of the San Diego Chargers. Svare had been my father's predecessor at the Rams, the coach who was drinking with Reeves the Christmas night Reeves decided to fire my father. I saw my father's mistake as a perfectly subtle, screw-you gesture to both Svare, his predecessor, and Prothro, his successor at the Rams. Of course, my father was not going to get away it. Commissioner Pete Rozelle called my father into the league offices in New York City. He made my father apologize to Prothro and Svare and pay a five-thousand-dollar fine. Dad then held a press conference where he defended his transaction. "There has never been a rule in the NFL against trading on credit," my father explained. "There has never been an NFL rule against trading for a choice you don't own at the moment but intend to have prior to draft day."

My father believed that by the time draft day arrived, he would have acquired the draft pick from another team. My father had a lot of faith in his trading abilities. He was known as the master draft dealer and trader in the league, eventually topping the charts with 133 trades. My father had not broken any rules. He had simply manipulated the rules to pull his power play, he said. League owners were not impressed. Immediately league owners called a special meeting, sat my father in a solitary chair, and berated him for his transgressions. A couple of owners thought my father should have been banned from the league. Several reporters noted that my father's heinous act would never be forgotten, that reporters would never forgive him, that this act jeopardized his future chances of being voted into the Hall of Fame.

In the end, my father got the player he had wanted because it would have been awkward to return a player to a team that had already traded him away. My father always found a way around the rules. When the league cut the number of men on team rosters, he tried to sign pro wrestler Andre the Giant, whose size and weight made him two men in one. When my father ran out of draft choices, he held free-agent camps every year, recruiting potential players from a crop of agent-free cabdrivers, carpenters, and bricklayers who had always dreamed of playing for a professional football team. At the 1971 camp, he signed Leslie "Speedy" Duncan, who went on to be the number one punt returner in the league that season.

My father walked away from the league offices feigning a joker's laugh, but when he returned to his New York City hotel room, where my mother and I waited for him, he was visibly upset. He motioned for me to turn on the TV for the evening sports. Someone in the Redskins organization had made the bookkeeping mistake, not him, Dad grumbled to the TV set. He would never say who that someone was. I never asked. I did not want to see my father as someone who blamed someone else for his mistake. And I never wanted to see my father as a cheater. My brothers often claimed our father cheated in their driveway basketball games. They said he denied all fouls called on him. "Uh-oh!" he'd say, stepping on a foot, and "Boy," he'd say, elbowing a rib, and "Hey!" he'd say, backing up into a gut. He always beat his sons. Even when he raced me in the beach sand, he never let me win. Most fathers would let their daughter win. Not mine. He was honest. He was faster than I was and he wasn't going to pretend to anyone, especially me, that he wasn't. He was a fierce competitor. He wasn't going to let anyone beat him. Not his children, and certainly not the league.

"George Allen has been caught, censured, and fined, but never stopped," the television sports reporter said that evening. "It's not just the spirit of the law he sets out to violate—Allen would never attempt anything so trivial—but the law itself."

Another reporter added, "Let the rule makers and the policy setters establish a new set of no-nos and Allen automatically begins scheming on how to beat it."

"Well, I hope you've learned your lesson," Mom said, snapping off the TV and going to sleep in my room next door so she could snore in peace.

That night, I couldn't sleep. At first I thought it was Mom's snoring, then I realized a fierce wind howled between the tall buildings. I got up out of the roll-away cot and peeked in on Dad. He was awake, too, standing at the window, looking out on Manhattan. It was snowing.

"Boy," Dad said, "isn't that something?"

Snow swirled in the wind.

"Hey, how about we order up some grilled cheese, milk shakes, and French fries?" Dad asked.

It was long after midnight. A deli delivered our grilled cheese sandwiches, milk shakes, and French fries, and we ate it all, alone, together.

"Isn't this great?" Dad said, sipping his shake.

It sure was.

It was one of the happiest moments of my life.

I played it down.

"Yeah, great," I said.

But it *was* great. It was all my father had to do to make me trust him again. If he had done something wrong, he would try to make it right. That night, he showed me he could enjoy a moment with his neglected family, if only given the chance.

Legends

THE TRENCH COAT, the khakis, the leather shoes. The gapped front teeth. The black-rimmed eyeglasses. The gruff voice. His record: five Championships in ten seasons. His name: Vince Lombardi. The ghost of Lombardi loomed above every coach in the National Football League. Especially over my father. Lombardi had been at the Redskins for only one year. His one-year Redskins record was above average but not exceptional. Then, while still under contract with the Redskins, he died. That left a mark on everyone who had met him in Washington. Lombardi died a martyr's death: trying to bring the Redskins a Championship. That, in itself, made Lombardi a football legend.

I saw my father as a legend-in-training. He had his own style: the Redskins cap, the windbreaker, the jogging shoes. He had his gestures: the way he paced the sidelines, tugged his cap, licked his fingers. Fans saw these movements as a secret sign language; I saw them as nervous tics. My father's ghost loomed over no one. But already his one-year record had beaten Lombardi's one-year record. Even dead, legends were competitors. Lombardi's photo was the first image you saw when stepping into the top sports restaurant in town, Duke Zeiberts. In the foyer at Redskin Park, Lombardi's portrait was hung between Williams's and Dad's. Dad had hung the portrait out of respect. And also as a reminder to beat the dead.

I was coached to not let on to anyone how much we hated Lombardi. I had never met the man, yet I was coached to not like any coach who had preceded my father at any job. That was our main enemy: not the opposing team, but the previous administration. When Dad arrived at the Redskins, he made sure to fire, trade, or cut any player unwilling to submit to the Allen plan. But there was one renegade player Dad did not dare cut:

the thirty-eight-year-old star quarterback, Adolph "Sonny" Jurgensen. From the moment my father joined the Redskins, Sonny upheld his former coach, the late Vince Lombardi, as the only coach who ever understood him and allowed him to play his kind of game. After sitting out last season with an injury, Sonny openly voiced his concerns that George Allen was the most difficult coach he had ever known.

Sonny was an outstanding quarterback, ranked in 1972 as the number one lifetime passer in the league. Sonny was confident, cocky, and calm. He graduated with honors from Duke, wore spiffy plaid blazers, and drove a convertible maroon Cadillac. His license plates bore his initials, SJ, and his jersey number, 9. He was known around town as a hotshot and a winner and the man Lombardi and Edward Bennett Williams adored. Everyone in Washington loved Sonny. Sonny was one of the few winners on the team when Dad arrived. There were others—Jerry Smith, Charlie Taylor, Chris Hanburger, Len Hauss, Harold McClinton—but none had the flashy style, the bright red hair, and the broad grin of Sonny.

In practices, Sonny refused to run the plays my father called.

In games, Sonny refused to run the plays my father called.

In meetings, Sonny refused to agree with the conservative offense my father insisted upon—a hand-off, keep-the-ball, low-to-the-ground offense.

Dad replaced Sonny, in the first-string quarterback slot, with Billy Kilmer. Kilmer was a thirty-two-year-old former New Orleans Saint we had often played against with the Rams. Dad had studied Kilmer in game films, noting his tenacious scrambling and his ability to withstand severe physical poundings from Deacon Jones. Kilmer's toughness had been established early in his career. Before his first season in the pros, he suffered a near-fatal car accident, almost losing his leg to gangrene and permanently damaging the nerves in his throwing hand. The nerve damage gave his passes a trademark wobble. Unlike the perfect streamlined spiral of Jurgensen's, Kilmer's lobbed high, and spun end-over-end. More times than not, Kilmer's passes landed in the receiver's hands. But even when the Redskins were winning, Kilmer walked onto the field at RFK and was welcomed by booing Redskins fans who had come to watch Jurgensen play. Kilmer never let on how much the boos hurt. He never let on how Edward Bennett Williams had mocked him one night at the Palm restaurant. He never publicized the fistfight that Sonny held off between

Williams and himself, the president and the quarterback. Kilmer simply walked onto the field the following week, threw his wobbling passes, and became, in the eyes of his teammates, the emotional leader of the Over-the-Hill Gang.

A Billy-versus-Sonny feud arose among Redskins fans. Bumper stickers read, I LOVE BILLY and I LOVE SONNY. A feud also developed between my father and Edward Bennett Williams: Dad liked Kilmer; Williams liked Jurgensen. A couple of nights before a game, Williams would telephone my father and suggest that my father start Jurgensen. "These owners want a puppet coach. Well, I won't be a puppet for Williams, or for anyone," my father would say after slamming down the receiver. Game day, Dad would start his first-string quarterback, Billy Kilmer. "If there were any doubt in my mind who I was starting, Williams's telephone call clarified that for me," my father later told me. "I'd start Kilmer."

Dad would start Kilmer, then sometimes, in the fourth quarter, when the Redskins were trailing by a couple of touchdowns, Dad would send Jurgensen in to save the game.

"Do your thing," he'd tell the star.

Jurgensen would go in, throw a couple of perfect passes, and earn another win for the Redskins.

The following week, Dad would still start Kilmer again.

Throughout his career, Jurgensen had been plagued with injuries. In the 1971 season, Jurgensen separated his shoulder in a preseason game. Even when Jurgensen recovered, Dad kept him on the sidelines. Jurgensen was supposed to finish his Redskins years in glory, with fans cheering him off the field, not standing on the sidelines, draped in a Redskins cape, holding a clipboard.

Like most of Washington, it would take me a few more years to understand and appreciate the man my brother Bruce said most resembled our dad. "Kilmer is all heart and guts," Bruce would remind me. Bruce was the team statistician; he saw everything that happened on the sidelines and in the locker rooms and at Redskins practice. "That's Dad," Bruce told me. "All heart and guts."

Now, as we headed into the 1972 season with Jurgensen recovered from last season's injury, Dad still decided to start Kilmer over Lombardi's number one star.

That season, Lombardi's widow, Marie, often attended the Redskins games, a guest in Edward Bennett Williams's box. Mrs. Lombardi, like the sidelined aging star quarterback, was a reminder that until someone greater came along, her husband's ghost would still hover over the Redskins, RFK Stadium, and the entire National Football League. I saw Mrs. Lombardi as a reminder of the past and a premonition of the future. Whenever I saw Williams guiding the silvery-blond woman into his box, I wondered if, even after my father's death, my mother might still want to go to football games. I wondered if Mrs. Lombardi was trying to resurrect her husband from the dead. I wondered if she was really rooting for the Redskins, just as I wondered if Jurgensen was really rooting for his teammates. If they were anything like the rest of the football world I had come to know, they were feigning affection while really hoping their own records would never be surpassed.

1972 *Championship Season*

IN 1972, MY father was certain the Redskins would go to the Super Bowl. Before the season even began, he had designed a Super Bowl VII ring: a square ruby stone, inlaid with a gold Redskins medallion, around which were fourteen diamonds (one for each regular season game) all set in eighteen-karat gold. My father hung a design of the Super Bowl VII ring in the trainer's room at Redskin Park. The trainer's room was where players were mended on cold metal tables. As a trainer assessed and tried to repair the damage with ice, tape, and needles, the player could look up and see the ring as a kind of golden carrot at the end of a long season of torn Achilles tendons, pulled muscles, and separated joints.

My father also left samples of the women's Super Bowl jewelry for us to see on the kitchen table. Daintier in design, sporting only one diamond, the ring was suitable for a wife's little finger. A bracelet with a gold charm of a Redskins headdress was suitable for a daughter. With these jewels, my father was trying to motivate everyone. For me, the bracelet held no incentive. After last season's ending, I wanted to see the Redskins win because a Redskins victory was a victory for me. The Redskins were no longer those guys who played for Dad. The Redskins were us, we, and me. Reporters had deemed the Redskins the number one underdogs in the league. My father said that what motivated him was his great fear of losing. What motivated me was my love of seeing the underdog win.

The Dallas Cowboys were the top dogs in the National Football Conference, having won the Super Bowl the previous season and the Eastern Division Title for the last six seasons. The Cowboys were the Redskins' most difficult opponent to beat to win the title. Everything we did that season was generated toward beating the Cowboys. We played them only twice during the regular season. Still, all our efforts remained on our biggest obstacle to reaching the Super Bowl: the Cowboys. Turning on a light switch, Mom would say, "Beat the Cowboys." Tossing an orange over his shoulder and trying to catch it, blindly, behind his back, Dad would say, "If I catch this, we'll beat the Cowboys." If he missed, he would say, "Two out of three." Dad had Mom and Bruce and Gregory and me take private tae kwon do lessons with international black-belt champion Jhoon "Nobody bothers me!" Rhee so we could learn how to break boards with our feet and our hands, all while saying "Beat the Cowboys." That season, Dad took his board-breaking skill to a team meeting and instead broke his hand. It wasn't the first time Dad broke his hand over the Dallas Cowboys. The other time was back in 1966, after Dad's first loss as head coach of the Los Angeles Rams. After that game, Dad was reviewing the Rams' mistakes when he slammed his fist on the table for emphasis and broke his hand in three places. We had always hated the Dallas Cowboys. And now, with the Cowboys in the Redskins' division, we hated them all the more.

Owner Tex Schramm was a former Los Angeles Rams executive and friend of Dan Reeves. Quarterback Roger Staubach, a former Heisman-trophy winner, was an off-the-field saint and an on-the-field scrambler. Head Coach Tom Landry was a Christian and a former World War II air force pilot.

"Football doesn't come first in my life," Landry once said. "The good Lord does."

Landry was a cool-tempered gentleman who paced the sidelines wearing a coat and a tie, a feather in his fedora. His expressionless game-day mug earned him the nickname "Ol' Stone Face." As a player he had once been a cornerback and a punter in the pros. As a coach, he perfected the flex defense and the multiple offense. He maintained a youthful appearance by staying in supreme shape. Once, at an NFL meeting in Waikiki, I spotted the rival coach strolling through the hotel lobby in a golf shirt, shorts, and sandals. He walked by, saying hello, without breaking stride. "He's so handsome," I whispered to my mother. "I know," Mom said.

Landry's players respected and feared him. His owner never once argued with him, or berated or belittled him. When the coach signed a ten-year contract with the Cowboys, it was the longest contract in the history of professional sports. Landry was the only coach the Dallas Cowboys had ever had. And unlike my Dad, he had never been fired.

"I wish it were just me and Landry—head to head—at the fifty-yard line," my father said at the start of the season. "I know it would come down to a wrestling match and I would win."

By the end of the season, my father's earlier prediction appeared correct: the Redskins would reach the Super Bowl that year. As I watched the Redskins' and Cowboys' team captains line up on the fifty-yard line for the coin toss at the start of the 1972 Championship game, I, too, knew that the game would come down to a wrestling match, and that we would win. We were on our home field, at RFK, and it was New Year's Eve, and there was never a better stage for my father to finally achieve his dream—to win the Championship—and to finally wear a Super Bowl ring. But that is about all I can remember. I wish I could remember a single incident of the 1972 season that led the Redskins to this Championship game. I can only remember a few isolated family dramas: bleeding stomach ulcers, emergency room visits, and a dead dog. These season events were drowned out by the more resounding words of Redskins fans cheering, "We're number one!"

When you win, you forget. Winning is a narcotic, an analgesic, a buffer for all the pain suffered to reach the final, victorious, score.

The final score: Redskins 26, Cowboys 3.

The rest I will never forget.

Redskins fans stormed the field. Fans bent the goalpost down onto the end-zone turf. They tore up bits of souvenir turf. My father was lifted high above all fans, transported like a king, on the shoulders of two mammoth Redskins. He was riding high, waving to all the fans who reached up to touch the man who had made Washington a winner for the first time in thirty years. His Redskins cap was ripped off his head. The Redskins band played "Amazing Grace." Fans chanted, "Amen, amen, amen."

Reporters began writing tomorrow's New Year's Day edition: "George Allen is the messiah," one wrote. Another wrote, "George Allen, a legend in his own time . . ." My father wasn't just my father anymore. He wasn't just a coach anymore. He was more. He was finally called a legend, and legends, I was made to believe, never really died.

"Let's get out of here," my mother said, and we waded through the sea of drunken fans to squeeze our way into the elevator. Down at the lower-level exit, we were pressed up against a cold concrete pillar by fans who had barged through the security doors. We squirreled around arms and legs to reach the Lincoln. Leroy was offering me a helping hand, when one fan stopped me, tugged at my coat, and asked, "Can I have your autograph?"

"Mine?" I asked. "You want mine?"

"Yes!" he shrieked. "Yours!"

He handed me his Redskins pen and his Championship souvenir program.

My hand shook as I tried to sign my autograph.

"Sign it," the fan told me, " 'George Allen's daughter.' "

I thanked the fan, because for a moment, standing in my own little shining spotlight, I had forgotten who I was.

Best wishes, I signed the program. *Your friend, George Allen's daughter.*

The First Family of Football

NEW YEAR'S DAY, we were all combed, and parted, and pressed, riding in the Lincoln to visit President Nixon.

"Now, let's see, each one of you," Dad said, "come on, let's see how you're going to shake the president's hand!" Dad made each one of us shake his hand firmly, look him straight in the eye, and say, "It's an honor to meet you, Mr. President." Mom made sure we knew proper etiquette. "Now, listen, all of you," she said, "whatever you do, don't steal anything!"

We did not steal anything at the White House. We shook the president's hand firmly, looked him straight in the eye, and said, "It's an honor to meet you, Mr. President." We watched the president open his Oval Office desk drawer to show us where he kept the 1969 Pro Bowl game ball Dad had given him at his inauguration. Dad and the president marveled at how the All–Pro autographs had not worn away through the years.

"Can I hold it?" Dad asked.

The president handed the ball to Dad.

Dad turned the ball slowly in his hands.

"There's Deacon," one of my brothers said.

"There's Merlin," another one said.

"Roman," said another one.

We all stood there, overcome with a sick melancholy, staring at this piece of our past in Dad's hands.

"You see," Dad said to us then, "the president took good care of this, and now he'll have it forever. You kids could learn a few things from the president."

Dad had given all my brothers autographed game balls. My brothers would toss the balls around, smearing the Magic-Markered autographs. Or they would leave the footballs in the grass in the sun, and the leather would crack. Or they would forget to put air in the footballs, and the pigskin would deflate. The president's ball looked as if it was kept sealed in plastic at night, then taken out, every morning, to be reinflated and cleaned and shined.

"That's what I mean by respect," Dad said. "You see, the president understands respect."

Dad shook his head in amazement and then handed the ball off to the president.

The president carefully placed the ball back in his Oval Office drawer. I wondered if he took it out during key meetings to impress foreign ministers. Or if he had closets full of trinkets people had given him, trinkets that he pulled out when the people came to visit, just to make them feel important like Dad did now, seeing his Pro Bowl game ball in the president's desk. I peered over the president's shoulder to see what else he kept in there, but he snapped the drawer shut and directed us out to the Rose Garden, where the entire corps of Washington press stood.

WE'RE WINNERS AT LAST! the *Washington Star* headline had read earlier that day. BOMBING RESUMED IN NORTH VIETNAM, read a smaller headline. Now the cameras flashed, making us tomorrow's headline photograph: THE FIRST FAMILY OF FOOTBALL.

We shook the president's hand again and said, "Happy New Year." The next time we would visit Nixon, he'd be resigned, driving a golf cart around the grounds of his beachside estate in San Clemente. But for now, the president was president, and Dad was the messiah.

We went home, our egos inflated, and found, taped to our front door, a note from the landlord: "Congratulations on a great victory! When you have a chance, let's talk about your move out of Merrywood."

"For cripes sakes," Dad started to say, and then Mom discovered a telegram tucked just under the GO REDSKINS doormat.

"Dear Coach, that was a great win yesterday," Dad read aloud. "Good luck in the Super Bowl, Tom Landry."

"Boy," Dad said, "is that class or is that class?"

"Class, my ass," Mom said. "He doesn't fool me. He only hopes we win because if we win it makes him look good."

The Super Bowl was two weeks away. No one wanted to talk about the Super Bowl yet. Not even Dad.

AT DINNERTIME, there was no happier Dad than mine. Dad drank his milk, ate his vegetables, and even swallowed his meat. Dad usually never swallowed his meat. He'd rather roll it around in his mouth, suck the juice out, then spit it on his fork and deposit the gray bloodless clump on the side of his dinner plate. He did this even at White House dinners. Meat slowed down a man's digestion, Dad always said, and that could stunt a man's momentum, his motivation, and eventually lead to an early death. But tonight, Dad chewed and swallowed and said, "Boy, is that great chicken!"

It was roast beef. No one corrected Dad. He was on a roll. He went around the table praising each of us. Dad said George's A+ grades were "admirable," he said Gregory's acceptance into the University of Delaware was "commendable," that Bruce's statistical help on the sidelines was "invaluable," that my long hair was "beautiful," and that Mom was "the most lovable woman in all the world."

"What are you, drunk?" Mom asked and poured Dad some more milk.

After dinner, we all gathered in the living room to watch the replay of the Redskins beating the Cowboys on every single channel. We had three TVs in the living room. Each TV was turned to a major network so that I wouldn't have to jump to switch channels. We watched, three times, the highlights of the Redskins beating the Cowboys. We also watched, three times, the highlights of Dad being carried off the field. Each time we saw the fan ripping the Redskins cap off Dad's head, Mom said, "That was your goddamn good-luck cap."

Finally, Dad said, "I'll get another gosh-darn good-luck cap!"

"Another one?" Mom said. "How are you going to get another goddamn good-luck cap?"

"Christ almighty!" Dad said. "You see how your mother is?"

Dad got up and went upstairs to bed. After a few minutes, he called our dogs Hilda and Dixie to be with him. Dad didn't know that Dixie had been run over by a truck earlier in the season. No one had the nerve to tell Dad. We shoved Hilda off the living room couch, and she made her fat way up the stairs, to sleep at the foot of Dad's bed.

"Your father has a lot to learn," Mom said to all of us then. No one seemed to be listening. My brothers were watching the rest of the sports. Dad's TV was blaring out the same sobering news: the Redskins were up against the team with the best record in the history of the National Football League—the undefeated, 16-0 Miami Dolphins.

Our Championship celebration had ended. The pregame Super Bowl panic had begun.

Super Bowl VII, Los Angeles Memorial Coliseum

"IF I HAD MY WAY," Dad said, "we'd stay at some cemetery." Instead, we were staying across the street from Disneyland at the Saddleback Inn, where clerks were dressed with ten-gallon hats and sheriff's-badge name tags that read "Howdy!" We had a suite and a fireplace with fake logs burning a cellophanelike flame. All along the hotel corridors, black-and-white WANTED posters hung of Kit Carson, Jesse James, and Wyatt Earp. Cowboys surrounded us, Dad noted. Maybe Commissioner Pete Rozelle had plotted this psychological contest on the Redskins. After all, Commissioner Rozelle had selected where the team would stay for the Super Bowl and had decided when and where the team would hold their daily press conferences. When my father complained about this, the commissioner re-marked, "George Allen would be happiest practicing on an aircraft carrier." Then Rozelle fined my father $5,000 for not reporting a couple of players on injured reserve in the play-off game against Green Bay.

"That bastard," Mom said, unpacking her massive suitcase stocked with cigarettes and antacid. "Couldn't he wait until the Super Bowl was over?" My mother believed that there was no greater enemy than Commissioner Pete Rozelle. She would always remind me that Rozelle had once worked with Dan Reeves at the Rams. Mom then began to list so many enemies and friends of enemies she had already seen in the Saddleback hotel lobby that, for a moment, I had forgotten who our real Super Bowl enemy was: the undefeated Miami Dolphins.

I liked the Miami Dolphins. I liked their tropical colors—aqua and or-ange. I liked their insignia—a dolphin wearing a football helmet. I liked the frivolous, partylike name of their stadium—the Orange Bowl. I liked their mascots—several jubilant dolphins splashing in a fish tank beyond the end zone. I even liked the Miami Dolphins' ball boys—all blonds, and one better-looking than the next. I would watch those ball boys on the side-lines and imagine myself as the future wife of any one of them, and then I would cut that fantasy short—what was I thinking, marrying into the Dol-phin camp? What was I thinking, marrying at all?! Still, I could not stop myself from liking the Dolphins' ball boys or their father, Miami's head coach, Don Shula.

Each time Dad was fired by the Rams, Don Shula was the first person to call and send his condolences. Shula had worked for a difficult owner already, Carroll Rosenbloom, who now owned the Los Angeles Rams. Shula worked under Rosenbloom at the Baltimore Colts. We once ate dinner with Shula, and I was impressed with his appetite. He ordered ribs and laughed and knew how to select wine. Mom said, "Not every coach is as boring as your father." Everyone admired Shula; he held the best coaching record of any active coach in the league. After the Champi-onship victory over the Cowboys, Dad told reporters, "The reason we beat the Cowboys was because we hated the bastards." Now I was finding it hard to muster up enough hate to beat the Dolphins. There was nothing to even *dislike* about Don Shula, or his team.

We watched our parents sourly unpack their bags. When one of us asked, "What's for dinner?" Dad said, "*Dinner?* What you don't seem to realize is that right now in Washington it's—" and then he paused to look at his watch and realized he had left his watch back in Washington. "Are we all staying in this same room together?" I asked, and Bruce told me to shut up, and George called Bruce an idiot, and Gregory said, "Daddy doesn't like that word," and I said, "What word?" and Mom yelled, "Shut up!" and Dad said, "Boy, oh, boy, we've got the biggest game in our life coming up and all you guys can do is argue? Boy, oh, boy, is that how we stick together? By arguing in front of Daddy?"

The vinyl couches folded out, Mom showed us. There were a couple of roll-outs for Bruce and me. A king-size bed for Mom and Dad. Mom hated sharing a bed with Dad. He always stole all the covers, she said, and then, when she was snoring, he'd throw pillows at her head to make her stop. My parents would never last in the same bed for the entire week leading up to the game. I knew it was only a matter of days before Dad had his own private room. I watched Dad unpack his shaving kit, his coaching shorts, and a new Redskins cap. When he put the cap on his head, the cap looked awkward: too small, too stiff, too new. Anyone could see the cap held neither a future nor a sense of history. Mom took the cap off Dad's head and bent the bill so that it would look a little more worn, a little more wise. Dad put it back on, looked in the mirror, shook his head, and said, "Boy, oh, boy."

Our room was the last room at the end of the "Wild West" wing of the hotel. We were the only Redskins family staying with the team. The other families were staying over forty miles away at the Airport Marina Hotel a couple of blocks away from an LAX runway. When Mom suggested that the Redskins wives ought to be allowed to stay with their husbands, Dad said, "I like those wives, but I would rather they be in Washington." The Miami players were saying how much they missed their wives, Mom reminded Dad. Maybe the Redskins would be better off with their wives beside them.

"My players are too old to be crying about their wives," Dad replied. "Anyway, they've got all their lives to be with those wives."

"Well, I'm sorry I came, then," Mom said. "If you didn't want me here, then why in goddamn hell did you invite me?"

Bruce gave Mom a look. George said, "Shut up, Mother," and Gregory said, "I'm calling *Surf Report*."

Dad said he had other things to worry about than the goshdarn Redskin wives. Dad said he was worried about the sun. How was the sun going to move across the Coliseum field? Had any of us considered that? Had any of us thought how hard it would be to block a punt or receive a punt or catch a pass in the midwinter sun? We all shook our heads no. Well, Dad had. Dad had hired a man to chart the movement of the sun at the Coliseum, minute by minute, kickoff to fifth quarter, if that's what the game would come to, sudden death, overtime. "You can't be overly prepared," Dad said.

Dad then reminded us how he had learned the importance of preparation long ago when he was an officer in the Navy Reserves and was visiting Princeton, New Jersey. We had heard the story countless times, but we all shut up to listen to Dad tell his tale. After attending Sunday mass in the university town, Dad learned that the great physicist Albert Einstein lived nearby. Dad said he was interested in Einstein because he had heard somewhere that Einstein was a checkers champion. Dad prided himself on having won several checkers championships, and that day, he decided to pay a surprise visit to the professor and challenge the genius to a match.

When Einstein appeared at the door, the scientist said he was not a checkers champion but that he would be happy to take my father on. "Did you bring a checkerboard?" the scientist asked. Dad didn't have a checkerboard. He assumed that Einstein, brilliant as he was, would have his own board. Dad was ashamed, he said, to have come so unprepared. Einstein then said he would love to visit longer but that he was busy working on a project that would stop the world war. Years later, Dad realized that Einstein was talking about the atomic bomb. More important, Dad reminded us all that day, "I have never since allowed myself to be so unprepared."

After his short reminiscence, Dad put on his new Redskins cap. It was slipping off his head. Dad said he was going to study the conditions of the practice field, a baseball field on the other side of Disneyland.

It was almost midnight, Mom reminded him.

Not to worry, Dad said: Double O had a flashlight.

TWO NIGHTS BEFORE the Super Bowl, Mom and I went to Commissioner Pete Rozelle's party on the *Queen Mary*. The *Queen Mary* was a broken-down ship docked for life in Long Beach, or Wrong Beach, as my brother Gregory called it. With stained carpeting, humidity-fogged windows, and moldy bathrooms, the once glamorous ship was now filled with cigar-smoking, drunken fans arguing over who would win— Redskins or Dolphins. Mom had pneumonia. A 103-degree fever. The chills. I was winded just hearing her cough.

We both sat on a bench beside the ship's grand staircase, watching the partiers pass by, waiting for Leroy to pick us up and drive us back to the Saddleback Inn. When someone walked past us, Mom coughed out a smile, and as soon as that someone was out of earshot, she would say to me, "That's that phony bastard." Everyone at the commissioner's party was a phony bastard: reporters, owners, especially the commissioner. I wanted to finally meet them all. I wanted to meet the owners who wanted my father barred from coaching. I wanted to meet the commissioner who was always fining Dad. Mostly I wanted to meet the reporters.

I wanted to meet the reporter who had described Dad as a "casket salesman," and the one who called him a "*Watchtower* salesman," and the one who had pondered: "What makes 270-pound hulks follow Allen around as if he were going to throw them a bone?" I wanted to meet the one who asked, "How can Allen get grown men to kneel and cry on national TV after they have won a lousy football game?" And the one who wondered, "Where does Allen's messianic image come from?"

I wanted to meet these writers who posed such questions because these were the same questions I wanted answered.

My mother held me back. She held my arm so tight that I was afraid, if I broke loose, she might collapse. She was sweating, coughing, and wheezing on a cigarette. I watched the reporters walk by us. What struck me most about reporters was this: they seemed to be the most humble men there. With their elbow-worn blazers, and their ankle-skimming trousers, these men appeared to take their deeds more seriously than they did their attire. Some of them stopped to greet my mother; others quietly stepped past us. I now saw these men as the gentler species, one that measured every step and every word. When a Christian kid at school talked about "the Word," I always thought she meant the word of sportswriters. With the act of creating the written word, these men could invent lives and also destroy lives. Seeing them now file out of the party, one by one, headed to their all-night desks in cheap hotels, I recognized the assumed power of the powerless. And for the first time I considered their profession—one that allowed them access into the locker room and into the press box and into all-male football parties—as a potential life for me.

Later that night, after my mother and my brothers had fallen asleep, I saw the words of these writers diminished. Their glorified image of the messiah stood before me—dwindled down to the silhouette of Dad. Dad was standing at the hotel window, looking out at the colorful lights of the "happiest place on earth." There stood the loneliest man on earth, I thought, sipping his milk. The figure I saw standing there was not that of a messiah, or an evangelist, or a god. The sportswriters were wrong. All I could see was my father; all I could hear was the stuttering sighs, between sips of milk, "Boy, oh, boy, oh, boy."

In the morning, Double O came to our room. He told us he was moving my father's bags out of ours and into another, more private and secluded room. "The coach needs his sleep," he said. As he took the last carton of milk out of the mini-bar, I could hear him chanting, "Everything's under control, everything's under control, everything's under control."

THE FOLLOWING DAY, after the game, my father told reporters, "I assumed the team knew what was taking place. And so I didn't try to motivate them. I didn't even give them a pregame pep talk." He added, "The Super Bowl was almost anticlimactic; beating the Dallas Cowboys was our Super Bowl."

The Redskins had lost to the Dolphins, 14 to 7.

Jack Kent Cooke was hosting a postgame Super Bowl party at the Fabulous Forum Club. The last couple of years, Cooke had been busy cheering his Los Angeles Lakers to an NBA Championship. My parents never even mentioned Cooke anymore. Once the contract had been signed and we moved to Washington, they had enough to complain about with Edward Bennett Williams. After the Super Bowl loss, my father wanted to pay his respects to the man who had brought him to the Washington Redskins.

When Leroy pulled into the Forum parking lot, my father told us all to wait in the car while he went in—it would only take a second. My mother shoved me out of the door after my father, telling me, "Follow him." I followed him like a guardian shadow, through the parking lot full of shiny expensive cars and under the golden awning of the private Forum Club. The place was packed. The air was thick with smoke. The laughter was frightening. No one reached out to shake my father's hand. No one stopped my father for an autograph. No one yelled, "Hey, Coach! Hey, George! We love you!" No one knew that now, more than ever, my father needed to be surrounded by fans. No one seemed even to recognize him. "Excuse me, pardon me, I'm sorry," my father said as he made his way through the crowd. In a far corner of the club, Jack Kent Cooke sat at a round table filled with men. When they saw my father, the table of men stood to offer him a chair.

Cooke remained seated.

My father remained standing. He had his hands in his trouser pockets.

"I just wanted to say, thank you, Jack," he told Cooke.

Cooke took a sip of his drink, swallowed slowly, and said in a gravelly voice, "George, dear." He cleared his throat. Took another sip, and said, "Dear George, don't be ashamed of a thing. Be proud of what you have done."

My father had his head down. He looked as if he was studying the pattern in the carpet.

Then he lifted his head and said, "Let me just say one thing: we will be back."

Cooke and the men nodded their heads in agreement. Still, I could see that each of them, in their unified nod, was thinking the same thing: you won't be back to the Super Bowl, George, dear; this was your last chance.

THAT NIGHT, my father had foreseen the end of his Redskins years. The following morning, he telephoned the Los Angeles Rams owner, Carroll Rosenbloom, to inquire about his prospects of returning to coach the team. "I quickly reminded George that he had five years remaining on his Washington contract," Rosenbloom admitted later. "George said he knew that, but he asked me to keep him in mind just the same."

On our way home to Washington, the Redskins' airplane was nearly empty. Some players had gone to Las Vegas. Others had returned to their off-season homes. A few had flown to Hawaii to play in the Pro Bowl. "It's a little sad, I guess, everyone going their separate ways," Diron Talbert told reporters, "but you get tired being together month after month after month. We haven't had a break from each other since training camp began over seven months ago."

Once home, we found another handwritten note from the president on the doorstep.

"Dear George," the note read. "You will be back."

My father handed the note to my mother. She put it in a shoe box filled with notes from the president. Then he went to bed. I went to say good night. He had already turned the lights off in his bedroom. I could hear him in there, still awake, thinking in the dark, adding up his mistakes, wearing himself out before another long off-season began.

"Dad?" I said. "Dad?"

He didn't answer.

I had always thought my father loved his players more than anyone else. But now, I think, I was wrong. That season, my father forbade Sonny Jurgensen to stand in the team photograph because Sonny was injured again and could not play for most of the season. Years later, Sonny told me that he was so hurt by that—that all his career he had wanted to be on a Super Bowl team and my father would not even let him pose in the photograph or stand on the sidelines at the Coliseum during the Super Bowl. That was Sonny's last season of his career. Sonny did not know if I, a woman, could understand. I told him I could. My father had not allowed me into so many banquets, games, camps, and locker-room celebrations, why would I expect him now to let me into his dark, sorrowful bedroom?

I went to my own bedroom, shut the door, and locked it.

First Love

CAL HAD PEROXIDE-BLEACHED BLOND HAIR, small thin hands, and a lazy eye. He was a California transplant, a supposed surfer, old enough to be in high school yet still in the eighth grade. Cal spent his school days smoking cigarettes in the girls' room, pressing girls up against the metal lockers, his tongue deep down their throats, and flipping off teachers behind their backs. He often loitered around classroom doors, in the hallways, and in the woods behind the school where a gully led to a creek. That's where everyone dropped acid. He didn't even seem to be enrolled in the school, except that every day after the last bell rang, I'd see his bald, goatee-faced father arrive in his shiny silver Mustang, pick Cal up, and peel out of the school parking lot. Cal didn't have a mother. She left them both long ago.

Cal was the best-looking lowlife my junior high school offered. He first talked to me after I made a comment about his surfing T-shirt. It had a crumbly, airbrushed picture of a guy swallowed up in a hip-high shore break. I knew the lingo. I said, "Catch a tube." "I'll tube you," he said, and he reached his hand down the back of my pants, yanked my hot pink panties halfway up my back, and screamed, "Wedgie!" The next day, he moved a carton of cigarettes and a stack of surfer magazines into my locker. I said he could. I gave him my locker combination—the true indication of commitment back then.

We made out all over the school: in the girls' room, in the boys' room, and in both the girls' and boys' locker-room showers. Cal taught me how to smoke filterless cigarettes, how to flick beer-bottle caps, and how to kiss without making a mess. Sometimes, when we kissed, I felt like an adult trapped in a kid's body. Other times, I felt like a kid trapped in an adult's body. Often I'd catch him making out with some other girl and he'd call me a bitch for spying. Then he'd make me something corny in shop class—a gorilla holding a bouquet of dried flowers that said DON'T LEAVE ME! Or a leather bracelet engraved with the words I LOVE YOU. If Cal had written "I luv you," I would have dumped him. But he wrote out the entire word, "love," and I believed he meant every letter. I promised to be his unto eternity. Or at least until school was out, when I'd return to California for the summer.

What I loved most about Cal: he cared nothing about football, the Redskins, or my dad.

All his other friends were equally uninterested. His friends were girls with oily faces and bare halter-topped backs. Girls whose parents were divorced, or dead, or missing in action. At lunch, we all sat on the hill of grass outside the cafeteria, sneaking cigarettes. Once, after Cal and I spent the entire lunch period demonstrating how to French-kiss, the principal led me to his office.

He made me dial my telephone number.

My mother answered "Hello?" and the principal tore the receiver from my hand.

He told my mother I was hanging out with the wrong kind of kids. "Fast kids," he said. "Kids growing up too fast."

He said from now on, he'd keep an eye on me. Because I was a nice kid, he said. There wasn't a worse thing he could have said about me. I was a nice kid. A nice kid. Then he asked, "How are the Redskins shaping up this year?" I knew the guy was a Philadelphia Eagles fan. He always dressed in Eagles green. The Eagles stunk. They landed in last place in the Eastern Division every single season, far behind the Cowboys, the Cardinals, the Giants, and the Redskins. He told my mother that I could not attend any future junior high dance.

I hadn't even been to a dance yet!

I cried so hard, the principal sent me to the nurse's office. Within minutes, lying on a cot in the dark, I heard Cal telling the nurse, "I have a stomachache. Can I lie down?" The dumb nurse gave him a cot. Soon we were going at it on the cot, in the dark, until the school bell rang.

Home, my mother said, "That Cal's trouble. He doesn't fool me with his 'Yes, ma'ams.' "

My mother despised Cal. She had seen him only a couple of times when he'd dropped by our house unannounced. He'd say "Hello, ma'am" to my mom, and before she could stop me, I'd be running out the door with Cal far into the woods behind our home, heading down to the Potomac.

Sometimes, when he dropped by during dinnertime, he'd appear in our kitchen window. He'd dodge in and out of the trash cans, making faces behind my father's back. Once, my brother Bruce spotted him and asked, "Who's that idiot?"

"My boyfriend!" I said.

My father stopped sipping his milk. He put down his glass, then he said, "Channel 2."

Cal had no respect for any kind of authority—parents, principals, football coaches. I respected him entirely for that.

Then, one day, he didn't show up at school. He was gone. He'd been expelled, one girl said. Another said he'd flunked too many classes. Another said he was caught making out with the school nurse. Yet another said he was sent to juvenile camp. When I came home weeping, saying that Cal was gone forever, my mother lit a cigarette. She said she was goddamn relieved. She said that was the best goddamn thing that had ever happened to me. There was no telling what more I might learn from that goddamn Cal, she said, dragging on a cigarette, picking her teeth with the edge of a matchbook.

No telling.

"IS THAT HOW YOU let her go to school?" my brother George yelled.

I was wearing my brother Bruce's baggy corduroys with an angora midriff sweater and mud-covered Adidas. My pants hung so loose and so low that my math teacher tied a rope through the belt loops, pulled them up, and threatened to send me to the principal's office if she ever saw me wearing my pants so low again. As soon as I left math class, I undid the rope and whipped it at every boy who dared ask me "What are the odds of the Redskins returning to the Super Bowl next year?"

"Do you think I have any control over what she wears?" Mom said, then offered George a gallon of milk.

George came home weekly from law school to raid our refrigerator of all its food.

"Send her to Madeira!" George screamed.

"I already have the application," Mom said.

Madeira was the nearby, private, all-girls school where girls learned girl things—like foreign languages, horseback riding, and how to braid long hair. I'd seen the Madeira girls—blond, horse-riding, confident. I'd rather go to a school with boys—keeping me brunette, terrified of horses, and insecure.

"Madeira's not the real world!" I screamed.

"Real world?" Mom replied. "You don't even know what the real world is!"

George took out a plug of tobacco and stuffed it in his mouth. He growled up a thick wad of phlegm and spit it into his hand for the dogs to come lick. He was dressed like a character on *Hee Haw*—cowboy hat, flannel shirt, blue jeans, and boots. Mom admired him more than any of her other children. He got straight As even when he acted like a hick. She went to stroke her son's strong arm, but he brushed her away with a loud burp.

"Go ahead," she said to me then, "hang out with losers, be like Gregory, you're only hurting yourself!"

Gregory had recently declared his college major: psychology. His lifetime goal was to help heal broken families as a family counselor, he told Mom. His University of Delaware friends, a group of surfers from Philadelphia, supported Gregory in his quest. They, too, sought to someday mend lives as social workers. Mom said such professions were noble but useless—"The only person to rely on is yourself," she often said. "How do you think I've survived all these years?" Now I was headed in the wrong direction, too, Mom told George. She recited my eighth-grade grades: an F in math, an A in fiction, Cs in everything else.

"Fiction?" George said. "What's fiction?"

Fiction was an elective class taught in a converted custodian's closet. My peers were a handful of downcast, tie-dye-dressed students. The teacher was a spinster who seldom said more than a sentence. As soon as the class bell rang, she'd draw the window blinds, turn off the lights, play cassette readings of Edgar Allan Poe stories, and watch us all quiver in our straight-back chairs. After the ghoulish tales ended, she'd flip on the lights, tell us, "Now, go home and write something that scares me." Then the bell would ring, and we'd run our separate ways. I wanted to explain to George and Mom that fiction class was a relief from the world of football where achievement was measured so mathematically exact—wins, losses, ties—that in fiction class, all I had to do was write something, anything, that made sense. That when I wrote, I was absolutely alone, and I could write for hours without anyone telling me to shut up. I wanted to explain all this to the both of them standing there staring at me. Instead I blurted out,

"How can smoking pot hurt me?

"How can inhaling aerosol deodorant hurt me?

"How can drinking airplane bottles of whiskey, cognac, and vodka hurt me?"

"She's going to Madeira!" George barked.

"I'm going to Langley!" I screamed.

Gregory and Bruce had gone to Langley High School. Why couldn't I? Langley had race problems, drug problems, and a football team. What did Madeira have? Horses, girls, and pleated skirts.

"You're going to Madeira," Mom said.

George filled up his huge sideline coolers and tossed them all into the back of his Redskins pickup truck. He left the refrigerator empty. Mom cried. She cried whenever any of her sons returned to college or law school. Then she turned to me, standing there in the driveway, watching the truck crest the hill.

"Stand up straight!" she yelled.

In spite of my other problems, Mom's biggest issue with me was my poor posture. I was always walking around with my arms crossed in front of my chest. I was walking like my father, she said, walking like I was ashamed. "What are you so goddamn ashamed of?" she'd ask. "You should be proud!" She led me back inside the house, sat me in a chair, jammed a knee between my shoulder blades, and yanked my shoulders back. "There!" she said, cracking my spine, "that's how a girl should stand!"

As soon as she let go, I caved back in. I ran to my room, shut the door, and lit a cigarette. I smoked until the sky grew dark. Then, when I heard Dad come home, I brushed my teeth, washed my face, and reappeared, the good-girl child he had always known, downstairs, in the kitchen to help Mom serve dinner.

At school year's end, I said good-bye to all my friends in junior high, went to California for the summer, and assumed I'd be dressed in a kilt and kneesocks and a pressed white blouse in the fall, headed to my new school, Madeira. But Mom never said anything about Madeira again. I guess there were too many pressing things to worry about other than me—the new house Mom was building and Dad's struggles to get the Redskins in the play-offs.

The Good Doctor

MY PROBLEM RESIDED in my head, the Redskins' team doctor explained, in a little gland in my brain. The pituitary gland. He showed me the gland in a full-length poster of the male human body that hung on his office wall, beside a team photograph of the Super Bowl Redskins. I stared at the tiny, oval-shaped gland and wanted it removed immediately. The gland was making me cry incessantly! The gland was making me bleed to death! The gland was making me want to be a cheerleader! I wanted to explain these things to the doctor, but how could I, when all off-season long the doctor was tending to more important things—like healing Billy Kilmer's stomach ailment, which had hospitalized him before the last game of the regular season? What was I going to say, here, in this room, sitting fully dressed on this padded table, about my little aches and big pains when the doctor had a handful of Redskins who couldn't even walk? Obviously there was nothing wrong with *their* pituitary glands.

"The pituitary gland controls your emotions," the doctor explained. "There's no controlling the pituitary. Only your desire to control your own emotions will help you control how you feel and what you feel."

"Now do you feel better?" my mother asked as we left the doctor's office.

"Sure," I lied, "I feel great."

"See, there's nothing to cry about," she said. "There's no reason to be *depressed.*" She looked over at me sinking into the seat beside her. She took one hand off the steering wheel and placed it softly on mine. She confided the true secret behind her sanity. "When you feel yourself getting upset, you need to *control* it, *ignore* it, *negate* it," she told me. "How do you think I've lasted this long with your father?" Then she leaned back, took a long deep breath, and began talking about her impending nervous breakdown. Mom was going through menopause. She dressed for summer in winter, smoked three packs a day, and spoke daily of her impending breakdown. She'd often ask me, "Are you trying to give me a breakdown?"

Whenever Mom said "nervous breakdown," I pictured all her tightly wound nerves breaking and snapping, leaving her emotionally inert and perfectly calm. I did not think that would be such a bad thing for Mom. A breakdown of her nerves might be just what she needed. She could stop worrying about us kids, stop yelling at reporters, and stop wondering about the length of Dad's coaching contract. After a breakdown, Mom could start all over, rebuilding her life and her emotional state just as she built houses—from scratch.

Driving us home from the Redskins doctor's office that day, she bumped every curb, ran red lights, and flicked ashes into the Cadillac's thick-pile carpet. She was driving worse than ever before. When I mentioned to her that she had just run her fourth red light, that she'd better be careful, that she might get a ticket and how would that look in the sports pages, she screamed at me, "Listen, when you're a mother and a wife and housekeeper, then you can tell me how to drive. Until then, mind your own goddamn business!"

I fastened my seat belt.

TWO YEARS PASSED.

For two years, I followed my mother's advice for maintaining a semblance of sanity. During those two years, President Nixon had resigned; we had moved into our new, desolate, fortress of a home; the Redskins had been knocked, twice, out of the running for the Super Bowl in the first round of the play-offs; Leroy had been replaced by a new driver, a hefty ex–D.C. cop named John; and my brother Bruce had left for college. Throughout it all, I learned to control it, ignore it, and negate it—until my father's sister was found dead.

George Allen's Sister

MY FATHER'S SISTER, VIRGINIA, had been found in the garage of her home in upstate New York, slumped over the steering wheel of her car with the engine running. A pile of paid bills, stamped and sealed in envelopes, lay on the seat beside her. Her husband discovered her around midnight in the house they shared with her mother. She was scheduled to leave the following morning for a vacation in Miami with her husband. The family doctor said that Virginia had agreed to go on vacation only if he would place her mother temporarily in a convalescent hospital; she never wanted to leave her mother unattended. The doctor said that Virginia was tired, overworked, and weak. She owned and ran a strip-mall diner. The doctor reasoned that she was on her way to the diner late at night to do some bookkeeping, had started the car to warm the engine, and had fallen asleep. Cause of death, he said, was cardiac arrest.

Suicide was immediately ruled out. It was an accident, the doctor said. Virginia wanted to live.

I heard the doctor's story twenty years after her death. But twenty years earlier, I had heard a different story from my dad.

Dad told the story only moments after he had received word of his sister's death. He told me that Virginia was found on the floor of the garage, beside a crowbar, apparently trying to open the garage door, which was frozen shut. He told me it was morning, that she was on her way to work, when the fumes overcame her. He told me that this should be a lesson to me: never start a car with the garage door shut. He also told me something that he had never before mentioned—that I reminded him so much of his sister, that I was thin, just like her, and conscientious, he said, just like her. He said that his sister was frail and couldn't open the garage door and was overcome by the engine fumes. You need to gain some weight, he said to me before packing his bags and returning to the town where his father was born and buried—Albany, New York.

I did not believe the doctor's story or my father's story. I did not believe that Virginia had wanted to live or that she had struggled to stay alive.

All her life, she lived with her mother, through one failed marriage, and then throughout her second marriage. I had met Grandma Loretta and Virginia only once. Virginia was quiet and reserved and barely smiled; Grandma was chatty and outgoing and giggled incessantly. At the end of every season, we would telephone the both of them, a customary annual call, to talk about incidentals like the weather. Grandma was, as many in Albany later told me, a "hardworking, whip-cracking, Irish Catholic." Virginia was "a perfectionist," "wound tight as a rope," and "constantly overstressed." Her only vacations were those imposed upon her. She often became so run-down and sick that she would be forced to take a few days off from work and rest in a hospital bed.

"She was lonely—she kept to herself," a neighbor told me.

"She was too busy working to make any friends," a distant relative said.

Virginia was also never one to complain. I imagine her to be the kind of person who would hide her own suicide. She would set everything in order, get her mother into a good, safe hospital, pay the bills, have her hair done (she had been to the hairdresser earlier that day), and then, when everything was in order, she would sit in her car and start the engine. I have always believed Virginia planned her own death and framed it as an accident.

I will never know what really happened. Her death was not investigated. Someone, maybe Grandma, maybe Mom, maybe Dad, maybe all of them collectively, decided that an investigation into the cause of death would be bad publicity for Coach George Allen.

Dad said a handful of people attended her funeral. She was to be laid to rest in a family plot in a Catholic cemetery, but a blizzard postponed the burial. Dad did not have time to wait for the snow to clear; he had to get back to Washington to prepare for the draft. Within twenty-four hours of leaving, he returned home from Albany with a handful of childhood photographs. There was one of Dad pulling his baby sister in a wagon, another one of Grandma and Virginia and Dad dressed for church, another one of Earl with his baby son in a field of grass. In all the photographs, my father had a distant look on his face that to me implied "I will escape." Virginia knew that she would never escape being an Allen, the depression that went with it, and the destiny to be buried not beside her husband, but alongside her own father. One photograph in particular moved me. It showed my grandfather Earl, with a zombielike expression, as his daughter stood beside him in an overgrown rose garden. Virginia had her arm around him, leaning her head toward him, as if holding him up. I had never seen photos of Virginia this young. I had seen only the adult Virginia, tall and gaunt and lean with frosted hair and black pencil-thin eyebrows. Here she was young, soft, and plump, with brown, wavy hair past her shoulders. I could almost discern a subtle grin. She leaned her head into her father's chest. Her posture seemed to say "Love me." His body appeared stiff, his gaze absent, his mind seemingly unaware that his own daughter was standing beside him.

Earl looked just like my father. I looked just like Ginny.

After her death, my father would unconsciously call me by his sister's name.

"Ginny, pass me the milk," he would say, or "Ginny, go help your mother with dinner," or "Ginny, don't frown so much—it will ruin your looks."

I never pointed out his mistake. I passed my father his milk. I helped my mother serve dinner. I tried not to frown.

Once, my mother spoke up and said, "She's not Ginny."

Dad didn't even look up at me. He simply said into his milk glass, "You're just like my sister."

His words, "You're just like my sister," shook me. Were these a compliment or a curse? I had often thought my life would end just like Virginia's: in a secret suicide that no one would ever have the time or the courage or the interest to try to understand.

Many seasons later, my father told me how he regretted never having visited his sister's grave. He had never even seen her headstone. Maybe someday we could both go there together, he said. I told him I would like that, though of course we never did. Several years after he died, I went to view his sister's grave. It took hours to find it, but with my husband's patient help, I finally found the grave in an untended site. My aunt is buried beside her father in an odd-shaped family plot in a crowded cemetery filled with dirt-stained, grass-covered, weather-worn headstones. I do not know why I had expected something more than the untended plaque of slate: VIRGINIA ALLEN SHATTUCK, 1920–1975. My father's grandparents are buried somewhere nearby in unmarked graves. I do not think my father could have stood seeing the place. He would not have taken pride in how far he had driven himself from this final resting place; he would only have shuddered at how easily anonymity could take those once closest to him.

Home

THE WASHINGTON POST published a full description of our new home—a secluded, private, three-story, seven-bedroom, eight-bathroom, five-fireplace, three-car-garage, 8,400-square-foot house set on six acres of rural Virginia land. The nearest neighbor was half a mile down the road. The design, the Post said, was southern colonial: handmade-tile floors in the entranceway, marble counters in all the bathrooms, and cherrywood cabinets in the kitchen. A massive stone fireplace graced the family room. The home had its own private well, a lazy creek running through the backyard, a large swimming pool, a half-size basketball court, and a regulation-size tennis court. Hand-painted tiles were set into the brick posts at the head of the driveway, naming the house VILLA ROUGETS, a rough French translation meaning "home of the Redskins." The place was valued at $650,000. I thought my mother would have been pleased with the attention. But when she read the Post's rendering of her home, she said, "Those bastards! First of all, it's not goddamn southern colonial, it's goddamn country French, and second, what right do those bastards think they have, publicizing our address to the whole shit-ass town of Washington?"

She telephoned Ben Bradlee. "How could you give out this kind of information?" she screamed into the receiver. "All anyone has to do is look at the Redskins schedule, see when George is out of town, and then come here and kill me and my daughter!"

My mother threatened to sue Bradlee if he did not pay for an electric security gate to keep out all the fanatic fans who would now surely be rushing to our doorstep.

My mother's threats did not shake Bradlee. Years later, he told me he did not even recall the conversation.

But I recalled the conversation and my mother's shouts into the telephone she thought was tapped. After she slammed down the receiver, she said, "I hope they liked hearing that one, those bastards!"

My mother was certain *The Washington Post* had tapped our telephone. She complained of hearing clicking on the other end of the line. She often asked me if I had heard the clicking, too, as if someone were listening in from another room. Day by day, game by game, season by season, she grew more deaf. She often thought the stove fan was on full blast. "Do you hear any buzzing?" she'd ask me. "Is that fan on again?" When I told her that I did not hear any clicking or any buzzing, that maybe the sounds were in her ears, she said it had nothing to do with her goddamn ears. She said it had to do with the *Post* tapping our phone lines, trying to learn what Dad was intending to do next. She said, How else would Edward Bennett Williams have caught my brothers using the Redskins' credit card to make long-distance calls to check the local surf report in Los Angeles?

She complained so much that my father finally telephoned a CIA investigator to check out the telephone poles around our house. My father did not think to *not* place the call from our house; he did not consider that the wiretapper might be listening in. The following day, my mother said, she saw a woman, dressed in a business suit and pumps, standing alongside a mysterious unmarked van parked beside the telephone pole at the end of our steep driveway. When my mother asked the woman what she was doing, the woman explained that she was a supervisor for Virginia Power and Electric Company, and before my mother could ask more questions, the woman loaded her crew into the van and sped off. A few days later, the CIA investigator presented my parents with a twelve-page report revealing that the telephone pole "may have been tampered with," that there were "fresh footprints through the thick thicket around the telephone poles," that there were several "loosened lug nuts," leading the investigator to conclude that there was "good concern for" but not a "certain case of" tampering. The investigator suggested that we not "go to the press" with this information because it would prevent the investigator from finding the culprit.

My mother fumed. "They don't want us to go to the press because the press is guilty!"

When I rolled my eyes, my mother glared at me.

"You think you know everything, don't you?" she asked.

I shook my head. I certainly did not know everything. I hardly knew anything at all, I told her.

"Don't you sass me," she said. "For your information, there's been death threats on your father, and kidnapping threats on you—so *there,* now you know everything."

It seemed a little far-fetched to me. Someone was going to kill Dad? Why, for sending Sonny Jurgensen into retirement?

"How in the hell should I know?" she screamed. "Did I make the threat?"

And why would someone want to kidnap me? I wasn't Patty Hearst, I had to remind Mom.

"Who's talking about Patty Hearst?" Mom snapped.

Mom looked scared, panicked, in her masterpiece of a house so large, and so empty, that our voices echoed throughout its several thousand square feet. It would take years to buy enough furniture to fill the entire home that sat on a hill so bare of trees that the house stood out, declaring, Rob me, rape me, vandalize me! At night, unknown cars would circle our drive. I would peek at the cars through the peephole in the front door. I would hear the engine rev, see the headlights flash, bright lights, low lights, and then the car would speed away, burning rubber down the smooth, new driveway. We had no curtains to hide us from what may have been lurking in the dark. At night, after stepping out of the shower, I crawled along the floor of the window-filled bathroom, certain someone was watching from the woods. Once, when my mother spotted me snaking naked across the bathroom floor, she asked, "What the hell are you doing?"

When I told her that I was afraid of what she had told me—of me being kidnapped, and of Dad being killed, of both of us being raped or robbed or murdered—she asked, "Did I say that?"

"Yeah, you said that."

"Well," she said with a sigh, "you can't believe everything you hear."

Now I was terrified even to answer the telephone. We had already changed our unlisted number three times in the past three years. Often, when I answered "Hello? Allen residence. Hello?" I would hear a quiet breathing on the other end of the line.

"Hello?" I would say.

"What do you want?" I'd hear my mother shout on another line in the home.

"I was answering the telephone."

"Well, hang up," she would say. "There's obviously no son-of-a-bitching bastard there."

The Future Was Yesterday

A FEW NIGHTS BEFORE the 1975 season began, Dad came home for dinner with Mom and me. We were watching sports when we heard a former Redskin say, "George Allen is the best coach there is, but he's an under-dealer, telling a person one thing and doing the other behind his back." Last off-season, irreparable knee ligaments had forced the player into early retirement. Now he sat, his face unshaved, his gut fat, on the flatbed gate of a pickup truck. "I'd pick George as a coach any time," the player went on to say, "but George Allen is the last person in the world I would want as a father."

"I treated him like a son," Dad said, bewildered, gazing at the TV set. "I thought so much of him."

Next the TV reporter cited Allen's treatment of his own son, Bruce. Last season, at a game in Philadelphia, a referee caught Bruce standing outside the Redskins sideline boundaries, heckling the Eagles quarterback, disrupting the quarterback's audibles. The referee blew a whistle, stopped the play, led Bruce to Dad, and asked Dad, "Is this young man a member of your staff?"

An admission would have been a fifteen-yard penalty.

Dad looked at his favorite son.

"He must be one of those people the Eagles gave us as ball boys," Dad told the referee. The referee blew the whistle, and the game resumed. In the following play, the Redskins intercepted the quarterback's pass.

Home, after the victorious game, I remember Bruce joking with Dad about the referee's call. Bruce did not mind Dad denying him as a son. Bruce did not want the penalty either.

Next, the reporter interviewed a player in a dark room. The player's voice was electronically distorted beyond recognition, his head an anonymous silhouette. "To be perfectly honest, a lot of people are sick of George," the player said. "I wouldn't be surprised to see George coaching somewhere else next year."

When my father arrived at the Redskins, he instituted a system of fines to keep players muzzled from speaking their feelings to reporters. Now players didn't care about the system, and many openly spoke out against my father. One first-string veteran with a guaranteed no-cut contract didn't even hide his identity. He stood outside the gates of Redskin Park and said, "If George Allen says, 'This is the biggest game of your life,' one more time, I'm going to vomit."

"That bastard!" Mom shrieked.

I poured Dad some more milk.

Dad just stared at the TV.

"A loss of faith creeps in with Allen teams after five years," the reporter said. "His dictums and discipline and players grow old and tired, and soon it's time for Allen to move on."

The TV station then showed a film clip of my father when he first arrived in Washington. "The future is now!" my father cheered, his fist punching the air.

"The future *was* yesterday," the reporter concluded.

Mom motioned for me to turn off the TV set.

Dad rubbed his eyes.

"Is it worth it?" Mom asked Dad. "Is this so-called success worth being constantly under attack?"

"Sometimes I wonder," Dad said, gathering his playbooks into his arms and trudging up the stairs to bed, "sometimes I wonder."

The previous season, in 1974, the Redskins had lost $500,000 in revenue. The Redskins were also number two in league fines: Dad trading draft choices twice, Dad not citing a player's injury, Dad not keeping his game-day helpers within the boundary sidelines. The Redskins' payroll, at $3.6 million, led the league. Edward Bennett Williams blamed the revenue loss on the way my father paid players top dollar. If a player asked for a $50,000 annual salary, Dad offered the guy $60,000. The way my father was spending money, Williams said, the team would be bankrupt soon. "The main thing is to win," my father often told reporters. "If you win, nobody cares how much you spend."

That night, Dad could not sleep.

My bedroom shared a wall with my parents, and I could hear Dad rifling through the medicine cabinet, looking for his sleeping pills. Dad's medicine cabinet was filled with all kinds of pills: pills to help him sleep, pills to help him wake up, pills to help the pills.

I could hear my father fumbling to open a bottle of pills, and then my mother yelling, "Bring it here, bring it here, here, I'll open it, there, it's opened, *there.*"

I heard the water faucet turned on.

I heard the telephone ring.

I answered the telephone in my room. It was Edward Bennett Williams calling for Dad. I stayed in my room, listening in on my extension.

Williams told Dad he would not renew his contract at the Redskins unless Dad started the new young promising Redskins quarterback Joe Theismann ahead of Billy Kilmer.

"Okay, Ed," Dad said, and then hung up the telephone.

"Does he realize what goddamn time it is?" Mom said.

"I should never have come to the Redskins!" Dad said. "I should never have gone into coaching!"

When my mother failed to find the words to console him, Dad said, "I hope I die tomorrow," and Mom said, "Well, tomorrow's another day. Get some sleep."

"Look," Dad said, "I do things my way, that's the only way I know how, the *hard* way, and when I die, I won't have any regrets!"

Then he walked past my bedroom and down the hall to Bruce's bedroom.

With Bruce at college, his empty bed was the only place where Dad could fall asleep. I once found Dad in there, curled around Bruce's childhood stuffed toy that Mom had made out of a torn athletic sock. Maybe

Dad sensed that the Redskins were about to have the worst season since he arrived here—three games would go into overtime, and we'd lose two of them—but what would make the season even more difficult for Dad was having Bruce away at college. Bruce was the only one who could comfort him on the way home from a loss, reading aloud the game's statistics. Now, as we headed into the 1975 season, I knew our drives home from the stadium would be quiet, and I knew that without Bruce there, Dad would need more and more pills to lull himself to sleep.

In the morning, Dad sat at the breakfast table, late for work, groggy and grouchy, his reading glasses tilted on the tip of his nose.

The sports headline read IS THIS THE END OF GEORGE ALLEN?

Mom tried to pry the article from Dad's hands, asking him, "Why do you even bother to read that garbage?"

Dad ignored her. Dad handed me the article. He asked me to read the last paragraph aloud. As I did, I felt as if I were reading his obituary.

"The only thing the Redskins have going for them," I read aloud, "is a new rookie quarterback named Joe Theismann. Still, whether Theismann resurrects the Redskins or not, there is still a major problem lurking at the Redskins: George Allen."

Mom yanked the article from my hands.

"Who wrote that garbage?" she asked, and Dad went upstairs to get ready for work. Mom tossed the article in the trash. On his way out, Dad saw it. He handed it to me and told me to flatten the crumpled pages so that the article might someday be placed in one of his ten-pound scrapbooks stacked high in his home office. Dad followed me as I took the coffee-stained article into his office, placed it on the floor, and with the palm of my hand began smoothing out the bad news.

Dad told me that he wanted me to have these scrapbooks someday. I looked at the daunting, big, black books, filled with criticism and praise. Maybe the brothers might want them, I suggested. I did not want to have to remember the victories and defeats again. But I could not tell Dad that. I could see that he was so consumed with the daily tallying of wins and losses, and so concerned with how he was measured by reporters, and so dependent on these sports pages to determine how he felt about himself each day, that for me to say "I don't want to remember" would be the equivalent of me saying, "Someday, Dad, I plan to forget all about you."

Dad stood over me, as I, down on my knees, straightened out the future memories that I now see, with or without scrapbooks, I would never be able to forget.

Then I felt Dad's hand pet the top of my head. "Have a good day," he said.

Before I could turn to say, "You, too," he had already slipped out of the room, gone, headed for another day at Redskin Park.

Walter, Sam, and Flynn

WHEN DAD NEVER CAME to watch me cheerlead, Mom told me, "It's only cheerleading, what do you expect? It's not like you're playing in the game." While cheering the football team on, I tapped a varsity player named Walter to be my boyfriend. Walter was a nice Virginia boy who wore wool cardigans and beige khakis and leather Top-Sider shoes. His black wiry hair was always neatly tamed and combed. He smelled like a gallon of Brut, the same postgame cologne my father wore. He seemed like the right kind of guy Dad would like for me to call my boyfriend. Except that he played offense. Dad preferred defense. Walter's true offensive talent came through one night when we made out in a field of grass behind the neighborhood Pizza Hut. After hours of rolling around, rubbing skin, we returned to his house. His parents were going to give me a ride home. We spent what felt to me like hours upon hours chatting away in the brightly lit kitchen, discussing quarterback Joe Theismann, before his parents finally drove me home.

The next morning, as I ate breakfast, my chin and cheeks raw from Walter's roughly shaved face, my mother stared at me. "What did you do last night, play rugby?" she asked. She got the clothes I had worn the night before and tossed them on the breakfast table. There were grass stains and mud stains all over the back of my white ski jacket and powder blue pants. Without a word, she carried them to the laundry room sink and began scrubbing the stains out.

I should have dumped Walter then—isn't it a guy's job to clean off his handiwork? Instead, I waited until he tore a knee ligament in a game. After watching Walter get carried off the field on a stretcher, his parents offered me his windbreaker as a security blanket. I cuddled in it like a baby as I tried to sleep that night. But I could not sleep. Here I was, already I could see it, married to a football player, crying over every single loss and bruise! The next day, Walter returned to school on crutches. He said the injury knocked him out for the rest of the season. I could not bear having to watch him pine around on the sidelines. Plus, without a boyfriend in the game, Dad would never come see me cheer. I decided I only had room for one football guy in my life—my father—and one football drama, the Redskins. So I broke up with Walter. In the cafeteria, during break, I told him he was too good for me: a line a guy once told me when wanting to back out of a date. Walter nodded his head; he agreed.

"I *am* too good for you," he said.

He was the first and last football player I ever kissed. I never even ever allowed myself to look at another football player again. Instead, I looked at the guy seated next to Walter when I broke up with him, his friend Sam.

Sam was from the Bronx, a tall, skinny white guy who secretly wished he was born tall, skinny, and black. He wore a bandanna tied around his cleanly shaved head like all the cool black guys. He tried hanging out with the black guys at school; they brushed him off. Often on dates, Sam never said a word. He only responded to my ongoing questions—Why won't you talk to me? What's wrong with you? Are you mad at me?—with the thumbs-up or thumbs-down sign. One night we were at a couples-only party. The parents were out of town, and the bedrooms were filled on a first-come, first-serve basis. We were left with the couch. We had the TV on, pretending to be watching the evening news while Sam slipped his hand up my sweater. He was fumbling around when my father appeared on the TV screen. The TV reporter was asking him, "Do you expect to renew your contract with the Redskins?" Sam quickly pulled his hand away. When I tried to encourage him to continue, he leapt off the couch. "That's your father," he squealed, breaking his thumbs-only silence. "So?" I said, reaching for his hand. "Don't you know who your father is?" he yelped. "He's George Allen!" A handful of boys darted out of the bedrooms. One sleepy-eyed stud said, "George Allen? So, he's not as tough as the Cowboys' genius, Tom Landry."

The sleepy-eyed stud was my next boyfriend, Flynn. Flynn had long blond Frampton hair, smooth Swedish skin, and a springy walk. He wore tight T-shirts that showed off his Brando-esque torso. His most popular shirt pictured a Wheaties cereal box that read SEX: BREAKFAST OF CHAMPIONS. He had a nonstop series of girlfriends, one more beautiful than the next, and was known around school as a sex maniac. When he wasn't driving his royal blue 1967 convertible Corvette, he was driving his mother's red Spitfire, or his father's light blue convertible Mercedes 450 SL. Flynn's Corvette went sixty-five miles an hour in second gear. The car's engine was so heavy that when he drove it fast around sharp turns, the rear wheels lifted and whipped onto the shoulder of the road. Cresting a hill, the chassis would be airborne, and for a moment we'd feel weightless, free. Riding with Flynn down the wild Virginia back roads, I felt more alive than ever. Once, tilting my head back and looking up at the sky through a blur of trees, I realized, So this is what adults mean when they say these are the best years of your life. Some nights we would just drive around aimlessly with the top down, and the heat blaring, and the radio playing some sad Neil Young ballad. Flynn's choice in music was the only giveaway to how troubled he really was. His parents were going through a divorce. That's all he told me. Often after eating dinner at my house, he would tell me, "It's like a home here. It's like a real family."

My mother welcomed Flynn into our family by serving him mounds of spaghetti. My brother George welcomed him by slamming a pool cue against his head. My brother Gregory welcomed him by offering him a free psychological analysis. My brother Bruce welcomed him by giving him the nickname "Meathead." My father welcomed him by asking him, "Are you out for any sports?" Flynn started to say, "Tennis," and then hesitated and, instead, said, "Basketball." Dad then challenged Flynn to a game of Horse in our driveway. Dad won. When Flynn left our house, Dad said to me, "I like that Flynn." When I told Dad that Flynn was a Dallas Cowboys fan, Dad replied, "I didn't say he was *smart,* I said I liked him."

But Flynn *was* smart. He let my father win.

One night Dad came to see me cheerlead Flynn onto the high school basketball court. Flynn was second string. I was an alternate cheerleader, the equivalent of second string. Our team had clinched the game when the coach sent Flynn in during the opponent's last-second free-throw shot. Flynn lined up for the rebound. He caught the rebound and then shot—at the wrong basket—and missed. After the game, Dad consoled him. "Look, Flynn," Dad said, "I did that so many times in high school, you get sent in at the last minute, you're all excited to play, and then you forget which basket is yours." Dad was lying. He was never sent into a game in the last minute. He was captain of his high school team through three championships. But he made Flynn feel better. Dad would have done the same for my brothers. That night, I thought Dad might have a word of encouragement for me about my cheerleading. On the way home, all Dad could talk about was Flynn's mistake. The next day when I complained to Flynn that my dad hadn't even said anything to me about my cheering, Flynn said, "You're lucky your parents even came." His own parents never went to a game.

I never told Dad about Flynn's drinking. I did not tell Dad about Flynn driving drunk, and passing out, and waking to find that he had flipped his car on its side, wedged between a bulldozer and a tree. I did not tell Dad that when we went to parties, Flynn usually passed out. Sometimes, I would find him in the shrubbery; other times, flat-out on the grass. His drinking never failed to put him to sleep. He slept through my first fully dressed, body-to-body, nonpenetrating orgasm.

I did not tell Dad any of that.

Even as I postponed the eventual loss of my virginity, Flynn never begged. He never complained. He stuck with me. I stuck with him. Our relationship lasted seven years.

Everyman

ALL SEASON LONG, my father continued to ask Williams to renew his Redskins contract, and Williams continued to make his late-night telephone calls to our home, to inform my father, "If you don't start Theismann, I'm not renewing your contract." Williams preferred the young, quick, hot-headed Joe Theismann to the old, slow, cool-headed Kilmer. Theismann could be relied upon for a perfectly aimed spiraling bomb. He could also be counted on to get overexcited and then, with his soaring adrenaline, throw an interception.

The Washington press mocked Kilmer's barrel-size beer gut, his conservative play-calling, and his wobbly passes. With sixteen years in the league, the thirty-six-year-old could be depended upon to lead the team, more often than not, to victory. Kilmer had led the Redskins to four play-offs in five years, and to their only Super Bowl. As the 1975 season neared its end, Kilmer played with a separated shoulder and a fractured foot.

"If Bill Kilmer had been born a horse," one local reporter noted, "they would have put him out of his misery long ago."

Even with his injuries, Kilmer's twenty-three touchdown passes were second only to Cowboy Roger Staubach's in the NFC. Still, the Redskins fans did not fully accept Kilmer as their first-string quarterback. For years, I had watched Kilmer walk off the field, hearing fans shout, "We want Sonny!" At last, I thought, with Sonny gone, Kilmer could walk onto the field hearing cheers. But now fans chanted, "We want Joe!" It was always sad to see Kilmer walk off the field after a poor pass or a failed third down and hear the Redskins fans boo him. Even worse was now having to watch Kilmer walk *onto* the field with the discouraging chant. When asked if he found the chant demeaning, the warhorse replied, "I don't really give a damn."

Kilmer often spent his off-seasons in a hospital, where, he said, he felt like the scarecrow in the *Wizard of Oz* getting unstuffed and restuffed and sewn back together again. This season Kilmer did not have to wait until January to be admitted to a hospital. In the thirteenth week of a fourteen-week season, in Texas Stadium, in the fourth quarter of play in a game that would determine whether the Redskins entered the play-offs, Kilmer was blindsided by a rush of Cowboys. He was lifted off his feet and shoved, separated-shoulder first, into the hard AstroTurf. The referee blew his whistle. Cowboys stood, hands on hips, looking down at Kilmer. Then one offered Kilmer his hand and lifted the quarterback back up on his feet. Kilmer held his arm close to his chest as the Redskins doctor walked onto the field. Joe Theismann was sent in. The camera remained on Kilmer, supporting his left arm with his right hand, shaking his head as if to say he was so sorry to the coaches and to his teammates and to all his Redskins fans. With his one working arm, Kilmer took off his helmet, bowed his head, and wept. He was not crying because his shoulder hurt. He was crying because he had let his coach, his team, and their fans down.

The next day, the Washington press finally applauded the quarterback. "Kilmer shared with his television audience the beauty of a man's emotional commitment beyond himself," one reporter wrote. Another, who had always criticized Kilmer's awkward gait, wrote, "There are searchers among us who are looking for a testimony of what it means to be a man. Yesterday, in Texas, there were searchers who were uplifted by Bill Kilmer's tears."

"This is a man who stumbles and falls, but this is a man who tries," wrote yet another. "Kilmer shows on every play that he's so human. There he is, the guy with the bad body, no classic style, scratching for everything he gets. Every man on the street identifies with him. With Kilmer, it's all in the heart."

Seeing Kilmer walk off that field, I saw strength in what he may have thought was weakness. I saw this as Kilmer's greatest, truest, most heroic moment, and it inspired me beyond anything my father or my brothers or my mother could ever say or do to teach me how to live my life. "Suffer and sacrifice," my father always preached. His philosophy was perfectly rendered when Kilmer wept before millions on national television. The Redskins went on to lose, 31 to 10. We were knocked out of the play-offs, but I had never understood my father better.

When Dad arrived home from Dallas, it was late, past midnight, and I did something I had not done since I was a child back in Chicago. I got out of bed and ran down the stairs to greet him. My mother was already waiting in the kitchen. Without a word, she sat him down in his dinner chair, and cut him a piece of rice pudding. She poured him his glass of milk. I watched my father eat his cold rice pudding, one hand on his stomach ulcer, the other on his spoon.

"How's Billy?" I asked Dad.

Dad looked up from his pudding, and for a moment, he gave me the kind of look I had only seen him give my brothers, a look that said to me that he understood that I could understand him.

"Oh, so-so," Dad said, "so-so."

I watched him eat and chew and swallow every single bite of that cold good-luck Redskins-beat-Cowboys rice pudding.

The Redskins ended the 1975 season 8-6, in third place. For the first time in my father's Redskins career, the team had not made the play-offs. The Christmas headline read AS THE SUN SINKS, WHITHER ALLEN? On Christmas Eve, Dad stopped by a nursery and bought the entire grove of leftover live Christmas trees to be planted in our yard. The trees were his gift to all of us, Dad said, for all those Christmases when he was not home, coaching in the play-offs. For Christmas, Dad would also give each of his sons a brand-new Redskins-sponsored car—for George, a Ford truck; for Gregory, a Dodge Colt; for Bruce, a Chevrolet Camaro. He gave me a personalized Redskins jersey that read JENNIFER across the shoulders. But the greatest gift was that brief moment of recognition that said to me, "You do understand me, don't you?"

Etiquette

FOR MY SIXTEENTH BIRTHDAY, my mother gave me a fingernail kit, a hair-curling iron, and a copy of *Seventeen* magazine's *Book of Etiquette*. Now that I was a young lady, she said, I needed to know how to groom myself. Mom said the first thing a boy sees is how a girl is groomed. I thought "groomed" sounded like something that was done to a dog, not to a teenage girl. It was 1976—no one was groomed. Not even store-window mannequins.

We were standing in her dressing room, before her three-way full-length mirror.

First of all, she said, look at your nails. Are they neatly filed and clean and smooth? My nails were broken and bitten and tobacco-stained yellow. Look at your hair, she said. Is it clean and brushed and parted neatly? My long, brown, straight hair was clean but not brushed and certainly not parted. Look at your eyebrows, she went on. Are they thin and delicate? My eyebrows were thick and bushy. Mom said boys care about these things. She said now that I was sixteen, going on seventeen, I should start caring about these things too.

She sent me off to my bedroom with my new book. She almost had me convinced. Then I started reading the book jacket.

"The teen who has everything," the book jacket read,

. . . can keep a beau

. . . is nice to have around

. . . has comfortable manners

. . . can write a good letter

. . . wears the right clothes

. . . can say "no" nicely

. . . knows how to travel

. . . has good manners on the road

. . . is charming on the telephone

. . . is a good hostess

. . . is a better guest

. . . understands boys

. . . gets along with grown-ups

. . . is popular at school

. . . does her share for other people

. . . knows the right present to give

. . . will get engaged and be able to plan the perfect wedding!

Q: How does she do it?

A. She read the book.

Q. What book?

A. *The Seventeen Book of Etiquette.*

The editor went on to explain that the book was designed for boys and girls. Yeah, right, I could see this on my brothers' bookshelves. The cover showed a girl with a white rabbit-fur sweater tied over her shoulders and a blue silk scarf wrapped around her hair. She wore pink lipstick, false eyelashes, and thick black eyeliner. Her bobbed hair was fluffed high on top and curled up at the ends. She looked like no one I would ever want to be. I breezed through the pages—how to talk politely to telephone operators, when to arrive at and when to leave a party, how to translate restaurant menus, how *not* to lend clothes. There was an entire list of "image wreckers," from the perils of a "slumped posture that forms one long blob from neck to hipbone" to "collapsing into a chair like a blob of putty." I couldn't read any further. I had no interest in containing myself. Sure, it's nice to be polite. Sure, it's nice to be considerate. But no one, and no book, was going to tell me how to walk, sit, or talk.

I put the book on my shelf, alongside my Redskins press guides and the belated sixteenth-birthday game ball Dad had given me for having missed attending my first Redskins home game ever, sick with mono and a 105-degree fever. TO THE REDSKINS #1 CHEERLEADER, the game ball read, JENNIFER ALLEN. BEST WISHES, GEORGE ALLEN. It was forged by the Redskins equipment manager, who delivered the ball to our home one

day, asking me, "Did we spell your name right this time, babycakes?" I knew the game ball wasn't a real game ball like the ones my brothers had. My game ball was made of soft white leather. The laces appeared to be made of the finest silk thread. I breezed through my NFL press guides. There was more I could learn about life reading press guides than I could reading some girl book. I could learn about pain and suffering and overcoming obstacles—the true things in life—not false things like the shape of eyebrows and the proper way to cross your legs. Who did Mom want me to be anyway? I had a boyfriend. I was a cheerleader. What more did my mother want? She wanted me to walk and talk like a girl? I was doing all I could to be a girl. Still, I was failing. I knew my cheerleading would never earn me a college athletic scholarship like George and Bruce and even Gregory, with his lame grades, had managed to earn. I knew that my average grades would not get me into a decent college with a decent football team. I knew I was not amounting to the girl she dreamed I would be—a Miss America. All I was amounting to was a poor-postured girl who never let anyone know, not even my boyfriend Flynn, what a true loser I really thought I was.

Boy, was I a fake. I had learned my lessons from watching sports reporting on TV. All those years seeing Dad lie to reporters, "We have a lot to look forward to"; all those years watching injured players put on a tough act, "It doesn't really hurt"; all those years watching reporters act as if they deeply cared—"Tough loss, Coach"—had taught me well. Never let on to who you are, or how you feel. I was a fraud, just like the best of them. But at least, I reasoned, I knew it.

Now I had to tell someone.

Mom always said that she was my best friend. So I might as well tell her the truth.

I stormed back into my mother's dressing room. She was plucking her eyebrows bare.

"I'm sorry I'm a girl!" I told her.

"I'm sorry I can't play football!"

"I'm sorry I can't earn a scholarship!"

Her response?

She put down the tweezers.

She rubbed her eyebrows.

Then she laughed.

"We don't want you to be a boy," she said. "You're our princess! Our doll babe! Our Miss America!"

Each word cut me in half.

I was now standing as high as her kneecap.

"I don't want to be a princess! I don't want to be a Miss America!" I cried. "I want to be a boy! I want to play football! I want to do something that matters!"

She laughed some more until the laughing slowly turned to crying.

"Boy," she said, "you're really abused, aren't you?"

I shook my head, no, yes, no.

"Most girls want to be thought of as a princess! Most girls want to be Miss America! Most girls wish they had parents who loved them as much as Daddy and I love you!"

She lit a cigarette.

"Boy," she said, "I must have done something wrong if you feel this goddamn bad."

Cigarette smoke streamed from her nostrils. I tried to sneak away. Her smoke curled me near to her.

"Well, I'm sorry," she yelled. "I'm goddamn sorry I can't make your father happy, and I can't make the Redskins win, and I can't make you happy to be a girl. I'm sorry, okay? I'm sorry I can't control every goddamn thing in this goddamn world to make every one of you goddamn happy!"

She shook her head. "Believe me," she said, "if I could control every thing in this world, I would."

I believed her. More than anything, I knew that if my mother could, she would control everything in this world.

I tossed the book down the stairs, slammed my door, and lit a cigarette.

Confession

ONE NIGHT, during the 1976 off-season, I came to dinner stoned. Or what I thought was stoned—I had smoked some oregano in a hash pipe that gave me a tremendous, throbbing headache and blurring bloodred eyes.

My father stared at me while he sipped his milk.

"Did you have a workout today?" he asked. "When was the last time you had a workout?"

To my father, a "workout" was running several miles to sweat away all sin, angst, and fear. "Did you have a workout today?" was asking me, "Did you go to confession today? When was the last time you went to confession?"

I had never been to confession. I had never even been baptized. I never even jogged an extra lap around the high school track.

"I had a good workout yesterday," I lied.

Dad did not have to look at me to know I was lying.

The following morning, he woke me up by having Hilda jump on my bed.

"Would you like to come with me to Redskin Park?" he asked.

I sprang out of bed, put on my Adidas sweat suit, my Adidas running shoes, and my personalized Redskins jersey. Dad dictated a note for me to write to Mom, "Took Jennifer to work today, see you tonight, love, Georgie Porgie," and tossed me the keys to the car. I tossed the keys back and reminded him that I didn't know how to drive yet. Dad handed me his playbooks, got behind the wheel, and drove me to Redskin Park. There weren't any cars in the parking lot. A black bird sat on THE RED-SKINS sign.

Dad parked the car, took out his private keys, and opened the triple-locked doors to the building. There wasn't anyone else there. Only us. Dad told me he was going upstairs to look at some films, why didn't I have a look around, the locker room's down that hall, and out the doors I'd find a practice field, and down that hall over there, I'd find the saunas, hot tubs, and showers. I should help myself to anything and everything, he said. If I needed him, he'd be upstairs.

He left me alone.

At first I was scared, certain that I would run into the ghost of Vince Lombardi. After I had checked out every corner of the locker room and equipment room and weight room and saw that no one was there, I grabbed an official NFL "Duke" football, double-tied my shoes, and stormed out the doors. I charged onto the grass practice field, dodging imaginary defenders. I threw bombs, caught bombs, and made game-saving end-zone interceptions. On the fifty-yard line, I did push-ups, sit-ups, and more push-ups. I jogged a couple of miles around the track and then came inside, to the weight room, where I punched the air out of a punching bag labeled "Cowboys." I drank water from the locker room's steel vat of "Holy Water." Dad had this water imported weekly from a source in Pennsylvania. The water tasted like any other water. I drank it, seeing myself filled with the Redskins' fighting spirit. I later learned that the water was actually tap water. Dad had told players that it was holy, infusing them with the spirit of God to fight all evil, and many of them believed.

Then I strolled through the locker room. Each doorless locker posted the player's name and number on the top shelf. I noted each player's preference in shampoo, razor, mouthwash, powder, deodorant, and lotion. I gathered up armfuls of toiletries and took them all with me into the showers. I ran from one shower head to the next, imagining, Did Billy Kilmer wash his hair here? Did Diron Talbert scrub his toes here? I used Billy Kilmer's shampoo, Roy Jefferson's razor, Diron Talbert's powder, and as the final touch—one I have savored for years—I squirted tons of Joe Theismann's baby lotion onto my freshly shaved legs. I then wrapped myself in some of the thousands of fluffy pink towels folded and neatly stacked alongside each stall. I wrapped my hair in one towel, like girls do, wrapped another around my hips, like guys do, and draped one around my neck, like Dad did.

In the equipment manager's den, I put on a brand-new Redskins T-shirt that hung to my knees, a pair of bright white socks that reached my thighs, and a gray hooded sweatshirt with PROPERTY OF REDSKINS printed across it that hung to my ankles. I tossed my former soiled self into a laundry bag, threw it over my shoulder, and headed upstairs to find my dad. I passed by the photos of those who had come before—Vince Lombardi—and those who would never come again—Richard Nixon—and he who would soon own the entire Washington Redskins—Jack Kent Cooke—and made my way up the stairs to Dad's office. The lights were off, the film projector was on, the door was open. Then I saw the flickering black-and-white images and knew that Dad was watching *The Impossible Dream*. "Those Rams special teams were prepared," Dad said without removing his gaze from the screen. Dad coined the term "special teams" for the kicking and punting and receiving squad. Dad called them "special" because these were players who seldom were treated that way. Dad once had the announcer introduce the squad as the starting lineup on *Monday Night*

Football. The act was considered radical and irreverent by the league: it placed special teams as high on the ladder as offense and defense, as a team that could score and win games, not just kick and catch and run for cover. Some of those players still remember it as a highlight of their career.

As we watched the Rams block Green Bay's punt, Dad said, "You know, all you have to do is believe in yourself, and you'll be able to do anything you set your mind to do."

He then started to rewind the film.

I felt Dad had just asked me a question: what are you planning to do with your life? He rewound the film slowly. He was waiting for me to give him some kind of an answer. So I told him, I was thinking maybe when I grew up I would become some kind of a writer.

"A writer," Dad said, placing the film in its canister. "A writer," he said again. "Let me make a note of that." He wrote a little note to himself, and the following day, when I returned home from school, I found a brand-new electric typewriter on my desk in my bedroom. A handwritten note was taped to it. "From the desk of George Allen," the letterhead read. "Good luck," the note read in my father's own handwriting. "Love you all my life, Daddy Pie."

A Future

IN 1976, every time the Redskins lost, I skipped school for a day, sometimes two. I couldn't stand the postgame ridicule anymore: George Allen sucks! The Deadskins stink! The Redskins are history! By the time I'd return to school, almost everyone had forgotten about the Redskins' loss. My attendance record was failing me in most classes. My father once saw my report card and told me, "I had a perfect attendance record in high school. I never missed one day of school." That's because he was running away from home. Me, I was stuck at home, lying in bed all day after defeats, feeling lazy and weak. My mother never forced me to go to school. She, too, stayed at home, watching her soaps, dressed in her bathrobe until dinnertime sports.

Most kids were considering where to apply for colleges ing if any college would even accept me.

A guidance counselor suggested that I enter the high "Alternative Learning Program." The counselor present independent-study program for self-motivated kids, but I knew ALP was for stoners and outcasts who couldn't pull it together to attend class five days a week. All I had to do was make it to an ALP class three days a week and keep a journal to indicate what I had done during those two days off from class. ALP consisted of a couple of classrooms at the end of a hallway cordoned off from the rest of the school by a chalkboard on wheels. A torn-up couch and some broken chairs were situated in the hall outside the classroom doors. Long after the class bell rang, you could always spot a handful of ALPers crashed out on the couch, feet up on the chairs, cigarettes tucked behind their ears. During class, you could find some more toking up in the bathrooms or in the smokers' lounge outside.

The ALP teachers weren't like the rest of the high school teachers. They wanted students to call them by their first name. They really wanted to be teachers, unlike the others, who seemed trapped in a profession they despised. If it weren't for my two ALP teachers, I never would have made it through high school without failing. My government teacher hated Nixon and couldn't care less about George Allen. My English teacher didn't even know the difference between Richard Nixon and George Allen. At the end of every week, she would sit down next to me on the couch and silently read my journal, grim daily entries of winning and losing, living and dying, smoking and drinking and driving. When she closed the journal, she gave me a pained smile.

Once, she gave me an assignment to write a story about whatever I wanted.

"Whatever I want?"

"Whatever you want."

"Does it have to be true?"

"No."

I could even change my name, make a pen name for myself, like George Sand or George Eliot, the teacher said. I listened to her talk about writers like Sylvia Plath and Ernest Hemingway who had killed themselves. And others like F. Scott Fitzgerald who drank themselves to death.

She seemed to be saying, The worse their life, the better their art; the younger they died, the more they were remembered. I told the teacher I wanted the writer's life. I wanted to be a writer.

"Well," she said, "start writing."

When I told my mother how excited I was over the idea of someday becoming a writer, she said to me, "What do you think I've been saying all this time? Why do you think I read the sports page aloud every god-damn morning? To hear myself speak?" She looked up to the ceiling and said, "Finally, someone has listened to me!"

Then she looked me in the eye and said, "Actually, I think you should become a TV sportscaster—then maybe you would brush your hair."

For my English assignment, I wrote a story about a girl who hanged herself in the locker-room showers. The story began in the third-person voice and ended, after her death, in the first-person voice of the dead girl.

I got an A+. My first A+ ever.

My career was launched!

I came home to show my mother my grade. She brushed me away. Sports was on TV. While I had been celebrating my possible future, my father had been contemplating his own with the Redskins.

"Unless Edward Bennett Williams renews Allen's contract," the TV reporter said, "Allen may have to end his last season here as a lame-duck coach."

"*Bien entendu,*" Mom said in French, and then for my benefit, she said to me, "Here we go again, here we goddamn go again."

Negotiations

MOM AND I SPENT the summer of 1977 at our house in Palos Verdes. In July, Edward Bennett Williams scheduled a press conference to announce that my father had renewed his contract with the Redskins. My father missed the conference because his mother had died and he had to travel up to Albany, New York, for the funeral. That's when he noticed that, for two years, his sister's grave had remained unmarked. He assigned the task to a distant relative and returned to Washington quickly so that he and Williams could appear together before the TV cameras.

"Yes, it's a great contract," my father told reporters.

"Yes, I am indebted to the Redskins," he said.

"Yes, my love goes first to the Washington Redskins fans," he added.

Williams, who stood behind my father, leaned into the microphone to say, "We're happy to have George Allen along for three more years."

On our television in Palos Verdes, I watched my father and Williams shake hands. My mother and I knew the truth. No agreement had been made. No contract had been signed. It was a sham. A media-drawing event. An attempt to make the team think, as Double O would say, "Everything's under control."

Once we returned to Washington, Mom told Dad, "Call Hookstratton."

E. Gregory Hookstratton was our lawyer, our friend, and also the legal counsel to the Los Angeles Rams.

Dad told Hookstratton, "Call Williams."

Hookstratton called Williams. By the time summer had ended, and we were back in our Virginia home, Williams had drawn up a new contract. It was a great contract, one that still gave my father complete authority to cut and trade players and negotiate player salaries without having to ask for Williams's permission. Plus, it offered Dad an even higher salary—$250,000 a year.

Mom read the contract and said, "He's conning you out of your stock option."

"Stock?" Dad said.

"That's right," Mom said. "We have an option, or we *had* an option, to buy five percent of the Redskins stock, and now he's removed it from this contract."

Mom was talking about Dad's first contract with the Redskins, a seven-year-old document that offered us the chance to own a piece of the franchise. Dad always said every coach dreamed of both owning and coaching a team just as George Halas had. Vince Lombardi had once purchased Redskins stock. When he died, Williams bought it back from Lombardi's widow, Marie.

Mom said, "Call Jack Kent Cooke."

It was now mid-season; the Redskins were 4-4. Play-off hopes were dim.

"Cooke will get the option reinstated," Mom told Dad. "Cooke's our friend."

Dad called Hookstratton and said, "Hook, call Cooke."

In the past few years, Cooke had been buying up more and more Redskins stock. In a few more years, Cooke would displace Edward Bennett Williams as the main stockholder and president of the Redskins. For now, Cooke and Williams owed more than six million dollars in interest on bank loans from the original purchase of the team. One reporter disclosed that Williams had been blaming my father for the Redskins' revenue loss. Actually, the loss of revenue was due to Williams's and Cooke's inability to pay off the loans, the reporter said. Cooke remained out west. He was too busy to deal with Dad's contract. He was about to enter into the most expensive divorce settlement in the history of the courts. When Hookstratton called Cooke, Cooke said, "Call Williams."

Reporters broke the story: Allen had not signed the Redskins contract. Allen might not return to the Redskins next year.

Williams explained why. Williams told reporters, "George is grumbling over the removal of a stock-option clause—he's had seven years to exercise the stock option." Williams went on, "I've tried to tell George that the option is worthless. Sports franchises are not very good investments these days."

Hookstratton disagreed. Hookstratton wanted the option reinstated. With the league's recent $530 million television contracts, the value of NFL teams had skyrocketed. Teams would now earn money, regardless of whether they won or lost or tied. Football was no longer about winning or losing, it was about making money. Hookstratton thought my father should have a right to earn a bit of that free cash. Hookstratton advised my father not to sign the contract. My father took his advice.

"Look," Williams told the press, "I've offered George Allen the best contract in professional football. He can take it. Or leave it."

That season, after every Redskins loss, we would come home, eat rice pudding, and talk about the 5 percent stock option clause. Boy, did that bug Mom and Dad.

"They're trying to take advantage of us!" Mom would shriek.

"Boy, oh, boy, remind me never to do business with a lawyer again!" Dad would say.

To me, it sounded like a stall tactic. I thought the stock option was something to argue over while trying to see if the Rams were interested in hiring Dad at season's end. After all, after this season, the Redskins' draft bank would be empty. The Rams owned all those draft picks Dad had traded to them when he first arrived here.

One night, after a Dallas Cowboys defeat, I listened to Mom and Dad rehash the pros and cons of staying with the Redskins versus returning to the Rams.

Mom pointed her lit cigarette tip at me and said, "By the way, if you tell anyone about this, you could get Daddy fired.

"If anyone asks you," Mom said, "you say, 'Yes, my father hopes to coach the Washington Redskins.' "

No one asked. Not even Flynn. He just watched me mark off the days on the surfer calendar hanging in my locker, counting the days until summer began, when I would return to California while Dad went to Redskins training camp. That's what I told Flynn. But I think he knew I was counting the days until the Redskins years would end.

By December, Flynn was kicked off the basketball team for failing grades, I was kicked off the cheerleading squad for smoking cigarettes in uniform, and the Redskins were knocked out of the play-offs.

Our season was over.

Dad was home for Christmas. Christmas night, he shared a beer with Mom and he asked my brother Bruce to put on that record, "What's it called?"

" 'Take This Job and Shove It?' " Bruce said.

"That's it," Dad said.

The record was Bruce's Christmas gift to Dad.

I watched Dad sip his beer and sing along to the words, "Take this job and shove it, I ain't working here no more." He tapped his foot erratically. He said, "Boy, is that a great song," and then had Bruce telephone a handful of his favorite Redskins to come over for a sing-along. When they arrived, Mom offered everyone a beer, and all the men went downstairs and played pool and chugged beers and slapped backs. By next season, most of these men would be cut, or traded, or knocked into retirement with career-ending injuries. For now they acted as if they were young rookies with promising lives ahead of them, singing, "Take this job and shove it!" The more they sang, and the more they laughed, and the more they drank, the more I finally came to understand what my mother called "false hilarity." These men were putting on the same fake front as my dad, singing and drinking and laughing. Dad and his men sang until their throats became hoarse, and I thought that there had never before been a sadder Christmas than this, with all of us, our family and Dad's football family, gathered together under one roof.

TWO WEEKS LATER, on Mom's fifty-fifth birthday, Dad was fired by Edward Bennett Williams. I heard the news from a reporter who telephoned to ask, "Is George Allen available for a comment regarding his firing?" Dad was not home. He was on his way from Dulles airport with Mom after having spent the day in Los Angeles at Rams owner Carroll Rosenbloom's home. "My father's out having dinner with my mother," I told the reporter. The reporter hung up. I disconnected the telephone. I turned on the TV. Edward Bennett Williams wasn't available for comment, the TV reporter said. Williams was hiding from the press at Ben Bradlee's home. By the time my parents arrived home, they had already heard the news. My brother Gregory, on his way to pick up my parents at the airport, had heard about it on the car radio and had to be the one to inform them, "We've been fired again."

The following day my father denied reports that he had been to Los Angeles to discuss a job with the Rams. Coming home from school, I found Dad in his pajamas, arguing with a reporter on the kitchen telephone.

"I take my wife out to dinner, and this happens," my father yelled into the telephone.

Mom was goading Dad. She was flashing him hand gestures—the twist of the knife, the eye gouge, the throat hold. I picked up an extra phone line in the den and listened in.

"But George," the reporter was saying, "we have photographs of you and your wife arriving at Los Angeles airport yesterday."

"It's nobody's business where I was," Dad barked back, then finally admitted that he was in Los Angeles with his lawyer, Hookstratton, to discuss the Redskins contract. Dad said on the flight home to Washington he and his wife had decided to remain with the Redskins. The reporter asked, "If that's true, why didn't you telephone Williams when you heard the news?"

Dad's reply sounded like a teenage girl after a breakup.

"I wasn't going to call him. He fired me! If he wanted to talk to me, he could call me!

"Listen," Dad said. "The only reason I haven't signed a contract is because of one man—Edward Bennett Williams. I haven't applied or approached anyone about another job since I've been here. I've given the Redskins, the organization, the players, and the community everything I have—my heart and my soul and my health. And this is what I get—*fired*.

"Listen," Dad went on, "Williams is a cold-blooded fish. He uses people. He doesn't care about people. He only cares about what he can get out of them. That'll be the same way with whoever else comes in here next."

My father was hanging himself. No NFL coach talked about an owner as honestly as that. Even I realized that Dad's accusations were turning off owners across the league from ever wanting to hire George Allen again.

"Listen," Dad continued, "Williams is a Jekyll and Hyde, anybody who deals with him knows that. One day he calls you and he's ranting and raving. The next day he's as meek as a kitten. That's his training. He's a courtroom lawyer! He's an actor!"

My father went on to call Williams "petty, mean, and vindictive." He recited a series of "cheap, low tactics" on the part of several other owners, whom he deemed "sickening, self-righteous men."

I could hear the reporter scrambling to write down every word, flipping page after page in his reporter's notebook.

Then I heard Mom pick up another telephone line. She blurted into it, "Our telephone's been tapped."

"Hello?"

"My wife's on the other line," Dad said. "She said our telephone's been tapped."

"By who?"

"You tell me," Mom said.

"Look," Dad said, "I've been stabbed in the back. Why don't you find Williams and ask him why he had to fire me like that?"

A play-by-play of the conversation was published in a *Washington Post* article titled "The Final Plays." Days later, when Commissioner Pete Rozelle read it, he fined my father $3,000 for his comments. Rozelle noted that the on-the-field successes of teams under my father's direction were "matters of record." Unfortunately, however, several aspects of my father's performance away from the playing field had made "a record that continued to be, at the very least, disappointing."

When Williams came out of hiding, a reporter reminded the Redskins president, "Seven years ago, you said, 'George Allen is the last coach I will hire.' "

Williams replied, "Well, I was wrong."

Williams added, "I offered George Allen the best contract in football. I waited for George to sign the contract. I gave George Allen my unlimited patience, and he has exhausted it."

Williams then billed us $14,847 for misuse of the Redskins credit card—buying steaks for our dogs, chartering a private jet to see Bruce punt, and making long-distance calls to Los Angeles.

Throughout the long afternoon, reporters telephoned, seeking a comment, and real estate agents called, offering to help us sell our home.

That evening, Mom read the late edition of the sports page aloud.

"Allen and his peculiar philosophy, sooner or later, wear out their welcome," one *Post* reporter wrote. "He is so megalomaniacal about winning, so insistent that victories are more important than life itself . . . that he shreds the last vestiges of illusion owners have about being involved in a sport."

"Allen is a man people love to hate," another reporter wrote. "He has gone through life with the hangdog, worried look of a man who enjoys misery. His life is devoted to the serious pursuit of winning football games. He is like a religious fanatic trying to buy his way into heaven with a won-lost record."

"Nobody is invincible, not even a winner," wrote yet another reporter, who noted that my father had the best record of any coach in Redskins history. "But ultimately," the reporter reasoned, "it was not how many games Allen won that counted. All that mattered was how few friends he had made, and how little grace he showed when he was in power."

The following morning, only forty-eight hours after the firing, my father was informed that he had to immediately remove himself and his be-

longings from Redskin Park. He had often prided himself on having designed the first team-owned athletic facility in the entire league. Now, entering the building one last time, he saw that the de-Allenization of the park had already begun. On the walls, his portrait beside Lombardi's had been removed. In the office, Shirley and Double O were helping our driver, John, pack and seal my father's belongings into several moving boxes. On his desk, Shirley and Double O had placed copies of their letters of resignation to Cooke and Williams. My father held a final meeting with the assistant coaches, the trainers, the secretaries, the equipment manager, and the few players who had come to clean out their lockers for the long off-season ahead. Moments later, my father said good-bye, and headed out the double-locked doors of the building and into the Lincoln. As the car pulled out of the parking lot, my father looked out the rear window. The last thing he saw, he later recalled, was two men, dressed in gray coveralls, changing the locks on the doors to Redskin Park.

FOURTH QUARTER

A Dream Come True

"THIS IS A DREAM COME TRUE," my father was telling reporters. "My wife and I were saying this morning how lucky we are. Los Angeles has always been our home."

My father shook his head and wiped tears from his eyes, while my mother stood behind him, smiling, nodding her head.

At the Century Plaza Hotel in Los Angeles, in the exact room where Dan Reeves once claimed, "George Allen is the last coach I will hire," Rams owner Carroll Rosenbloom now stepped up to the microphone-laden podium to say, "George Allen is the last coach I will hire."

I watched the press conference, alone, during the dinnertime sports in Virginia. The day before, my mother had flown west with my father. She wanted to assess the winter storm damage to our Palos Verdes home. A summer drought followed by relentless rains had caused the backyard to landslide into the canyon. The goalpost was spared.

Two weeks had passed since Edward Bennett Williams fired my father. During that time, no other owner sought my father. My father was not worried. He had one job in mind: to coach the Rams. His lawyer, Hook-stratton, had helped him secure it. For now, my father appeared elated, and so did his new boss, Carroll Rosenbloom.

Rosenbloom was the acne-scarred, Gucci-tailored owner whom the NFL had once investigated for placing bets on his former team, the Baltimore Colts. After the league found him innocent, he bought the Los Angeles Rams from Robert Irsay, who had purchased the club immediately after Dan Reeves's death. In 1972, Irsay transferred ownership to Rosenbloom in exchange for the Colts. Under Rosenbloom, the Rams often finished top in their division. Lately, they would enter the play-offs, win in the first round, then lose to the Cowboys in the NFC title game. Rosenbloom now said Allen was the only coach who knew how to beat the Dallas Cowboys. If the Rams could beat the Cowboys, they could reach the Super Bowl. This will be an easy job, Rosenbloom continued, there is nothing to rebuild. No one to trade. No one to cut. All Allen has to do is beat the Dallas Cowboys.

My father nodded his head, yes.

My mother clapped. She stopped clapping after she looked around the room and saw that she was the only one applauding her husband's probable success.

When asked to divulge the contract terms, Rosenbloom avoided citing any details.

"I'm fascinated by the thought of what George Allen can do just coaching," Rosenbloom said.

But the terms, reporters urged, how much, how long?

"We discussed a year-to-year contract," he explained, "but we finally agreed on a week-to-week contract."

The roomful of reporters laughed.

So did my father. Looking back, I now see he looked like a fool, laughing at the joke made at his expense. At the time I thought, he is finally learning how to laugh. He has finally learned how to crack a smile.

My father then said he "relished" the idea of just "coaching and teaching." He said he wanted to "debunk the myth" that George Allen is "difficult" to get along with. He even promised to employ a multiple-set offense, and to open training-camp practice to fans. More than anything, he said, he was happy just to be coaching.

"I just want to coach," my father said. "All I want to do is coach."

My father's new title at the Rams was simply "head coach." I thought it was a step down from his title at the Redskins. Now he would have no general-manager responsibilities, no authority to fire assistant coaches or even trade draft choices. More than anything, my father's new Rams contract clearly indicated what he would *not* have. My father had not read the contract. If he had, he might have noticed that the contract devoted three pages to the terms for termination, citing that if the coach was "terminated," the Rams would pay the coach his annual $200,000 salary in deferred increments of $50,000 for ten years. If, after the termination, the coach earned $50,000 a year or more elsewhere, the Rams would not be responsible for paying him a single cent. My father had not only not read the contract, he had not signed the contract.

The TV reporter called the union of Rosenbloom and Allen the marriage of the NFL's odd couple. Allen had spent his career alienating owners. Rosenbloom had spent his career alienating coaches—especially former coach Don Shula, who had a seven-year winning record of 73-26-4 for Rosenbloom's Colts. Rosenbloom knew he wasn't winning any popularity contests by hiring George Allen. A recent *Sports Illustrated* poll had voted my father the most unpopular coach in the NFL. Ten years earlier, when his career was just getting under way, *Esquire* had called my father the NFL's "sweetheart coach."

"Can you live with George Allen?" a reporter now asked Rosenbloom.

"Hell, yes, I can live with George," Rosenbloom said. "I can live with him if he wins."

The press conference ended with owner and coach shaking hands. The TV reporter concluded the program by referring to my father's return to the Rams as "the second coming."

Sports was over. Weather came next. The weatherman quipped, "By George, he's born again!"

I shut off the TV.

THE FOLLOWING DAY, the Washington sports-page headline read, RAM PLAYERS PROTEST ALLEN COMING.

The hiring did not surprise the team. One player said, "The rumor's been going around the locker room for a couple of weeks. The guys who were here last time he coached the Rams told us it isn't going to be a lot of laughs."

"Don't think there hasn't been lobbying against him coming here," a Rams executive who chose to remain anonymous added. "There is tremendous resistance to Allen coming here. The remarks he made about Ed Williams when he got fired are reminiscent of the things he said here when he was fired by Dan Reeves in 1970—Allen can't open his mouth without lying."

"I can't believe Carroll Rosenbloom would do such a thing to his team," said Rams defensive linebacker Isiah Robertson. "I can't play for George Allen. I want to be traded!"

My father probably wanted to trade Robertson, but he did not have the power anymore. There were probably a couple of assistant coaches he wanted to fire, too. Yet all he could do was come to Virginia, and ask Shirley and Double O to return with him, back to California and the Los Angeles Rams. My mother helped him pack his bags. As I watched her pack his playbooks and his whistle and his brand-new Rams cap, she explained that she and I would remain in Virginia until after I finished my school year, and that by summer, she hoped to have our house here sold. Until then, my father would sleep on his old couch in the Rams offices. He would survive on his usual diet of vitamin shots, milk, and peanut-butter sandwiches. He'll be fine, my mother said, and my father agreed, he'd be perfectly fine. Just fine.

The day he arrived at the Rams office, the local Los Angeles morning sports-page headline read, GEORGE ALLEN HAS BEEN WELCOMED TO LOS ANGELES WITH A GUN TO HIS HEAD.

Homecoming

IN AUGUST, for the first preseason game, we sat in the exact same Coliseum seats we had sat in years before, surrounded by the same fans. During the national anthem, Mom turned to me and, with a confused look, asked, "Am I here now or then?" Everything seemed exactly the same until the game was under way. Players dropped passes, missed tackles, fumbled balls. The first-place Rams were playing like last-place Lambs. Halftime, the fans booed the team off the field. I had never heard my father's entire team booed before. Dad's secretary, Shirley, met us in the women's room and said, "I'm going home, something's wrong, I can't watch."

We lost.

The locker-room tunnel was nearly empty. No fans. Only a couple of Rams executives smoking cigarettes. I recognized one from the Dan Reeves era. He looked the same as he had years before—same wide, long sideburns, same buck-toothed dentures, same year-round golfer's tan. The Brownie Lady was nowhere to be seen. My mother asked the executive if he had seen her and he replied, "That old bag with the bum eye? She croaked a long time ago."

When Dad stepped out of the locker-room doors, no one ran to get his autograph.

Double O followed close behind. I waited for him to say "Everything's under control." But all he did was hand me a Xerox of the game's statistics.

Dad walked to the team bus. The bus was headed back to the Rams training camp.

"Don't you want a day off?" Mom asked Dad.

Dad shook his head no.

Dad had not taken one day off from work since he had taken the Rams job seven months earlier.

That night, he returned to his twin bed in his dorm room on the same run-down, suburban, college-training-camp campus. There, he continued his campaign to take the Rams to the Super Bowl. The following day, in the cafeteria, he noted the illogical location of saltines in the buffet line—saltines should be next to the soup, not next to the dessert. In the offices, he complained about the decor—torn carpet, broken water fountain, a painting of a sunset—how were those things going to help the team beat the Dallas Cowboys? On the practice field, he yelled at players to pick up their discarded Gatorade cups. He then enforced a three-practices-a-day work schedule, refusing to allow players off the field until each play was performed "perfect." He also installed a "Don't Walk On Grass" rule: "We run on grass. Only mailmen walk on grass." At meetings, he set up a contest for the neatest-kept notebook. The winner would receive a free gallon of milk. At night, he did bed checks, and after everyone had gone to sleep, he telephoned the front-office executives at home, insisting that the men now work on Saturdays.

A few days later, several first-string players walked out of camp. One player said, "I can't work with George Allen." Another one said, "His system is too complicated." Said another, "Allen should be cited for violating human rights!"

"I'm worrying about doing a good job to keep my job," Dad told reporters, "and these guys are acting like they own the team."

It was the first time I ever heard my father say that he was worried about keeping his job. I was worried more about his state of mind—why would Dad publicly admit this fear?—than I was worried about him keeping his position at the Rams.

The second preseason game was against the San Diego Chargers, who hadn't had a winning record in eight years. Before kickoff, nine Rams players called in "sick."

Mom and I called in "sick," too, staying home, listening to the summer-night game on the radio. We sat in the unlit den together, envisioning the eight dropped passes, the missed field goal, the mere fifty-four total yards in offense. The final score: Chargers 17, Rams 0.

It was Dad's first shutout in 133 games.

"It's just a matter of time before the players grasp my system," Dad told Rosenbloom after the defeat.

But Carroll Rosenbloom did not have the time.

Hired to Be Fired

THE NEXT DAY I picked up the upstairs telephone to call *Surf Report* when I heard my mother telling someone, "No, I haven't told Jennifer yet."

I hung up the telephone.

I ran down the stairs.

I knew the news was about my father. I thought he'd had a heart attack.

"No, he's been fired," she said.

I ran out the door and got into our new Rams Pinto. She ran into the driveway, waving me down, yelling, "Listen, listen!" I sped away down to the DEAD END sign of a windy beach road. I shut off the engine. I turned on the radio, found the *all*-sports-*all*-the-time radio station, and heard Carroll Rosenbloom say, "It is my feeling that I have made a serious error in judgment in believing George Allen could work within our framework. It's been extremely difficult for him to adjust to a new situation."

Rosenbloom was speaking from the Rams training camp, the radio reporter said, where, moments earlier, he had fired the new head coach, George Allen.

"We thought it would be wonderful if George only had to coach, not worry about things like cutting the grass," Rosenbloom was saying. "But we were wrong. When George came here he *did* worry about the grass. It was beginning to eat at George. I was beginning to worry about George's health. He gave up every drop of blood to his club. I wasn't going to sit back and see him destroy himself. George was his own worst critic. He gives himself no rest and no peace. He worked so hard it frightened me. He stayed up until two A.M. He rose at six A.M. He even thinks football when he's in bed. He is one heck of a coach. But I think he needs to take a rest."

Did it come down to a difference of opinion? the radio reporter wanted to know.

"If anybody thinks George did any wrong here, he's crazy," Rosenbloom said. "We never had a cross word. George has not done one single thing he could be reprimanded for. I am extremely fond of George Allen. When you've gotten to know somebody so fine, you don't want to hurt him. This time it hurt me."

It was the most complimentary firing I had ever heard.

"This is the shortest tenure of any coach in the history of the National Football League," the reporter noted.

"Allen isn't available for comment," the reporter added. "The coach is busy packing his bags."

I shut off the radio, flipped back the car seat, and lit a cigarette.

IT WAS NIGHT. Mom was in her bathrobe, sitting alone in the dark den. The French doors were open wide toward the pool patio. A strong summer wind sucked the curtains out the doors. The green pool light cast waving shadows across the room, making my mother appear to be underwater, drifting, floating. I could hear the telephone's incessant busy signal. The receiver was off the hook, hanging by its long cord off the den desk, and spinning slowly in the wind.

Without even looking up at me, Mom began replaying the day's events.

"When he called and told me, 'I've been fired,' I hung up on him," she said in a monotone. "The telephone rang again. I answered it, 'Are you kidding me?' He said he wouldn't joke about a thing like that. Then I hung up on him again."

I put the telephone back on the hook.

Mom said, "Keep that goddamn thing off."

I took it off and sat on the couch, waiting with Mom for Dad.

LATE INTO THE NIGHT, Dad arrived wearing his Rams cap with the "GA" initials embossed on the brim. The cap was tilted on his head. He stumbled into a chair and asked, "Hey, why's it so dark in here?" and then moved his hands across the wall to find the light switch. I stood up to kiss him but he stopped me, saying, "Close your eyes and hold out your hands." He then placed three turquoise stones in my palms. "Those are for good luck," he told me. I wanted to hand them back and tell him, "If anyone needs good luck, it's you, Dad."

Dad looked over to Mom. She still had not moved from the chair. He put the receiver back on the hook, forced out a laugh, and said, "Well, sweetie, I guess you won't have to worry about me coming home late anymore."

No one laughed.

The telephone rang. It was a reporter. I handed Dad the telephone.

"Listen," Dad said, taking off his cap and running his hand through his hair, "I would do everything the same. I did it my way, and that's the way it will always be. I had something to offer here, and it was rejected. I'm not the loser, see?"

Dad had been fired twice in six months; if he wasn't the loser, then I wasn't sure who was.

After Dad hung up, Mom said, "Can I ask you a question? Did you ever sign that goddamn contract?"

"Contract?" Dad said. "Contract? Signing that contract is the least of my worries."

I poured Dad a glass of milk.

Dad waved the milk aside.

"Right now," he said, "I just feel empty, like someone has cut out my heart."

Then he went upstairs to bed.

The Movers

THE FOLLOWING DAY Mom was downstairs in the same robe from the night before, reading the morning headline aloud to Dad—RAMS DITCH ALLEN—when the doorbell rang. It was the movers. They were here with all our belongings from Virginia. We peered at the imposing sight: two full-size moving trucks parked in the street ready to be unloaded into a house half the size of the one in Virginia. Dad took one look at the trucks, shook his head, and said, "I guess I made a mistake leaving a great job at the Redskins."

"Would you like us to come back tomorrow?" the movers asked.

"What's tomorrow?" Mom said.

"Tuesday," a mover said.

"Tuesday," Mom repeated. "What's Tuesday?"

"Tomorrow," the movers said.

Dad waved his hand. "What the heck," he said. "You're here, do your job."

Mom and Dad stood near the doorway watching the movers move every box in. A box marked RAMS would pass by, and Dad would say, "Do you think we should move back to Virginia?" and Mom would say, "Over my dead body. We're staying here!" Another box marked REDSKINS would pass by, and Mom would say, "Do you want to return to Virginia?" and Dad would say, "Heck, sweetie, I thought we were going to stay here." My parents were measuring the lesser of two evils: was it worse living in a place where you had been fired after seven successful seasons? Or was it worse living in a place where you had been fired after two preseason losses?

My parents could not decide.

The movers kept moving boxes in. The movers carved a walkway through the boxes so we could still get from room to room. Throughout the house, we made our way through a tall tunnel of boxes marked GAME BALLS and TROPHIES and PLAQUES. None of us could even begin to open up one box. Before leaving that day, the movers offered to help us unpack the boxes. My parents were unable to answer. I told the movers no thanks, tipped them well, and sent them on their way. Then I looked at all the sealed boxes and reasoned that my parents would now have something to do in the coming weeks besides rooting for every single team to lose.

In my bedroom, boxes were stacked as high as my head. I opened every box carefully and unwrapped each object slowly—a snow globe, a stuffed animal, a crayon drawing—and then tossed it into the trash bag. I threw away everything that meant anything to me—kindergarten drawings, my entire twenty-eight-NFL-city snow-globe collection, carnival stuffed animals my brothers won—into the bag. Mom, who had broken several toes kicking boxes while trying to maneuver to answer the telephone, now stood on one foot in my bedroom doorway, saying, "This is not the time to be doing this. Stop it." She tried to stop me. No one could stop me. Not even Dad standing in my doorway, saying, "Maybe you should wait until another day."

It took me only a couple of hours to toss out my entire life. This is so easy, I thought. I can simply erase everything by throwing it all way. When I was finished, my bedroom was devoid of most memories. All I kept was my Redskins game ball, my photograph of Roman Gabriel, and my electric typewriter. Now I can start all over, I thought, staring at my near-empty bedroom.

"We probably made a mistake bringing Jennifer back to California," Dad wrote, years later, in his self-help book, *Merry Christmas, You're Fired.* "We could have let her finish her senior year in Virginia and graduate there. We had friends she could have stayed with. It simply never occurred to us how much the move would disrupt her life. And of course we could not foresee how much that disruption would be compounded by the firing. It really hit her. I was the one who lost the job, but her loss seemed just as great."

I did feel a loss when my father was fired. I had lost my faith in football. When I lost that, I lost my faith in my dad. And that was my greatest loss of all.

SOS

TELEGRAMS ARRIVED:

DEAR COACH, STAY STRONG AND KEEP LOOSE . . . THERE ARE OTHER PASTURES. GOD BLESS. FRANK SINATRA.

Fan letters arrived:

"Dear Coach, hang in there. Look forward to seeing you coach where they'll appreciate you!"

Reporters telephoned:

"Got any plans?"

Dad had no plans.

Mom ripped the telephone receiver from Dad's hand, and responded to reporters' questions in French. *"À vaincre sans peril on triomphe sans gloire,"* she told one. "If one wins without danger, one triumphs without glory." When the reporter asked for a translation, she told him, "You're the writer, look it up."

Double O retired.

Shirley quit.

My brothers came home. George took a break from his job as a law clerk for a district judge in Virginia and searched Dad's files for the Rams contract. Gregory took a break from surfing and unpacked boxes to help Dad set up his office downstairs. Bruce took a break from tryouts at Baltimore Colts training camp to help Mom field reporters' telephone calls.

All the while, Dad remained in his pajamas, robe, and slippers, standing out on the balcony, looking out at the view stretching miles and miles over Los Angeles and the ocean and the Santa Monica mountains. He didn't shave. He didn't even dye his hair.

"Nice view," I once mentioned to Dad.

Dad raised his chin. He scratched the graying beard on his neck.

"Nothing's as nice as Redskin Park," he replied.

ONE DAY, at breakfast, after reading the sports pages aloud, Mom announced that she had an idea. My brothers stopped eating. Dad stopped sipping his milk. I stopped brushing my hair. Mom said she thought Dad should start a coaches' union. A coaches' union, she said, where coaches could gather and make a stand against NFL owners. Mom noted that in the past year, eleven out of the twenty-eight coaches had been fired or forced to retire. As she talked, she was rolling and twisting the sports pages into a tight tube. "How many other professions get rid of over forty percent of their top employees a year?" Mom asked us all.

Dad shook his head.

George burped.

Gregory bit his nails.

Bruce shrugged his shoulders.

"By the way," Mom added, shaking the rolled-up sports pages at Dad, "I'm still waiting for your answer. Did you ever sign that goddamn contract?"

"Sweetie," Dad said, "to tell you the truth, I can't remember."

George said he could not find the contract anywhere.

Mom then telephoned our lawyer, Hookstratton, to see if Dad had signed the Rams contract. Hookstratton said that Dad had signed it just before the firing, and that the Rams would honor the financial terms of the contract. He then reviewed the Rams' deferment program: $50,000 a year for the next ten years.

"Oh, they say, 'We'll pay you,'" Mom said, slamming down the receiver. "But what goddamn good does that do? What does it do for mental attitude, pride, and self-esteem? How can you compensate for that?"

"It's your own damn fault for being so stupid," George yelled at Mom and Dad. "Why did you trust Hookstratton? He's the Rams' legal counsel! Didn't you ever think that Hookstratton might have a conflict of interest?"

"There was a seal down at the beach yesterday, Dad," Gregory offered.

Bruce added, "The Rams will never go to the Super Bowl without you, Dad."

"That's it!" Mom said. "We fire Hookstratton for allowing you to sign that contract."

In a few days, Mom fired Hookstratton. George returned to Virginia, Bruce to training camp, and Gregory to the surf. Then Mom hired a lawyer to help us sue Carroll Rosenbloom for making Dad sign such a terrible contract.

The lawyer sat at the head of our dinner table. When I first saw him I thought he was an NFL owner. He wore the same kind of dark, expensive, perfectly tailored suit I had seen a handful of East Coast owners wear. But unlike most owners I had met, this guy listened. That's when I figured he must have been a lawyer, a man hired to listen to my parents. He listened to my parents talk about contracts and deferment of earnings and the unfairness of the league's hiring/firing system. He listened to Mom's fears— if Dad took another job for more than $50,000 a year, the Rams wouldn't owe him a cent! Mom didn't want Dad to take another job, because she didn't want to let the Rams off the hook. But, then again, she didn't want Dad moping around the house, either.

Sitting with his arms crossed in front of his chest, and his gaze set at the blank screen of the kitchen TV, Dad began recalling the day Rosenbloom fired him in his training-camp dorm room:

"Sit down, George," Rosenbloom had said.

My father sat on his twin bed.

Rosenbloom sat on my father's desk.

"What's wrong with the team, George?" Rosenbloom asked.

My father recited the problems with the team: lack of discipline, too much arrogance, poor attention spans. When my father finished, Rosenbloom suggested that my father retire, take a vacation, have a little rest from football.

"It was strange," Dad now told us all. "It was like having a good talk with a professor, and then realizing that he's telling you that you've flunked the class."

The lawyer nodded his head as if he understood.

Dad said he had refused to retire, and then Rosenbloom said he had no other option than to fire my father.

My mother lit another cigarette. Dad sipped his milk.

The lawyer jotted down some notes, tucked them into his briefcase, and then politely removed himself from the table.

I followed Mom and the lawyer out the door. Mom whispered to the man, "What am I supposed to do with George?"

"Find him a job," the lawyer said.

Several days later, I found a package containing a several-hundred-page document on our doorstep. The services were stamped, "Free of Charge," and the return address was the law offices of F. Lee Bailey.

When I asked Mom if that had been F. Lee Bailey sitting at our kitchen table, she said, "Who did you think it was, Zorba the Greek?"

Mom and Dad then had me type a letter to Carroll Rosenbloom, requesting a number of things: could we please keep the Rams Pinto and Rams Cutlass until we have the time to shop for our own automobiles? Could we still please keep the Rams gas card while Dad searched for another job? Could you please reimburse us for the life insurance we paid for ourselves during the last six months? Could you please pay us for a secretary in our home to help us respond to the thousands of fan letters we have received? Could you please tell players and executives in your organization to stop back-stabbing George to the media? And lastly, should the Rams beat the Cowboys and reach the Super Bowl, could you please pay us a share of the profits for George having given the Rams his cherished and most private playbooks?

A few weeks later, the Rams paid for the life insurance, repossessed the cars and the gas card, denied us a salary for a secretary, apologized for any defamation of the image of George Allen, and, lastly, refused to credit my father with any future Rams victories.

(Eventually, the Rams sued us in Los Angeles Superior Court for breach of contract because my mother would not show the team my father's earnings. "They owe us our money," she said. "We don't owe them anything!" Once in court, my father had to show how much he had earned that year—more than the Rams' annual deferred contract pay of $50,000—which gave the Rams no financial responsibility at all.)

That first season after he was fired, Dad earned $50,000 from CBS Sports as a broadcaster. Mom thought it would be good for Dad to get out of the house, shave, and change his pajamas. Dad said CBS Sports was a glue factory for retired coaches. The only good thing was getting to second-guess coaches the way he had been second-guessed all these years, Dad said. Game days, I'd listen to him announcing a game—"That's why the Rams will never make it to the Super Bowl"—and I'd cringe. Dad could not hide his emotions. Every victory was a potential loss of a future job.

Sundays when Dad did not announce, I would watch him watching football, in silence, immobile, in our wooden rocking chair. For the entire game, he would not move from that chair. He would not say a word until the referee fired the final gun, and then he would stand up and say, "You see that referee?" Dad was pointing to some frail, shriveled-up ref. "That guy cost me an undefeated season in 1952."

One day, after watching the Kansas City Chiefs beat the Cleveland Browns, Mom said, "Look at Hank Stram."

Hank Stram had announced the game.

Stram was the frustrated, toupéed former Kansas City head coach who had twice taken his team to the Super Bowl, losing once, and then, a few seasons later, winning at last. When the Chiefs failed to reach the Super Bowl again, Stram was fired while still under contract. Stram sued, collected little, and spent the rest of his seasons analyzing games for TV broadcasts.

We watched Stram adjust his hair, then say, with a forced smile, "So long from Kansas City!"

"Let's not sue," Dad said.

"Goddamn right," Mom said.

Back to School

AT PALOS VERDES High School, I would see kids I had known from childhood, vaguely recalling a bucktooth or a pair of knock-knees, and I would shout out "Hi!" but they would just keep walking, talking to their friends, not noticing I was even there.

One day a boy I had slugged in grade school said "That's George Allen's daughter" to another kid.

The other kid looked at me. "George Allen?" he asked. "Who's George Allen?"

As the football season went on, I would arrive at school late, to avoid the other kids in the hallways talking about dates and parties and colleges. I would spend break in my car smoking cigarettes. I would spend lunchtime in my car smoking grass. In PE, I was the last chosen for sides in any game of any kind. I did not blame them for not choosing me. I wouldn't choose me either. I stood around with my arms held close to my chest, unable even to talk anymore, my tongue too tied from smoking grass. One day, in chemistry class, some boy I had never seen before said hi to me. I was elated. Somebody noticed me! "Hi!" I shouted back. But then I noticed the boy was talking to some girl lighting a Bunsen burner behind me, flipping her long blond hair across the flame of gas. I thought of all the kids I must have ignored back in Virginia—kids who were not cheerleaders or jocks or daughters and sons of vaguely important men— kids who would have loved for someone just to say hi to them. What a jerk I must have been. Back in Virginia, I resented being known solely as George Allen's daughter. Now I saw it was worse not to be known at all.

The only place I really fit in was creative writing class. The teacher applauded my sappy, sentimental poems. He would read my words aloud to the class, giving each phrase a weight I had not even intended. He could barely make out my handwriting and saw words that were not there. After class, he would hand the poems back and tell me, "Type these up so I can read them." I would come home and type out my self-pitying poems about "lost love" and "lost dreams." Each poem ended with the same pathetic line: "leaving me to drown in the sorrows of tomorrow." A few were published in the school's literary journal under my new pseudonym, "J. Allen." When my mother read the poems, she said, "You better watch what you write—don't you realize whatever you write reflects on your father?"

My father? Who was my father?

My father did not even exist anymore. He was not the George Allen I used to know. I was beginning to wonder if I had ever known who he was. I was beginning to see that my words now reflected on no one but me.

The End

"MEL, MAYBE THIS IS the end of me. Maybe no one else will hire me," Dad was saying to Mel the reporter on the telephone. Mel was a friend who shared the same birthday as Dad and who often affectionately referred to Dad as "coachie-pie." "Maybe they'll say I'm too old. Maybe they'll say anything," Dad went on. "I've been voted Coach of the Year four times. Five of my former assistants are head coaches. And I haven't got a job."

As Dad talked in the den, Mom sat in the kitchen, listening in on the other line, the receiver cradled in her neck. The rooms were adjoining with just a low counter between them, so that Mom could watch Dad while he talked and Dad could look to Mom for direction. Often, she wrote notes to give to me to messenger to Dad. Mom was like those mutes who sit in the broadcast booth, frantically writing out facts on index cards for the broadcast star to read. Most of her suggestions were motivational—"Sound positive! Don't let him know you're depressed!" Some were instructive—"Tell Mel 'I'm not looking for another job. For the first time, I'm enjoying my life, relaxing, with my family.' " Dad took Mom's scribbling from my hands and nodded his head at her approvingly, and then went ahead and said what he truly felt. "Mel," Dad said, "I even miss my enemies. Used to be, I could pick up the paper and find someone putting the zing on me. Now no one even mentions me."

Mel offered some suggestions. I heard every word because Mom had a special hearing-aid switch that flipped the volume up on the telephone so loud that anyone could hear from a room away. Mel said, "Maybe the Rams have hurt your reputation. But look on the bright side. Maybe the Rams won't make it to the Super Bowl."

"Mel," Dad said, "my problem isn't the Los Angeles Rams anymore. My problem is figuring out each morning how to pass the day. For thirty years, I have worked seven days a week during the season and six days a week during the off-season. How many miles can a guy run? How long can a guy sit there reading a book?"

Days when Dad wasn't announcing a game, he searched for ways to spend his time. One day, he drove a hundred miles to attend the funeral of a tackle he had coached at Whittier College some thirty years before. Another day, Dad waited for hours in a hospital for a former player who had undergone knee surgery to be wheeled into recovery. Yet another day, he made a surprise appearance on the Jerry Lewis telethon to donate the game ball his players gave him during the '72 Championship season to raise $5,000 for Jerry's Kids. Frequently, he drove down south to visit Nixon in his San Clemente home and talk about the days when they both ruled the free world. But those diversions never fulfilled him. Dad would come home, telephone Mel, and ask him, "Mel, what did I do wrong?"

Mel would know exactly what to say.

"You'll be back, George," Mel would tell Dad. "Don't worry, you'll be back."

Dad would thank Mel, hang up the telephone, and head downstairs to his office.

Mom would shove me down the stairs. "Go check on your father," she'd say. "See what he's doing down there."

I never wanted to check on my father. I was afraid I would find him watching *The Impossible Dream*. Or maybe I would find him autographing one of the several hundred unsigned black-and-white photographs of George Allen, Head Coach, Los Angeles Rams that the Rams had returned to us after the firing. I guess I was afraid to find out who my father really was. All those years I had read the sports pages seeking an answer to the question Who is my Dad? Now, I had every chance to see him sitting at his desk, as he tallied up his lifetime coaching record.

Rams five-year record before George Allen: 19-48-3

Rams five-year record WITH George Allen: 49-17-4

Redskins seven-year record before George Allen: 42-51-5

Redskins seven-year record WITH George Allen: 67-30-1

He had piles of notes like these, along with other statistics that he had configured in his spare time.

When my father saw me standing there, he would ask me to place a telephone call. His address book, once an example of supreme organization—beside every man's name Dad had listed his home address, his home phone, wife's name, his children's names, his work phone, his work address, his secretary's phone, and his secretary's name—was now an example of perfect disarray. Names were not alphabetized. Area codes were missing. Some numbers had no names. Searching for a telephone number, I would come across more of Dad's notes to himself. They were too personal to ignore. I felt as if I was reading his journal, reading things he wrote while waiting for a call to be returned, things he wrote while waiting to place another call.

Job security—never wanted it—rather accept the risk

But now, I'm having trouble

Everything I worked for and gained has been destroyed

Like taking an instrument away from a musician

Hired to be fired from the start

I just wanted to coach

I sure liked doing a good job
Who will hire me now?
Try to think of yourself as a winner
Have to do something with my life!
God is testing me
God is teaching me patience

When I finally found the telephone number, I would dial the number myself and tell the wife or the child or the secretary that Coach George Allen was calling, and I would be told, Yes, he already received that message, sorry the call has not been returned yet, he would certainly return the call to Coach George Allen as soon as possible.

I would tell my father that the man would call back as soon as possible.

Once, after one of these aborted calls, my father said to me, "When you're fired, suddenly, Mr. Big Shot can't return your calls."

THE 1978 SEASON WAS OVER. Coaches were fired. Coaches were hired. Coaches retired. Christmas came and went, uncelebrated, unnoticed. Perpetually seated by the telephone in the den, Dad waited for a call from an owner, or an assistant coach, or even an equipment manager to offer him a hint of a new coaching position.

We watched the Rams play the Dallas Cowboys in the Conference Championship. The winner would go to the Super Bowl. The Rams lost, 28 to 0. In his address book, my father wrote, "Vindicated! I could have beaten the Dallas Cowboys!"

Still no owner called. Only reporters called, asking, "How does it feel to be out of a job another year?"

"I'm not the loser here, you see?" Dad told more than one reporter. "The Rams missed an opportunity when they fired me."

Mom shook her head. Dad was always too honest, she said.

At the end of another year, Mom went to bed alone, while Dad and I stayed up watching the live TV celebration in Times Square. Dad sat with the telephone beside him, his address book in his lap, writing more notes to himself: *Eroded confidence. Can't go through another season. Said I was difficult to get along with. Harmed me. Some owners hire anybody. 1979 belongs to George Allen.*

A Good Laugh

TO CHEER IN THE NEW YEAR, the Beverly Hills Friars Club "fried" Dad. Arriving home from the event, Dad told us he had never laughed so hard in his whole life. He said it was the best time he'd had since the Redskins beat the Cowboys on New Year's Eve. He then showed us a letter Milton Berle read aloud earlier that night.

Dear Coach,

> *I wish I could be with you on this wonderful occasion at the Friars, but I had a previous commitment with the Rams cheerleaders.*
> *While the Friars are giving you something to cheer about tonight, I am giving the Rams cheerleaders something to cheer about . . . one at a time.*
> *In all seriousness George, I really would like to be with you tonight, but I am having a private meeting, off the record, with the Vice Premier of China, Ten Hsaio-Ping, who, as you know, is visiting this country. I am trying to get you a job as a coach of the Peking Patriots since you have run out of teams in this country who will even talk to you.*

> *Love and Kisses,*
> *Francis Albert*

Dad shook his head, rubbed his eyes, and said, "Boy, is it good to laugh!"

We all laughed.

We all wiped our eyes.

It was the funniest goddamn letter we'd ever read.

Dad had the letter framed.

Mom hung it up in his office.

A couple of days later, the telephone rang. It was an NFL owner calling to discuss the last coaching position open for the 1979 season.

"I'll meet with you anywhere," Dad said.

"I'm headed to Los Angeles," the owner said. "We'll meet tomorrow. Call me at this hotel."

The following morning, Dad had a haircut and a barber's shave, then had Mom help him dress: Parisian double-breasted suit, Parisian silk tie, Parisian wing-tip shoes. Dad had me telephone the hotel to talk to the owner, but the owner was not registered, the hotel clerk said. Dad had me telephone the team's headquarters. Sorry, the owner was not there either. Dad had me telephone all the major hotels in L.A.—Bel Air, Beverly Hills, Beverly Hilton—but the owner was not registered at any of them. A few days later, the owner hired another coach. A few days after that, a former Redskins associate wrote Dad a note. The associate now worked for the same owner who had never showed up for the meeting with Dad.

"It's too bad about you not getting the job here," the associate wrote. "It's strange. Nobody even mentions you, don't know why."

Dad said, "Take the Sinatra letter down."

I raced down the basement stairs to take the Sinatra letter down from Dad's office walls. Mom then placed the letter in a closet.

"Don't worry about anything," Dad said to Mom, who was crying, knowing she was about to spend another long season with her husband home, fired, indefinitely. "Don't worry," he said, flipping through the pages of his telephone book, "nothing will be all right."

A few more days later, Dad was on an airplane, headed to the annual NFL meetings at some five-star resort hotel. He wasn't invited. That didn't matter. He had the third-best record of any coach in the history of the league and that gave him the right to crash any league gathering. For a week, Dad hung around the hotel lobby, casually bumping into owners. He later wrote that he had his *"hat in hand,"* with his *"tail between legs,"* as he approached every owner's handshake. He even approached Commissioner Pete Rozelle and told him, "Hey, Pete, it's amazing, guys that have losing records are getting jobs, and I never had a losing season—as you know, I rebuilt two franchises and won a Championship. I'm the only coach in the history of football who has coached as long as I have who has never had a losing season. Everywhere I go, people say, 'George, when are you coming back?' So why don't I get any job offers, Pete? What the heck's going on? If anyone can get me a job, it's you, Pete."

The commissioner replied, "Sorry, George, I can't control what the owners do." The commissioner patted my father on the back and said, "George, I can't get owners to agree on anything, much less who to hire."

Dad returned home from the meetings even more depressed. In a note in his address book, he wrote, *I've been blackballed, blueballed, and greenballed out of the NFL.*

What Georgia Needs

IN MARCH, when Rams owner Carroll Rosenbloom drowned while swimming off the coast of Florida, his widow, Georgia, became the new owner of the team. Immediately, Dad wrote Georgia a letter of condolence. "Dear Georgia," he wrote, "if there's anything I can do, let me know . . ." In his address book, he wrote, *You're exactly what Georgia needs—someone who can take charge and has kindness and thoughtfulness, too. She doesn't know who she can trust. No one in the Rams organization can do it or has done it. No one can be counted on. Need leadership and discipline. Need someone who knows the situation.*

Why would I take a job that isn't exactly right? To prove I was right the first time.

Rosenbloom's sudden death made Dad think, he said. Dad said he wanted to "forgive and forget," he wanted to move on, and the only way was to get on the telephone. As I dialed Edward Bennett Williams, I read in the margin of Dad's address book, *Biggest raping in history of sports. Didn't even have a chance. Didn't even have one regular-season game. Real shame that a guy can't do what he wants to do. In my heart, this is my life.*

As I dialed George Halas, I read, *Listen, I have nothing to prove. I don't consider getting dismissed after two preseason games as to warrant turning everything inside out. There was no mystery to what happened to me. There were people in the organization who back-stabbed me. I could have taken it easier. I could have had a few drinks, relaxed, shortened the meetings, and whether we won or lost, people would have said, Hey, that George, he's a pretty good guy. But that wouldn't have been George Allen. That wouldn't have been me.*

As I dialed Georgia Rosenbloom, I read, *Why should I be bitter? Don't have to be bitter and have self-pity. I'm not the loser.*

George and Jack, Part II

IN 1979, EDWARD BENNETT Williams continued to sell off his remaining shares of Redskins stock to Jack Kent Cooke. Williams wanted to place all his time, money, and effort into his new team, pro baseball's Baltimore Orioles. Dad had me telephone Cooke daily, but I could only reach Cooke's secretary. After weeks of our trying, Cooke's secretary telephoned to offer Dad two free tickets to a Los Angeles Lakers basketball game, plus a pregame dinner invitation with Cooke at the Forum Club.

Mom did not want to go. Mom had lost her voice. Since the firing, she'd been keeping up a steady rate of three packs of cigarettes a day. She now wrote us notes to let us know what she was thinking: "Just because I can't talk doesn't mean that you guys can't talk to me," and "When I don't talk, no one talks, and all is too quiet." That day she wrote Dad a note that read, "I'm tired of being Mrs. George Allen, take Jennifer instead."

Dad took me.

Dad sat me beside Cooke at his round table of men. Everyone laughed at everything Cooke said. They laughed at things that weren't even funny, like when Cooke informed my father that the two swans, George and Jack, had died. They were highbred swans, Cooke told them all, what did we expect, a long life span?

All the men laughed.

Dad did not laugh. Dad said, "Oh, that's a shame." He looked as if he had just been told that Hilda had died. Hilda had recently died of heat prostration at the beach. When it happened, Dad said, "Should we bury her in the backyard? Should we have a funeral? Should we make a pillow out of her fur?" Now, after hearing of the swans' deaths, Dad offered a similar suggestion: "Did you bury Jack and George at your ranch?"

Cooke ignored the question. Instead, he directed his attention at me, the only girl at the table. He asked me what I planned to do with my life. I told him I planned to go to college.

What was I going to major in?

I thought poetry sounded too vague so instead I said, "Humanities."

"Humanities?" Cooke said. "What's humanities?"

Just then, a waiter interrupted to inform Cooke of an important telephone call.

Cooke excused himself and, moments later, returned, telling us he had to take a flight back east. He apologized to my father. "Sorry, dear George," he said, "maybe we can talk some more next time."

"Maybe next time," my father said.

There wasn't a next time.

A Room of My Own

EVERY DAY AFTER SCHOOL, as graduation neared, my father would stand in my bedroom doorway and ask, "Do you like your room?"

I would be sitting on the floor, typing out another poem, and I would not even turn around to look at him. I would not even give him a grunt to let him know I had heard his question.

"Do you like your room?"

In this one simple, awkward question, I heard many questions my father was asking me:

Do you like your life?

Do you like yourself?

Do you like me?

I also heard a series of pleas:

Talk to me.

Be with me.

Help me.

All those years I had wished to have some time with my father, and now I had it. But I did not want anything to do with him. I was pushing him away just as the NFL had. Maybe I could not bear to see that we were going through the same things—loneliness, low self-esteem, depression. Maybe I refused to see what my mother once told me long ago and what she continues to tell me to this day: that out of all the children, I am the one most like my father. Maybe, I thought, I would deny him for all the time I thought he had denied me.

I would wait to hear my father's slippers quietly pad away on the soft carpet. Tomorrow, he would try to ask me the same question again: "Do you like your room?" Tomorrow, I would refuse him just the same; he'd go away.

After my father was far down the stairs, I would break down, face in hands, and think, Loser!

But my father was not the loser. I was.

A Family Decision

ON FATHER'S DAY, the local sports headline read, GEORGE ALLEN—THE MAN NOBODY WANTS.

My father had me read the sports pages aloud. Years of watching game films late into the night had worn out his eyes. My mother still had not regained her lost voice. My parents sat at the kitchen table, listening to the words I read, holding on to each syllable of their life as it unraveled before them.

The reporter interviewed my brother Bruce, who spoke from the sidelines of Arizona State University, where he was an assistant coach. Two torn ligaments on the inside of the right knee, a misplaced bone on the outside right knee, and seven torn ligaments on the right ankle had hindered his tryouts at last summer's Baltimore Colts training camp. At twenty-one years old, he decided to become a coach instead.

"It's a family decision," Bruce told the reporter. "We decided no more coaching for Dad this year."

Is your father retiring from coaching? the reporter wanted to know.

"I told Dad to retire after last year's firing," Bruce answered. "I don't want him in there again. He doesn't need the frustration."

Had anyone offered his father a job? the reporter asked.

"Sure," Bruce lied. "He's got eight coaching offers! It's tearing at him not to take them, but the only way my father's going to take a head coaching job again is if he's general manager and head coach and part owner of a team."

Mom scribbled a note she passed to me to read aloud: "That will teach those bastards."

I waved Mom's note away.

In the next paragraph, the reporter revealed that the coach had blown his son's charade. The reporter fact-checked this claim of eight coaching offers.

"No, I haven't had any pro offers, only college offers," Dad told the reporter. "No, no NFL team has offered me a job."

Mom dropped her head into her hands. Her cigarette set a bit of her hair on fire. She motioned for me to stop reading. Dad motioned for me to keep reading.

How does the coach feel about his son coaching?

"I tried to talk Bruce out of coaching," my father told the reporter, "but he's stubborn like his father."

Seems like Bruce Allen is following in the footsteps of George Allen, the reporter concluded.

"I wouldn't wish that on anyone," Dad said.

I folded up the sports pages and asked Dad if he wanted me to save them for his scrapbook.

At first he said no, then he said, "Yes, save it for Bruce. It's time for Bruce to start his own scrapbook."

In the coming months, Bruce would be hired as the new head coach of Occidental College, a small private college in Los Angeles. At the time, he was the youngest head football coach in the country. Bruce's team went on to finish the season in last place with a 2-6-1 record. Bruce quit coaching and never returned to coaching again. To this day, he says he has no regrets.

End Zone

THE GAME WAS OVER. We had won, 6 to 0. Playing in Deacon Jones's position, as the left defensive end in a high school "Powder Puff" football game, I had done my job well: two sacks, one rushing-the-passer, and one batted-down ball. Standing on the dirt track, I watched the other girls' parents pat them, good game, on the back. I was waiting for Dad to come congratulate me on my winning performance. He was still standing in the end zone. He appeared to be reviewing the game's high points with our coach, my former kindergarten boyfriend, a guy who had a future before him—he would soon attend the Air Force Academy—unlike my boyfriend Flynn, who remained on the East Coast, repeating his senior year of high school at a private, all-boys prep school.

I prepared for my moment of recognition.

I straightened my jersey, number 75.

I straightened my socks, red-striped hand-me-downs of my brothers.

I had finally done it, I thought. I had finally played football on the one field where all my brothers once played.

My mother stood behind me, beside the bleachers, where runaway pom-pom strings, faded programs, and empty peanut bags circled in the wind around her feet. She waved me close to her. She spoke in a raspy voice. "This was so good for your father," she said.

And I thought, yes, this must have been good for Dad to see that his only daughter could sack a quarterback.

Then she said, "Your father told me that he realized how many things he had missed all these years while he was busy coaching." She coughed, stopped to take a breath, and said, "Your father realized how much he missed never seeing your brothers play high school ball."

I looked at Dad. He still wore his Rams cap with the "GA" initials. He still wore his Redskins golf shirt with the curled collar from too many machine washings. The hem of his coaching pants, an inch or two too short, clipped his ankles, showing off his athletic socks, mismatched, one gold, one blue. And here was my mother, still standing as she always stood, patiently, waiting for her husband to walk off the field.

This was supposed to be my day, my game, my victory.

This was supposed to be my dream come true, my only triumph of gridiron fame.

I tore off my jersey, tossed it on the bench, and walked off the field.

Several days later, I graduated from Palos Verdes High. One college had accepted me—the University of California at San Diego, perched on the cliffs of a cove called Black's, an all-nude beach. I went through the motions of my graduation ceremony, vaguely listening to the speeches, mostly glad that I would never have to walk those school halls again. Days later, while helping Dad dial another telephone number, I found my graduation program on his desk. I did not even recall my father attending the ceremony. I was surprised to see that he had. On the page that listed my name, my father had written some notes. I thought maybe I would find some secret message Dad had written to me, some thought he had about his daughter's success— I had finally earned straight As. But all I found was more of Dad's ruminations about his past, his present, and his future.

If your contracts, your future careers, sending children to school and college, giving your family and wife the things she wants, having the niceties of life by winning games isn't enough, Dad wrote, *there's no use.*

And below this, on a page citing the school's victory song, Dad wrote, *What will I do the remaining days of my life?*

How do I make this day count?

What is true greatness?

FIFTH QUARTER

Sudden Death

My earliest childhood memory is of my father coming home with a game ball in his hands. I remember climbing out of bed and running down the stairs to greet my father. I remember my father tossing the ball up in the air, and my brothers, below him, reaching, stretching to catch the prize possession of the Chicago Bears 1963 Championship game. I also remember my mother crying.

"Dad's home!" I cheered. "Daddy's home!"

I was almost three years old.

Years later, I learned the facts behind the day's events. I learned that the Chicago Bears had beaten the former world champion New York Giants 14 to 10, that the victory was credited mostly to my father, who built a defense that secured five interceptions and one fumble that wintry, December day. I learned that as an assistant coach, my father's earning of a game ball was unprecedented in the history of the National Football League. And I also learned that my father saw this as the height of his career—the precise moment when the Bears gave him the game ball, and he gained national recognition on TV. There, in the postgame locker room, my father was congratulated by his fellow Bears as the players sang the highest song of praise: "Hooray for George! Hooray at last! Hooray for George, he's a horse's ass!"

Years later, we sang this same song to our father when he lay at rest.

Some thirty years after the Bears Championship victory, my father died on New Year's Eve. He was seventy-three and had recently completed his last season coaching, trying to resurrect the perpetually losing California State, Long Beach, football program. In the final game of the season, his team won, earning a final 6-5 record—considered, for statistical purposes, a winning season. After the game, his players doused him with an ice-cold bucket of water. My father remained in his wet clothes for several hours afterward, conducting interviews with reporters wanting to know "George, why did you take this job?" and "George, how does it feel to be coaching again?" After the Rams firing in 1978, my father was never hired again by an NFL team. Returning to college coaching, he told reporters, was returning to his "first love."

The following day, my father noticed a shortness of breath, and my mother convinced him to have a physical. The doctor discovered an irregular heartbeat and a case of viral pneumonia. My father was ordered to slow down, stop jogging, and start eating. A pacemaker was suggested, but my father protested, saying he didn't have the time—it was the off-season, after all, time to start preparing the team for the coming year.

Within a few weeks, my mother found my father on the floor in the den. He was dressed in his pajamas, his robe, and his slippers. A college bowl game was on the TV. She telephoned my brother Gregory. Gregory telephoned everyone else—including the press, the paramedics, and the church. Soon, across the nation, the announcement was made during all the holiday football games: George Allen was dead.

Overtime

MY FATHER LEFT NO WILL. He left no directions regarding our inheritance. He left his dresser drawers full, and his electric razor recharging, and his 16-millimeter highlight films stacked in chronological order so that, I thought, we could take what we needed and donate the rest to an archive interested in preserving the memory of George Allen. So far, everything has remained as it was—except for his football rings. My mother found those in his dresser drawer: three big gold rings studded with diamonds and rubies. My mother had me help her decide who received which ring. We gave George the Washington Redskins Super Bowl ring, because he was then a U.S. congressman living in Washington, D.C. We gave Gregory the four-time Coach of the Year ring, because he was then a pastor and a counselor, a kind of coach to those interested in God.

We gave Bruce the 1963 Championship Chicago Bears ring because Bruce was the son Dad often referred to as "Bear Boy Bruce," and also because Dad believed the ring held a kind of good-luck magic on the football field. After giving the boys the rings, we dressed for the funeral.

My brothers planned the three-part service—the burial, the funeral, and the memorial—and it began at kickoff, 1:06 P.M., and ended at approximately 4:06 P.M., final gun, game over.

My brothers planned what my father would wear for burial—coaching pants, coaching blazer, striped coaching tie—and what he would hold—a game ball—and what his pockets would contain—my brothers' business cards for posterity and a felt-tip pen for autographs.

My brothers planned who would carry the casket: Deacon Jones, Billy Kilmer, Dr. Jules Rasinski, and themselves.

My brothers planned who would speak at the memorial in the church: themselves, along with Reverend Tom Skinner, Roman Gabriel, and Billy Kilmer; Willie Brown, an all-pro cornerback and former assistant coach at Long Beach State; the president of Long Beach State; our father's best blocking end from Whittier College; and an actor who had known our father for a couple of years.

My brothers planned which highlight films would be shown in the church.

My brothers designed the memorial's souvenir program, complete with our father's lifelong record so that everyone could remember, as many told me that day, that "George Allen died a winner."

My brothers planned it all themselves, and along the way, they decided that I would not be a part of any of it.

Years later, I asked my brother Bruce, "Why wouldn't you guys let me speak at Dad's memorial?" Bruce answered me quickly: "You weren't strong enough, and anyway, those guys didn't want to hear what you had to say. They wanted to hear what Gabriel and Kilmer and everyone else had to say." Then he added, "Besides, we weren't honoring a father, we were honoring a coach."

IN BETWEEN MY LEAVING home for college and my father's death, I did some things that I had been told daughters of football coaches are not supposed to do. I kissed a girl, I befriended a death-row inmate, and I stopped watching football. I wrote a book containing so much profanity that *The Times* of London called it "obscene in every sense of the word," and my mother refused to keep it on the bookshelf in the den. My mother also told me that she hid the book from my father, fearing that he would be too disturbed to read his daughter's vulgar use of language.

My father often introduced me to his friends as a "journalist." I saw his inability to see me as a "fiction writer" as the equivalent of me seeing him as a baseball coach. But I never corrected him. After all, he had never read a word I had written. I told myself I did not care anymore what my father thought. But that lie passed away when my father did, when I found myself, days after his death, down in his home office, rummaging through his notes and his playbooks and his scrapbooks, trying to resurrect some kind of relationship we may have had in the past. I did care what my father thought of me. If only I could find some sense that in all his work he had thought of me or remembered me.

It was hard to find anything that let me know what my father had thought of me. One day, crammed in the back of a desk drawer, I found a Father's Day card I had made for him in grade school. Another day, I found a third-person tallying-up of his W, L, T record. Some days were easier than others. The easy ones were those when I would leave my father's office altogether to spend some time sitting alone in a nearby church. If I closed my eyes, I could imagine my father in the pew beside me, quiet and still. There, in church, I came to know what my father had known long before I was born, that there was a peace to be gained in this place where many gathered on game-day Sundays. There, I came to realize that by coaching, my father was fulfilling what he thought he was born to do. "My prayer," my father once said, "is that I can do what God put me on earth to do: coach."

The hard days were those spent alone in his office when I would find only half-written, incomplete notes. One note, written a day before his death, haunted me for years:

Bad news today—votes came in for Hall of Fame, I didn't make it again.

George Allen, he has a better Won and Loss record of 10 of the 11 coaches in the Hall of Fame.

George Allen, he never had a losing season.

George Allen, he won at every level of competition—Morningside College, Whittier College, Chicago Bears, Los Angeles Rams, Long Beach State.

George Allen, he deserves to be in the Hall of Fame, consider the opinions of: The note ended there.

I spent hours trying to fill in his missing words, hoping it would fill in some missing part of me.

Then, one day, I found a note in his office that read, *I thought nobody wanted me.* It was one that I could have written. I finally realized that my father's struggles were similar to mine. We both felt unwanted. Knowing this, I felt more complete.

The Final Score

MY MOTHER STILL LIVES in the house she built on the hill overlooking the ocean. She keeps the shades drawn to slow the sun's fading of the furniture and rugs and the portraits of my father that hang on all the walls in the den. She still keeps my father's clothes in his closet. His cardigan is draped over a wooden butler rack; below it are his slippers. A collection of his toothbrushes remains in a milk glass under his bathroom sink. His office in the basement is as he left it. My mother does not want to move a thing. She says she likes to feel that he is down there, studying game films, missing yet another family dinner. The early drafts of this book were written in his office. My mother often barged through the closed door to ask me, "Are you going to put those books back where you found them? Do you plan on leaving those papers all over the desk?" Once, I took one of his seventeen game balls, and my mother immediately noticed. "What happened to the Bears ball?" she demanded to know. It had been missing one day.

My mother spends her mornings reading the sports page and then running herself ragged at the gym. She spends her afternoons collapsed in Dad's TV chair. Evenings, she watches sports on the new kitchen TV. The old black-and-white unit no longer works. It sits in the garage. She cannot bring herself to toss it out. Nor can she throw out the countless closed and sealed boxes dating back to our move from Chicago in 1966. She still holds a feud with the late Dan Reeves, and the late Edward Bennett Williams, and the late NFL commissioner Pete Rozelle. She still adores the late Jack Kent Cooke. A few years ago, when Cooke built a new Redskins stadium and named an entire luxury-box level after my father, she chose to attend the opening-day ceremonies over my son Roman's baptism. "I'm still Mrs. George Allen, you know?" she reminded me. Recently, when I was pregnant again, my husband and I decided to not learn the baby's gender before it was born. During the pregnancy, whenever my mother and I argued, she would yell at me, "You *deserve* to have a girl!" When I gave birth to a son, Deacon, she confided, "You're lucky you didn't have a girl. Boys are so much easier!"

My mother quit smoking when she was diagnosed with breast cancer more than ten years ago. While she was receiving radiation treatments, my father learned how to pour his own glass of milk. He also learned how to serve my mother breakfast, lunch, and dinner in bed. After she recovered, she said, their life began. "Your father finally learned how to have fun," she has told me again and again. Some days she is furious at him. "I am *so mad* at your father!" she will tell me. "Wait until I get my hands on him!" She is kidding. She is not kidding. She misses my father terribly. She dreams of him often. She keeps Post-its on the refrigerator that Dad once wrote: "I'll be home early tonight, we'll have a nice dinner together." She keeps thinking that one day he'll show up and tell her it's all been a joke. Mostly, she wishes he would just come home. She says she imagines that once she is buried in the plot my brothers purchased beside my father's, she can resume her nagging. My father will probably like that. He once told me that he believed a wife's job was to keep the man in line. With a rolling pin if necessary. This year, my parents would have celebrated their fiftieth wedding anniversary.

We kids have all gone on with our lives. We have entered professions my father had once predicted for us. For all his time away from us, my father still had the intuitive perception to see what we could and would become. My brother George became a statesman. During his inauguration as the governor of Virginia, George reserved an empty chair for our father on the podium. My brother Gregory became a psychologist, and a Christian minister to wayward youth. Gregory believes our father is in heaven, and in this way, of all of us, he seems most at peace. After a short stint as a college football coach, my brother Bruce became an NFL agent and then an executive of the Oakland Raiders football team. Bruce reads the sports pages aloud to our father at his gravesite. He leaves a copy there, he says, in lieu of flowers.

At Christmas holiday dinners, when all my brothers come home, we head downstairs to shoot some pool. The pool table is covered in a sheet of plastic. After we've shot a few racks, Mom will come down and yell at all of us, Will you put the plastic back on? Will you turn off all the lights? Will you draw the blinds? We put the plastic back on, we turn off all the lights, we draw the blinds, and, later, we leave our mother as she wants to be left: with her memories of my father and her life as the wife of Coach George Allen.

At the end of a game, you can spend years reliving every mistake and every missed opportunity. Years spent studying, Why didn't I do that differently? The same is true for the end of a life. I always thought that when someone died, the relationship ended. Now I know a relationship continues long after death. I feel closer to my father now than I ever felt when he was alive. Writing this book helped. Getting married and having a couple of sons helped too. My father would have liked to have seen his grandsons grow up, and I bet he would have liked my husband. My husband never played football because of years of childhood hip surgeries that put him in body casts for six-month stretches at a time: the two positions he played then were not offense and defense but faceup or facedown. My husband may not know a great deal about football—in fact it's the only topic where I feel I know more than he does—but he does know what it means to live with pain and to keep on playing. My father would have said to me, That Mark, he has character. That Mark, he reminds me of one of my Redskins. And I would have had the chance to finally say, You're right, Dad, you're absolutely right.

A few years ago, I found *The Impossible Dream* and had it transferred onto videotape. I put it in a safe place because I want my sons to be able to watch it someday. It's not as long as I remember it. It lasts only a couple of minutes. The black-and-white images are grainy. The soundtrack crackles. Many of my father's favorite plays crumbled apart in the editing room because he had worn out the film, running it through the projector in slow motion, reverse, and freeze-frame. Those were the plays that moved my father the most: the fingertip catch, the long bomb, the savage sack, and the end-zone interception. The clearest surviving moment is the footage that my father never paused to replay. Yet this will be the most vivid scene my sons will see when they watch it with me: we'll see my father—their grandfather—being lifted onto the shoulders of his men and carried off the playing field, sobbing, victorious.

ACKNOWLEDGMENTS

Paul Zimmerman, the all-pro sportswriter, graciously assisted me in fact-checking this manuscript. For his help and his humor, I am, and will forever be, indebted. Mel Durslag, another star writer and close family friend, gave me the keenest advice, insisting that I write only what I saw and what I felt, that anything short of that would be pointless. My mother-in-law, Claire, provided strong arms to rock crying babies, and a prayerful heart to calm all fears. My brother George sat with me for hours by the pool one day, measuring out parcels of his past, all the while reminding me to remain faithful to the facts. My brother Gregory offered an open ear on our long walks along the cliffs. His wife, Christine, wrestled on the lawn with Roman while I wrestled with the words on the page. My brother Bruce telephoned often to make sure I was busy writing. Whenever I was feeling particularly discouraged, he'd write me a fatherly "Keep fighting," signed, "your hero." Lastly, I wish to thank and acknowledge my mother. For years, she has openly shared her memories of her life with my father. Rain or shine, my mother has been an enormous cheerleader for me, urging me to "get on with my life," and goading me, daily, with these simple words: "When are you going to finish that goddamn book?"

ABOUT THE AUTHOR

JENNIFER ALLEN lives in Los Angeles with
her husband, the author Mark Richard, and
their sons, Roman and Deacon.

ABOUT THE TYPE

This book was set in Bembo, a typeface based on an
old-style roman face that was used for Cardinal Bembo's
tract *De Aetna* in 1495. Bembo was cut by Francisco Griffo
in the early sixteenth century. The Lanston Monotype
Machine Company of Philadelphia brought the
well-proportioned letter forms of Bembo to
the United States in the 1930s.